Petra's Ashes

A Transcendental Journey

A MEMOIR BY
PETRA NICOLL

LUMINARE PRESS
WWW.LUMINAREPRESS.COM

Petra's Ashes

Printed in the United States of America

Cover Design: Claire Flint Last
Front Cover Imagery: Bojan Certic, Artist

LUMINARE PRESS
438 Charnelton St #101
Eugene, OR 97401
www.luminarepress.com

ISBN: 978-1-944733-04-9
LCCN: 2016952451

To my mother,
who will always be in my heart.

Contents

Introduction

I am an accumulation of those who went before me—and the people, places and events of my life today—and those yet to come. My desire in writing this book is to inspire others in this world who perhaps ask the same question that I did.

Why am I here and what is my true purpose on earth?

For me, adulthood had many twists and turns, filled with light and darkness. And it was quite magical, how life events would propel me to identify the repeated life patterns, and to fully accept myself for who I had become—and to utilize my gifts as I discovered my purpose on this earth.

Life laced with chaos and unmet emotional needs, eventually led me to a place of being filled with deep love and contentment. It took me some time, and much soul searching to fully understand the impact of these things that were significant parts of my life.

It seemed as if there had always been a plan.

There was much drama and trauma—a near-death experience at the age of nine, the sudden and tragic death of my mother, suicide, depression, and realities of war impacted and influenced my life. I was led to the Masters of the Far East, the Shamans of North America and Mexico, who awakened me to the realization and the vision that I had been given—to become transformed and more intuitive—which guided me on a journey that I now use as tools to help others.

What have I learned?

Like the caterpillar becomes the butterfly—it took a metamorphosis to evolve to where I am today—to become transformed, more intuitive, and yes, even psychic, as I moved into a life of deep introspection, and acceptance of what is—a transcendental journey that spanned decades.

Recognizing that life is a gift that has been given to us, it is in our hands to make the best out of it—and dare to believe that we can. Being true to ourselves and soul-centered removes us from the collective mainstream, as it opens the door to our humanity, finally to reveal to you, and to me, the nectar of this wildly delicious and messy life that moves steadily towards a finish line and leaves you, and those you touch, radically free.

What is my wish for you?

Through my story written on these pages, my intent is to inspire *you* to find the courage to extract and tell the story inside of *you!* In doing so, evolving personal acceptance, greater knowledge and understanding, and full recognition of YOUR purpose on this earth is seen in full, living color.

Through the ups and downs in life, you'll find lessons are learned that will make you a better person. Each experience—good and bad—makes you grow. Get along in life, and surely, things will start to become easier for you. And my wish is that you live for today, enjoy every moment, and capture the best that life has to offer you.

And to quote Maya Angelou—

"My mission in life is not merely to survive, but to thrive; and to do so with some passion, some compassion, some humor, and some style."

Best wishes,

Petra

1

Comatose

It was early December of 1970, one of the coldest winters Bavaria had seen in years. Temperatures dropped down to twenty degrees below zero. We lived just outside of Munich, Germany, in my hometown of "Markt Schwaben," which was entirely covered by a blanket of shimmering snow.

The plows could barely keep up with the heavy downfall, which greatly amused us children who were always ready for the next adventure. For us, deep layers of fresh fallen snow created the most magical winter wonderland Bavaria had ever seen—or at least that we had ever seen, and our days were filled with play and laughter. I remember this time fondly; I was just nine years old, full of energy, dreamy-eyed and bursting with youthful innocence, anticipation and joy.

It was my favorite time of the year. I could barely contain myself as I waited for all of the celebrations, keeping myself busy with snowball fights and building snowmen alongside my friends. The Christmas season was lavished with merriment and mystery.

The celebrations began with the four "Tapping Nights," "Klöpfelnächte," along with the nights before "Nicolas' Day" on the sixth of December. And, in only three days' time, it would be Krampus Day, dedicated to one of the companions of Saint Nicholas in some parts of Europe. These traditions ran deep, creating eagerness and delight.

In Austro-Bavarian folklore, Krampus is a horned, human-like figure, who, during the Christmas season, punishes misbehaving children. This year, I was quite sure that I had been a good girl and would not be getting any of his attention.

I was equally confident that Saint Nicholas *would* be visiting. I'd been good and would be receiving some hefty gifts for my outstanding behavior. To end with Saint Nicolas was the most rewarding and light-hearted of the ceremonies, often causing us to nag our parents, begging them to get us the presents sooner than was even possible.

I couldn't wait to be old enough to go with my big brother and his friends to the village, where we'd find men disguised in Krampus costumes, where children run from them as they are being chased. It was a longstanding tradition; folklore I wanted to take part in.

Even though I had been suffering with a cough this season, and wasn't feeling very well, I wasn't going to miss the festivities of the day. I pretended I was quite well, even though my chest was hurting and the occasional wheezes let loose.

On this particular day, my brother had lost his gloves on the way home from school and my mother was in a hurry to drive him to town. She had to buy a new pair before it got dark and the roads too slippery. When my mother returned, I begged her to let me stay at my aunt's house for the night.

I just loved any and all opportunities to spend time with

Maggie and her new, and handsome, husband, Jürgen. I remember Mother not being very happy about me staying, due to my persistent coughing. But I didn't give in, repeatedly urging her to let me go stay overnight, and finally got my way.

Their home was a bright and colorful place filled with a medley of refurbished antique as well as modern furniture. Their guest bed hadn't been delivered yet, so I had to sleep on the white, leather couch in the living room. I wasn't able to get warm, and the cold shivers running down my spine kept me awake. My hacking cough didn't let up all night and only got worse.

They say that the lungs are one of the last organs to mature in the womb. When I was two years old, I had had several episodes of whooping cough and colds affecting my respiratory system permanently. My lungs were already quite weak. I had been, after all, a premature baby, born too early, weighing maybe five pounds.

The next day, Maggie took me to our family doctor. Dr. Holley had his office on Bahnhofstrasse and had known me since I was young. He was aware of my whooping cough history and, so, was quite upset when he heard my cawing and barking noises. With sternness, he ordered my aunt to take me out of the freezing cold and back home immediately. That was no place for a girl in my condition during the thick of winter.

I faintly remember being in his office. My violent attack was so severe that I regurgitated a golf ball-sized lump of mucus, solid and scary green in color. He prescribed some medicine called "Lebertran," cod liver oil that tasted so putrid that it made me gag with that horrid fishy taste. He claimed it was sure to relieve my symptoms. "You will feel better by evening," he stated confidently. I wasn't quite so sure.

Bundled up in my favorite cozy blanket, my mother, in

her sweetest voice, whispered she loved me, kissed me on the forehead and gave me the Lebertran. In her gentle way, she lovingly tucked me in on the living room couch, and left with my brother to do some necessary errands. She assured me they would be back as soon as possible, since the center of our little town, Markt Schwaben, was only five minutes away from our house. She was in a hurry and had to go.

It was only three o'clock in the afternoon and already getting quite dark, with huge snowflakes falling outside and getting heavier by the minute. Extremely exhausted from coughing all day, I lay on the couch feeling content enough just to rest. I enjoyed the warmth of the house as I watched the fluffy snowflakes dance on the wind outside, eventually falling onto the moonlit balcony in front of me.

I slowly drifted away into sound sleep. Out of the blue, I remember waking up with such a terror, my body jumping in uncontrolled panic. I found myself desperately gasping for air. I sounded like a barking seal at the circus, or maybe something worse, as I flailed around this way and that, just trying to get comfortable. My cough seemed to become worse, and my sleep was restless.

In between coughs, I was making a strange crow-like noise. It reminded me of a wheezing sound I heard from my friend who I had watched have an asthma attack, scaring me to death. My chest below my rib cage sank inward with each breath I tried to take. I knew something wasn't right when I touched my ribs and felt how displaced they seemed. Gradually, as I lay on the couch, I started to withdraw from my body, drifting away from consciousness.

Barely, conscious, my body shifted and jolted in spasms again.

Out of dazed desperation, mustering all my strength I stood up, raising my arms above my head, frantic to open up my air passages so I could breathe. Each time I attempted to breathe inward, my airways tightened even more. I finally gave in.

Suddenly, everything turned quiet as the snowflakes falling.

A beautiful humming began to fill my ears—very peaceful and quiet; fear and terror left me. I fell to the floor and rolled under the glass coffee table. Eventually, how much time had passed, I don't know, but the chest pain stopped, and I began drifting toward a bright light—not of this world. I slipped out of consciousness, withdrawing from my body.

More time passed… and I heard my mother's voice calling my name from a distance, "Petra!" She pulled me from under the table, and I was aware of being in the living room and, once again, I felt the unbearable tightness in my chest as I gulped for oxygen.

She screamed at my brother, Wolfgang, to keep me upright, commanding him to keep me moving, and not allow me to lay down where I might become unconscious again. My mother told him to help me walk around the house a bit. In my delirium, I must have climbed the stairs for some reason, and almost fell down the stairs when my brother took his attention off of me for one minute. My poor brother! Immediately, I heard my mother call for my dad to drive us to the nearest hospital in Steinhoering, a town fifteen kilometers from us.

No air to breathe.

At fourteen years old, my mother had been hospitalized in this old place, Kinderkrankenhaus, also known as Children's Hospital. She had contracted the polio virus and was paralyzed for two years. The worst part, besides the pain, my mother had told me, was the disturbing emotional ache of being locked away there. Unable to hug her own mother or sister, except through a dingy, institutional window, made her feel like a prisoner—afraid and alone.

Later, I would learn more about this hospital—one with its roots in dreadful Nazi evil.

It was in 1935, when a most feared Nazi, Himmler, created a secret Nazi program called "Lebensborn" that took place in this hospital. Deemed racially pure, young women were taken from their families and isolated in those cavernous walls to *meet* SS officers, to become pregnant, so that they could bring more "racially pure" into the world. Nazi authorities believed that these Lebensborn children would be purebred Aryans, perfect future SS-leaders (given to the SS to train from birth); these children would become the new nobility that would dominate the world. At least, that was the plan.

I knew none of that horror at nine years old. I have tried to imagine what it must have been like for those poor women. I cannot. But I do know that for my mother, Steinhoering was always a dark time, a dark place, even though she was sent there after World War II.

For me, now, in this time and place, I had been admitted into a room, and placed in-between the hospital's sterile sheets to be cared for. I had no fear or disturbed or scared feelings, instead I felt light and peaceful, in a state of altered consciousness.

Personally, I can't say I recall much about the space itself, since I was so sick when I blacked out. I don't recollect the car ride or being carried into the hospital room either. However, I do remember hearing that same soothing, humming sound in my head; it faintly reminded me of a gentle breeze on a warm summer's day, nature's music, I would experience as I would run through the fields and play.

My awareness was not of being in my body, rather I

floated upward. Still light and peaceful, I came to some kind of altered consciousness at Steinhoering. Not in my body, I started to float, hovering on the hospital ceiling, not in my bed at all, which felt strange. I suppose words are hard to come by to describe it completely.

During this experience, I witnessed my body from a distance, observing its every move, as *my Spirit,* without notice, moved along the walls of the old hospital.

How was this possible?

"What is happening to me?" I faintly recall asking.

I continued to watch from above, high on the ceiling. My father stood down there next to me, leaning against my motionless body, holding my hand close to his heart, his tears falling on my lifeless face. I could feel his sadness and aching heart. I knew he didn't think I was going to make it.

Maybe this was a part of the Steinhöring legacy, the giving and taking of innocent lives. Yet, I wasn't worried. I wasn't "Petra" in her hospital bed; I was hovering above them, an unaffected observer.

My mother, in her red fox coat, sat in the dank corridor. She was on a bench, reading something, black pen in hand, her face pale. She appeared numb with dismay, a horror no mother wants to endure. Somehow, in my out-of-body state, I knew she was signing a document to consent to a dangerous surgery.

I remember thinking… *Poor Mummy, watching me on the edge of death in the same dreadful place she had to remain while ill in her childhood.*

Momentarily, I felt as if I was slipping into her body, mind and spirit—I could intensely feel her sorrow and despair. Her potent emotions came over me in a vibration of dread and sadness.

I then *traveled* into an operating room, where two doctors in their light green, baggy scrubs, and several nurses, vigorously scrubbed and washed their hands. I had a bird's-eye view. Wherever my attention focused, there I was. I could see clearly. I felt what everyone was feeling, as if I was able to slip inside their bodies and read their minds. Experiencing their every emotion, every shift, didn't seem odd or scary; I felt calm and neutral, unemotional, as I moved through the corridors processing the dynamics of life below.

I remember trying to get their attention, thinking I had called out to my father, "Pappi, Pappi—I'm up here!"

Then I said something like, "Don't cry—I'm alright, you don't have to worry about me." I continued, "I'm up here, I'm up here-look up, I am on the ceiling! I am fine!"

But my Pappi only continued to stare at my lifeless body and couldn't hear me calling out.

What is happening to my spirit? Why is my body lying there, yet I am on the ceiling looking down at my body with such a sense of calm?

I recall feeling this inner knowing that everything was perfect on those cream-white walls, when, suddenly, my spirit shot through a tunnel much like a vortex of clouds, illuminated by a bright white light.

I was flying like a bird, up, up through the sky. I felt this strange energy project me through the light with such enormous speed. It was as if I was enveloped by this brilliant ray inside and out. The sun was hugely magnified in a way I'd never seen before. I felt safe. It was otherworldly and intoxicating to my spirit.

I eventually found myself in an edifice that appeared like a gigantic library with a multitude of floors and books reaching into the vast sky. The joy, love and peace prevailed inside me. Feeling free and incredibly warm from the inside out, the humming sound reverberated throughout this tall library.

It all seemed strangely familiar.

In an instant, I stood next to seemingly wise old men. They reminded me of the ancient Babylonians, dressed in simple cloaks of white and brown, or the Franciscan monks in Bavaria.

One had a hefty, old book in his hand. He read from this leather-bound book. As I stared at their handsome, weathered faces, I felt like I had known them before, and they knew me. I felt I recognized one man in particular. He had the most peaceful and kindhearted face.

There was a bluish light emanating from him, and his eyes were so blue and bright that I wanted to get lost inside of them. I recognized him as Jesus the instant I set eyes on him. I could not conceive of a more loving face and eyes. Jesus and the other elders were talking about my fate, united in their care and concern. We were ONE.

They weren't talking like humans talk. Their conversation-telepathic consciousness; I could somehow perceive their thoughts and deep messages of love.

Not a little girl anymore, I felt timeless and *one* with them. No identity, no borders-I felt truly at home in their affection, their compassion.

I asked them if I could stay. But, no.

They smiled at me the way a loving father smiles at a daughter.

And then it all went blank.

The following morning, I woke up in the Intensive Care Unit in a huge room with old, wooden floors. There was only one other young child, in a meager crib-with a strange mushroom-like growth on his mouth.

His abnormality frightened me. I closed my eyes so I

didn't have to see it. Now, awake, I felt the pain and suffering in this old hospital that reeked of rotting wood and iodine. It felt nothing like home. The peace I had just experienced-gone-and I didn't like it.

When I looked away from the child, I heard the *creak* of a heavy door, like that of a medieval castle. High-heel shoes echoed down the corridor-and then, the familiar voice of my mother.

I could barely make out what she said: "Herzilein, Herzilein, you made it; I could not live without you!"

She kissed my face, and stroked my hair. My aunt held my hand; I tried to speak, but I couldn't utter a sound or open my eyes. I heard my mother relay to my aunt that I had suffered a serious attack of the croup, but the doctors didn't have to do surgery. Instead, they spent a great deal of time suctioning off a half liter of mucus. To be safe, the attendees had wanted to keep me for a few weeks.

What happened? Why was I back and how long had I been gone? I had no idea.

My limbs, my entire body was exhausted. Then it happened again.

The peace returned, as if God himself was holding me in his arms. It seemed I floated in a warm liquid, and the soothing, humming sound, like Tibetan chant, was all around. I was terribly sick, my mother still worried, but my trance-like state seemed to envelop me in such a deep bliss that I have very little memory of what went on around me for the rest of my recovery.

I often reflect that it must have been really difficult for my mother to visit me in that place, with the many painful memories she must have endured, even though she didn't always show it or talk about it. Even so, I knew.

And how hard it must have been for my big brother seemed pretty clear to me, too. After all, he had to watch me suffocating and delirious, when he was just over ten-and-one-half years old, a young boy unable to do anything more to help.

When I returned from the hospital, my brother told me he had been so scared; he was sure he had almost lost me down the marble stairs, with me so wobbly and unpredictable in my feverish state. I remember the very concerned look he had in his eyes when he told me he thought I was going to die in that old hospital building; he was so glad to have me back. I will always remember his caring words.

There is nothing he could have done differently. Yet, to this day, I wonder and, I hope, that he does not carry any guilt or shame about any of it in his heart.

And yes, life went on as usual. One morning at breakfast, not long after I returned home from the hospital, I told my mother about the light and about Jesus, when she gently put her index finger on my lips and said, "Shhhhhh… we will never talk about this; little girls don't talk to Jesus, and if you do they will put you away in an insane asylum."

Never to be spoken of again to my mother, I knew I was lucky to be alive, that was for certain. Decades later, as I researched the suspect history of Steinhöring, I often wondered if there was a reason that both me and my mother had experienced such severe illness in that place. And, we both survived.

Had there been a purpose to this coincidence?

The Nazi SS called the space "Lebensborn." Difficult to translate, I find that it means something like "fountain" or "source" of life, which is pretty ironic considering how the Nazi's operated there—how its purpose had been to give birth to people who might go on to control and exterminate others. Their plan, fortunately, didn't work.

I learned Himmler tried desperately to use his control of the Nazi security services to get large numbers of children in his army. This "stock" was considered genetically superior, mostly from the occupied countries. Increasing births within the Reich was proving difficult, so Himmler decided to 'harvest' genetically valuable 'material' from others. (I always found this so sick and disturbing.) That meant non-Reich women were sent there without their consent. How sad it must have been to be a Polish mother, removed from your family, only to serve as a baby factory.

Decades after my hospitalization, when I was on my own and out of the country, I went on to work with Jewish clients, who would help open my eyes to what had happened in Nazi-controlled Europe. I had no idea about the hospital nor most of what happened in Bavaria and Germany. Mostly, I wasn't told a thing. When I found out about the Nazi's later in life, I wondered—was shocked really—about why nobody talked about the hospital, its roots, nor much about Nazi Bavaria at all.

I learned that after the American Army liberated Germany in 1945, there were over 300 orphaned children housed in Steinhöring. The building remained a Children's hospital until 1971. It is amazing to me that I was hospitalized there during the last year of its existence.

Was I part of its transitioning? I surely hope so.

The heavenly encounter I experienced, and having my life saved, seemed only to confirm my suspicion that there was a reason for being there in its waning days before it no longer served as a hospital, especially in the way the Nazi's intended.

Before the war, Steinhöring was a former Caritas Catholic Charity children's home. The Nazis took all church charities and controlled charitable giving. The general physician at

Steinhoering, Dr. Ebner, was the Lebensborn physician. He became the medical director for the entire Lebensborn program and SS Oberführer.

I also learned of his mass killings of handicapped children, and was devastated. I felt this for all the children, but I can't help but think of the rare instance of talking about the war, when my mother would tell that she would have been killed if she had had polio earlier than she did, while the war was still happening. Now it makes sense. She wouldn't have been "genetically" superior; she was ill and couldn't walk. There was no room for the sick or weak in Steinhoering during the war. It was a shocking revelation.

No wonder my dear mother was so horrified to be locked away in Steinhöring. Clearly, she knew more than she ever told me about the place. The significance of her being stuffed away there to "recover" for several years is not lost on me. Maybe my alternate experience I tried to share with her helped release some of that burden she felt. I don't know; I will never know.

Today, the building is an "In-Home Care Facility" for one thousand handicapped people, with a staff of 400 employees. When I hear that Steinhöring is used to house and assist so many needy people, it makes me feel as if maybe, just maybe, it can free itself from its confusing and sometimes morbid past.

And, maybe, I wasn't the only one who got free from the walls of the hospital on its last waltz.

Something unexplainable had shifted inside of me. It was good. I was changed. I couldn't fully comprehend why I felt different, and strangely detached from my family, and my life as it was before. I suppose it was odd that I, as a nine-year-old girl, wished I could go back to the place of peace and love forever—*it* was home.

2

Geschichte

Growing up in Bavaria

There was no denying it, here I was, recovering back at my home in "Markt Schwaben," the only home I had ever known. *Why did I feel so removed from it all? Hadn't I always loved this place? Why did it feel strangely foreign to me now?*

Our life here was filled with family trips to Munich, including wonderful old buildings and museums to explore. And the famous Oktoberfest celebration with cavernous beer halls, including the Hofbräuhaus, founded in 1589—it was a festivity that was a huge part of my family's life, for as long as I can remember. *Yes, I loved it—didn't my childhood memories remind me of that fact?*

I wish you could see and experience Bavaria like I did as a child: In the walkable "Old Town," in the very heart of Munich, a most impressive building rises from the central square of Marienplatz—one of the world's most famous clocks, the fabulous Gothic Rathaus or town hall, with its memorable glockenspiel show. (A glockenspiel: Glocken: *bells* and Spiel: *set* is a percussion instrument composed of a set of tunes, keys arranged in the fashion of the keyboard of a piano. In this way, it is similar to the xylophone.)

The Munich Glockenspiel, with its variety of entertaining dancing figurines, included my childhood favorite, a Bavarian knight battling a French jouster—and of course, the Bavarian Knight always wins.

I was fascinated with this building, and the clock which consists of forty-three bells and thirty-two life-sized figures. Different tunes are played in the clock's forty-three bells. Every day, when I was a child and still today, the Marienplatz square is crammed with tourists and locals with their chins aimed skyward, watching one of the city's most loved oddities, the Munich Glockenspiel, or carillon. This chiming clock was added to the tower of the Neues Rathaus, or New Town Hall, the year the building was completed in 1907.

During spring and summer, three times each day, with bells chiming, actors re-enact two stories from the 16th Century—much to the amusement of mass crowds of tourists and locals. The Munich Glockenspiel recounts a royal wedding, jousting tournament and ritualistic dance—all events which have etched a mark on Munich's popular folklore. The show lasts about fifteen minutes and concludes with the golden bird emerging from the top and chirping three times. How well I remember to the third or fourth floor of the Hugendubel bookstore across the square, with my brother, so that we could get a better view of the knights on their horses.

Real life history tells the tale of a wedding that was a huge imperial occasion. The Austrian archdukes arrived on a train of over 1500 horses, and more than 600 oxen were cooked for the revelers. On the day of the nuptials the bride was collected from the nearby town of Dachau by no less than 3500 mounted riders. The wedding party lasted two weeks. The groom, Wilhelm V, became famous as the man who founded the Hofbrauhaus, and rather infamous for leading massive witch hunts across his domain.

The crowd highlight was the Kröndlstechen, or crown joust, which took place right on Marienplatz square, and is now a big part of the Glockenspiel show. And in honor of the happy couple, there is a joust with life-sized knights on horseback, representing Bavaria in hues of white and blue, and the Lothringen area in its reds and whites. As a child, I delighted in seeing the Bavarian knight win every single time. When I was 13-16 years old, I often walked by the Rathaus and many of the galleries and fancy boutiques, to watch and listen to the Glockenspiel at Marienplatz.

On the lower level of the Rathaus, you can see the red-coated city's coopers (barrel makers) do a ritualistic jig known as the Schäfflertanz. According to myth, 1517 was a year of plague in Munich. The dance is popularly thought to have begun in the devastating plague year, but it actually dates back further. Legend says the coopers started the dance to give Munich's residents the all-clear that the plague was done and dusted. Bavarian Duke Wilhelm IV ordered that the dance be re-enacted every seven years, to keep the deadly disease in the collective memory.

The next Schäfflertanz is scheduled for February, 2019, and I might have to fly to Munich just for that! You can see a couple of cooper statues in more detail at the entrance to Schäffler Strasse, west of the Marienhof Park at the back of the Neues Rathaus.

München (as written in German), is the capital and largest city in the German state of Bavaria, sitting on the banks of River Isar north of the Bavarian Alps. The Munich (as written in English) metropolitan area is home to 5.8 million people. A major hub, my family and I would frequently visit this thriving arts center with its advanced technologies, finance, publishing, culture, innovation, education, business and tourism. The name of the city stems from the Old/Middle High German term, "Munichen," meaning "by the monks" of the Benedictine; this was the order who ran a monastery at the place that was later to become "Old Town" in Munich.

As a child, I was also blessed to experience Bavaria's high plateaus and smaller mountains, where my family took frequent family outings. Outside the city, in the spectacular Alps, once, when I was just eight years old, my grandfather took my brother and me hiking. We were picture-perfect in our lederhosen, little hiking shoes and backpacks.

It was hard work for a little girl to hike the steep trails of Wendelstein, and of course then, I didn't appreciate the panoramic views people travel the world to see. I recall one particular hike as a child; I was about one-third my way up the mountain when my legs got wobbly and my breath shallow—I got so tired, and began to make every excuse I could to get out of going any further. As we know my lungs weren't the strongest.

Grandfather enticed me by promising that he had hid some of the most delicious drinks and treats inside his backpack, and that an angel would be waiting for us at the top of the mountain. He painted such a detailed picture of what the angel looked like and how good the food tasted, that his words cajoled me into keep putting one little foot in front of the other: I could almost see the little angel he had described dancing atop the food at the top of the mountain. The wonder of dining with angels made every strained step seem possible. When we arrived at the top of the mountain, we found a cross and a bench and I asked, "Grandpa, where is the angel?"

"The angel had to talk to God and will be back later," he replied, getting out of his angel's promise. Like always with Grandpa, once again, we had fallen for his sometimes-outlandish stories and tricks.

It's not like I didn't like hiking or walking, no—I did join the Mountain Club in our town when I was eleven, and went climbing and skiing almost every weekend. In fact, I joined the ski race team of the local club and even had my own trainer for a while. Outdoors was a huge part of the culture during my growing up years. I learned to appreciate the beauty of nature, and took part in festive days filled with giant bonfires and Bavarian folk dances—and I adored the fun and friendly people. I have many magical memories of the people and places I was allowed to visit and experience in my childhood.

One winter, my family went skiing at an Italian Glacier, known for its dangerous black ice. My father had all of us kids, including our neighbor, Arne, and my girlfriend, Petra, get in the trunk of his black Mercedes—to ensure the car was heavy enough to make it up the mountain. Fortunately, we made it safely!

Growing up was a different world—I loved all the rituals, customs and beauty of Bavaria, with its natural splendor, which for a child can be an outdoor wonderland.

Picture me in the North Country: the basalt knolls and high plateaus of Bavaria. And in the northwest, the wooded sandstone hills of the Spessart. To the southeast, the landscape varies from the stratified land formations of Swabia Franconia, to shell limestone and red marl of the hill country of the Franconian Rednitz Basin, and the Limestone Mountains of the Franconian Jura along the Danube River, which divides Bavaria north and south.

On the eastern edge of Bavaria, are the Bavarian and Bohemian forests, and in the north, is the Franconian Forest. South of the Danube is a plateau containing the capital, Munich, and beyond it are the Bavarian Alps. In the wooded peaks of the Bavarian Alps you find beautiful steep ridges and high plateaus in the west. They reach their highest point at Zugspitze, at 9,718 feet; the highest point in Germany. Bavaria has a harsher climate than most of middle Europe, hence my childhood winter wonderland.

I lived near the Bohemian Forest. Before Chernobyl, and the radiation fallout it caused, Grandfather would take us mushroom hunting in the Ebersberger Forest. We'd get up to leave by 5:00 a.m. and come home around 9:00 a.m., just in time for breakfast with the family. We'd walk in with our basketful of fresh mushrooms, *and voilà*, my mother would cook up our baskets full of tasty mushrooms, preparing and serving them in a parsley cream sauce with Bavarian dumplings. This was my most favorite tradition with the family. Both of my mother's sisters, my cousins Chrissi and Alexandra, and my grandfather were invited on these occasions.

Mushroom hunting was serious business, and the cosmos around me charming and magical—and at other times quite strange. My grandfather surprised me with how "intense his love of the mushroom" was the day he spotted a Steinpilz, or King Bolete, mushroom on the side of the forest. Before he could pick and be off with it, a man on a bicycle jumped on him, wrestling him for that much sought after type of mushroom—a fungus of all fungus! Granted, Steinpilze are a rare find, but still, when I was just six years old, it was unusual, and a little frightening, to see this battle fought out between the man who had leaped from his bicycle and my grandpa.

Mushrooms grew abundantly in the woods. I suppose many would say that the King Bolete is truly the "King of Mushrooms" that grows in that region of Bavaria and must have been worth fighting for.

It was rarely dull when I was with my Opa Egal. He was my mother's father. Another day, my heart raced like a hummingbird (maybe not quite 1200 beats per minute, but close) when we were chased out of the forest by a wild boar with huge tusks. It seemed kind of strange to me, when my Opa (grandpa) climbed up to the top of a tree, while yelling: "Kids! Run for your lives!" Since it turned out okay, it was funny, but he did make me and my brother promise that we would not tell our parents.

"We are the sum total of our experiences. Those experiences—are they positive or negative—make us the person we are, at any given point in our lives. And, like a flowing river, those same experiences, and those yet to come, continue to influence and reshape the person we are, and the person we become. None of us are the same as we were yesterday, nor will be tomorrow."

—B.J. Neblett, American author

Historically, the people in Bavaria, in the north are descendants of the Franks, and in the southeast, they are residents of old Bavarian stock, and in the southwest they are people of Bavarian Swabian descent. The majority of Bavaria's inhabitants still live in small towns. Only about one-fifth live in cities of 100,000 or more.

The Sudetenland is the German name (used in English in

the first half of the 20th-Century) to refer to those northern, southwest, and western areas of Czechoslovakia, which were inhabited primarily by ethnic German speakers, specifically in the border districts of Bohemia, Moravia, and those parts of Silesia located within Czechoslovakia. The name originated from the Sudetes Mountains which run along the northern Czech border, as far as Silesia and contemporary Poland—extending to areas well beyond.

The word Sudetenland did not come into existence until the early 20th-Century, and did not come to prominence until after the First World War, when the German-dominated Austria-Hungary was dismembered and the Sudeten Germans found themselves living in the new country of Czechoslovakia.

The *Sudeten crisis* of 1938 was provoked by the demands of Nazi Germany that the Sudetenland be annexed to Germany, which in fact took place after the later infamous "Munich Agreement" which reconstituted Czechoslovakia after the Second World War; the Sudeten Germans were largely expelled, and the region today is inhabited primarily by Czech speakers

A large percentage of the Bavarian population was composed of these refugees and their kin at the beginning of the 21st-Century. In the 1960s, the industrial areas received large numbers of migrant workers from southern Europe, from countries like Hungary and Poland.

A shift in religious affiliation took place after the Second World War, with a heavy influx of Protestants flooding in. At the beginning of the 21st-Century, most Bavarians were Roman Catholics, and the Evangelical Lutherans were the second largest religious group.

The government worked hard to attract industries; Bavaria

showing a higher rate of industrial growth than the rest of Germany. As a result, Munich is now, as I write this book, the largest industrial center in Bavaria and is the focus of high technology industries and transportation.

The Allgäuer Alps, near the Austrian border, where I used to go skiing with my family, and the Mountain Club, are very popular tourist destinations still to this day. Incredible resorts, spas, and healing springs attract young and old alike.

One of Bavaria's most popular tourist spots is the Neuschwanstein Castle, the famous "fairy castle" built for King Ludwig II of Bavaria. The region is also known for its many charming villages, which feature generously adorned churches, public buildings, and old homes. If you go further north, you get another scenic area known as Franconian Switzerland, containing caves and the ruins of medieval castles.

Folk art and culture remain important in Bavaria, and traditional crafts are still practiced to this day. Popular festivals happen throughout the year. Richard Wagner was a 19th-Century German composer, theatre director, polemicist, and conductor who is primarily known for his operas (or, as some of his later works were later known, "music dramas").

Unlike most opera composers, Wagner wrote both the libretto and the music for each of his stage works. Initially establishing his reputation as a composer of works in the romantic vein of Weber and Meyerbeer, Wagner revolutionized opera through his concept of the *Gesamtkunstwerk*— "total work of art"— by which he sought to synthesize the poetic, visual, musical and dramatic arts, with music subsidiary to drama. He described this vision in a series of essays published between 1849 and 1852. Wagner realized these ideas most fully in the first half of the four-opera cycle *Der Ring des Nibelungen* (*The Ring of the Nibelung*).

His compositions, particularly those of his later period, are notable for their complex textures, rich harmonies and orchestration, and the elaborate use of leitmotifs—musical phrases associated with individual characters, places, ideas or plot elements. Wagner had his own opera house built, the "Bayreuth Festspielhaus," which embodied many novel design features. "The Ring" and "Parsifal" were premiered in Bayreuth, and his most important stage works continue to be performed in an annual festival run by his descendants. Until his final years, Wagner's life was characterized by political exile, turbulent love affairs, poverty and repeated flight from his creditors. His controversial writings on music, drama and politics have attracted extensive comment since the late 20th-Century, especially where they express anti-Semitic sentiments which I didn't really understand as a young child, and which contributed to the population's ideologies. The effect of his ideas can be traced in many of the arts throughout the 20th century; his influence spread beyond composition into conducting, philosophy, literature, the visual arts and theatre.

Bavaria is well-known for theatres in all the larger cities, as well as orchestras, opera companies, museums, and art galleries. I so loved all of these as a child. I remember searching for answers to my many questions in the messages and themes of the operas and theatre plays by Wolfgang von Goethe and many others.

My rich Bavarian history, with its talented craftsman, and diverse arts and culture, fills me with respect and wonder of my homeland. I realize today that most people on earth are searching for their roots. We all seem to have an innate hunger to find out where we came from—it has an enormous influence on all aspects of our life, and our purpose and place in the world. The older I get, the more fascinated I am with my heritage. I suppose I did not fully appreciate how Bavaria influenced me until recently.

"The more you know of your history the more liberated you are."

—Maya Angelou, American author and poet, memoirist, and civil rights activist. (1928–2014)

The Celts were the first known inhabitants in the area of what is today called Bavaria. When the Romans conquered the region in the beginning of the Common Era, they divided the southern part into Raetia and Noricum, building forts along the north to keep out the Teuton armies. Flourishing Roman colonies arose in the south. The Romans were overcome in the 5th-Century, due to repeated Germanic attacks. The lands were eventually settled by Germanic tribes from the east and north who mixed with the remaining Celts and Romans.

The tribe that gave the territory its name was the Baiovarii (Bavarians), which settled in the south between 488 and 520 C.E (Common Era or A.D.). In the 7th and 8th-Centuries Bavaria was Christianized by Irish and Scottish monks. In 788, Charlemagne incorporated Bavaria into the Carolingian empire for a short time.

Bavaria became a part of the Holy Roman Empire in the 10th-Century. During that period Bavaria was constantly ravaged, and all but depopulated by the Hungarians. At the Battle of Pressburg, now Bratislava, Slovakia, on July 4, 907, the Hungarians inflicted a disastrous defeat on the Bavarians, but Hungarian ambitions in Bavaria were checked permanently in 955 by Otto I at the Battle of Lechfeld, just south of Augsburg. That defeat ushered in an era of cooperation between Bavaria and Hungary, culminating in 996 with the marriage of the Bavarian princess Gisela, and the Hungarian prince who would be crowned king as Stephen I. In 1180 the Holy Roman emperor Frederick I Barbarossa gave Bavaria to the Count Palatine Otto of Wittelsbach. That marked the start of the Wittelsbach Dynasty, which was to rule Bavaria until 1918.

Otto was succeeded in 1183 by his son Louis I, who was the real founder of the Bavarian principality. He recklessly used every means to extend his power. He founded the cities (Landshut, Straubing, Landau, and Iser), and also won the Palatinate, a region in Southwestern Germany covering an area of 2105 square miles, of the Rhine (1214). His son Otto II increased the area of his lands mainly by purchases. These efforts and succeeding duke's attempts to consolidate their power were fairly successful, but were soon corrupted by partitions that, for 250 years, made the political history of Bavaria little more than a chronicle of territorial divisions, family feuds, and petty squabbles. By the late 14th-Century the family's various branches had divided Bavaria into three separate duchies, which had the effect of temporarily eclipsing the power of the dukes. The government of the country and the control of its finances passed mainly into the hands of an assembly called the "Landtag," or "Landschaft," which had existed since the beginning of the 14th-Century. The towns, assuming certain independence, became strong and wealthy as trade increased, and the citizens of Munich were often formidable antagonists to the dukes.

Throughout the 18th-Century, Bavaria was ravaged by the wars of the Spanish Succession and the Austrian Succession. In 1777 the Bavarian succession passed to the elector Charles

Theodore of the Palatinate. Bavaria and the Palatinate were reunited. In the War of the Bavarian Succession, Frederick II (the Great) of Prussia successfully prevented Austria from incorporating a large part of Bavaria to which it had laid claim.

In 1813, shortly before the Battle of Leipzig, Bavaria rejected Napoleon, and in 1815 it joined the Germanic Confederation against him. It retained much of its territory and political gains, making it the third largest German state, after Austria and Prussia.

Under the German constitution of 1871, Bavaria received a larger measure of independence than any of the other constituent states of the German Empire. Meanwhile, Louis II had begun showing signs of mental instability, and his extravagant building projects like Neuschwanstein Castle had drained the Bavarian treasury. In 1886 he was declared insane, and an uncle, Luitpold, became regent that same year. Luitpold died in 1912, and his son Louis III became king.

At the end of World War I, an independent socialist, Kurt Eisner, deposed the Wittelsbach dynasty on the night of November 7–8, 1918, and proclaimed Bavaria a republic. King Louis III fled, thus ending the rule of one of the oldest European dynasties. Eisner was assassinated in February 1919, and, in the subsequent chaos, revolutionary councils carried out a "Red Terror" and formed a short-lived soviet republic that ended in May, 1919, when German army units and citizen defense corps recaptured Munich and instituted a similarly ruthless "White Terror" against the communists.

The Bavarian political scene remained unsettled, however, and in 1920 and 1921 there were unsuccessful right-wing coups. The National Socialist movement of Adolf Hitler got its start in Munich, and in 1923 Hitler and General Erich Ludendorff attempted their unsuccessful *putsch,* an attempt to overthrow the government, in that city. The Beer Hall Putsch, also known as the Munich Putsch, and, in German, as the Hitler putsch or Hitler-Ludendorff-Putsch, was a failed coup attempt by the Nazi Party leader Adolf Hitler—along with Generalquartiermeister, Erich Ludendorff and other Kampfbundleaders—in an effort to seize power in Munich, Bavaria, during November, 1923. About two thousand men marched to the center of Munich, where they confronted the police, which resulted in the death of sixteen Nazis and four policemen. Hitler himself was wounded.

After two days, Hitler was arrested and charged with treason. From Hitler's perspective, there were three positive benefits from this attempt to seize power unlawfully. First, the putsch brought Hitler to the attention of the German nation, and generated front page headlines in newspapers around the world. His arrest followed by a 24-day trial, which was widely publicized and gave Hitler a platform to publicize his nationalist sentiment to the nation. Hitler was found guilty of treason and sentenced to five years in Landsberg Prison. The second benefit to Hitler was that he used his time in prison to produce Mein Kampf, which was dictated to his fellow prisoner, Rudolf Hess. On December 20, 1924, having served only nine months, Hitler was released. The final benefit that accrued to Hitler was the insight that the path to power was through legitimate means rather than revolution or force. Accordingly, the most significant outcome of the putsch was a decision by Hitler to change NSDAP (NAZI Party) tactics, which would demand an increasing reliance on the development and furthering of Nazi propaganda.

When the Nazis came to power in 1933, they built their first concentration camp in March 1933, at Dachau, near Munich, forty minutes from my house in Markt Schwaben.

The fanatical Nürnberg rallies, held annually from 1933 to 1938, gained worldwide notoriety. Many Bavarians supported Nazism, but others, especially in the rural areas, opposed the regime's anti-Catholic policies.

After World War II, Bavaria became part of the American occupation zone. The Palatinate was detached and joined to the new Rheinland Pfalz state. Under the Basic Law (constitution) of West Germany of 1948, Bavaria became a state of the Federal Republic. The postwar era saw Bavaria dramatically transformed from a largely agricultural society to an urban industrial one, as Germany's Wirtschaftswunder "economic miracle" took hold. A distinct and robust cultural identification began to take place.

3

Großvater

Grandfather Egal

Everybody has a life story, and many characters that have parts they play in impacting and influencing our lives. It might be said that my grandfather Edgar Geisberger, a.k.a. "Egal," had two significant, yet conflicting sides to him. He was one of my heroes. Though not a perfect man, he influenced my childhood in countless ways, with vivid memories that still delightfully dance in my mind.

Talented as a poet, painter, musician, and storyteller—his business was the local taxi business in Markt Schwaben. He had three daughters. My beloved mother, Elfriede, was the eldest, with Irene in the middle, and Margot the youngest. All three of them were redheads, and inherited their fair complexion and freckles from their father.

Grandfather was, indeed, a character. The traditional Bavarian hat he wore was his signature look. Bavarian olive-green wool, with a large edelweiss hat brush—or sometimes a pheasant or ostrich feather on the side, the bigger the better since it was a sign of high standing. Stylish, he wore his hat in a slanted sort of way that made him look like a Jaeger or hunter—and made him appear even taller than he already was at 6 feet 5 inches. All this contributed to making him and his oversized feet comical. I had to crank my neck just right, to get a sneak peak of his face—and then, I just couldn't wait to sit on his lap to hear more stories when the time was right. One of my fondest memories as a little girl was to sit on top of his long legs in his lap, and together singing the children's song "Alle Meine Entchen." It stretched my imagination—especially since a young girl needed to be rescued.

He entertained his way through life when my brother and I were with him. His 1967 Mercedes had an *interesting* windup handle on the front of the hood. One day, as he struggled to get the car started, he was singing at the top of his voice, whistling in-between—which as kids, cracked us up, as he joked around. His play and fun brought such joy into our lives. We loved him.

As I grew older, I could see my grandfather's contradictions. Not just my grandfather, but for me, a girl growing up with men of that time who were influenced by societal rules, and who completely bought into the chauvinistic ideas of Bavarian men—but at the same time, were brilliant and so well liked by the public.

Grandfather tried so hard to hide his demons from me, but didn't always succeed. I learned very early on, while the Bavarian lifestyle was magical and festive at times, much of the socializing involved beer drinking and schnapps—Grandfather was no exception.

Most Bavarians would never admit to having a drinking

problem; it was an accepted, integral part of the culture to have a few beers every night. Sometimes, though, it got out-of-hand and created a lot of tension for me. Being so young, I witnessed boisterous, disrespectful behaviors that hurt my little innocent heart as a child.

On several disturbing occasions, I saw my grandfather aggressively push my grandmother, Anna, as he'd stumble through the kitchen. In one instance, when I was six years old, I was particularly upset when Egal slammed my grandmother into the cabinets in his drunken trajectory to get where he felt he had to go. It was as if she were invisible. I was confused and upset as I watched poor grandma walk into the nearby bedroom, sit on the bed and cry quietly.

I felt so totally helpless, but I still followed her in to console her by wrapping my arms around her, and soothing her with, "Es wird in Ordnung sein—*it will be okay*."

I was so angry at him! I remember wanting to take a cast iron pan and hit him over the head with it, just so he would learn a good lesson. I was only a child, but I knew better—you weren't supposed to treat people like that, especially a man treating his wife so uncaring and disrespectful. I remember my little self as I confronted him and demanded to know, "Why did you push grandmother and why are you always so angry with her?"

Of course, I was only six, and he never answered me. My inquiry was met with a blank stare, and total silence. I felt powerless and couldn't help this to change—and it bothered me to no end. It was then that I made the decision, to never let anything harmful happen to anyone ever again. Yes, I know. It was idealistic. But what else can you expect of a sensitive young girl? I could not stand to see my grandma suffer—or anyone for that matter. No, I decided right then—I was going to defend the weak, helpless and poor. It is amazing how this one particular incident with my grandparents influenced my whole life—my conviction to fight for people who could not defend themselves imbedded in me at that young age.

The subtle, and not so subtle, violence was hard enough. What hurt my youthful and innocent heart the most was how grandfather Egal kept grandmother on a financial shoestring. She wasn't allowed a budget, and had to constantly ask for money from him for anything she wanted and needed. This didn't feel right, and it made me very sad, and obviously affected my mother, too. As she raised me, she always made sure that I understood how to be independent and strong—and was taught not to depend on a disrespectful, dominating man. My mind was made up—never would I let a man treat me that way.

But in my grandparents' days, it was common practice for men to control most things in the family. Bavarian women (probably many women worldwide), in early 20th Century, were treated as second-class citizens until after the war. Life changed for them when their roles expanded out of necessity—because the men were gone, fighting the wars, in World War I and World War II. Traditional roles slowly began to evolve.

Sadly, much of her life, my grandmother seemed melancholy and heartbroken. I thought she didn't want to be among us anymore. I really felt that she would have been fine simply disappearing—she acted invisible most of the time, which said a lot about how she was treated and how she felt about herself. Oddly, her best escape happened at the age of sixty, when she developed Alzheimer's, dying from it when she was just fifty-four. Her anguish must have been too much to bear. Seeing her always downhearted was surely too much for me to see.

My grandmother's health declined rapidly, and she was taken to the mental hospital. During her last years, I knew that she was receiving electrical shock therapy, which was customary back in the 1960s and 70s. I now know that treatments for most any mental or emotional "disorder" were barbaric. Looking back, I can't help but wonder if some of the tactics didn't come from the Nazi years, something I'd think more about many years later.

I recall how sometimes, to my dismay, my drunk grandfather would joke about how he married this "wife" of his just because he thought she had money. He was going to get some of the action. He was sadly mistaken. She never got the money he presumed she would get. When grandmother's father died, her poor mother, a farmer's woman, was swindled out of the inheritance. With no inheritance coming, grandfather made sure we all knew he had made a serious mistake and should have married somebody else.

That's the way it went at my Grandpa Egal's house, and how he acted when he wasn't being a loving, adventurous grandfather with us children. I couldn't always make sense of his sporadic outbursts, nor his quick switch from a jolly old man to brutal husband, being verbally abusive and physically aggressive. I felt that it was deliberately cruel and unkind, the things he'd say to my grandma, and he made his snide remarks in front of everyone so they would be sure to hear it. It's as if he wanted to hurt her with the added insult of publicly shaming her.

I loved my grandpa very much, but I also felt deep compassion for Grandma. I was confused and bewildered by how he could be so humorous and loving, with a broad array of talents, and yet, so dark and destructive at times.

My grandfather's actions left me with conflicting fond

and frenetic memories. One such one was on Christmas Eve of 1971.

Grandmother was already gone, and Grandfather was living on the top floor of a two-story building. I remember getting so excited when he announced to the youngest of the family that he, along with my parents, and aunts and uncles, were getting ready to call in the angels. *Oh, the angels!* Grandpa often used the "angels" as a way to get us to do what he wanted us to do. And it always worked!

We were raised good Catholics. So especially at Christmastime, we were confident that the angels would descend from the heavens and bring gifts wrapped in Christmas paper and big ribbons—all that were on our wish lists. Grandfather asked us to patiently wait outside the living room until we heard the sound of the heavenly bells ring. When we heard the long-awaited chime, we'd know that our guests had come and gone. After that, we could jump back inside the room to discover the Christmas Eve gift that was left for us!

This was quite the test for me. In my heart I didn't know: was I supposed to first look for the angels *or* the presents? Interesting, when we enacted this ritual, I found myself most often wanting to see the angelic beings, rather than open a present that was waiting for me. That particular Christmas, in the midst of the excitement, as the living room door opened, my brother was the first to enter; I was right behind him.

What we saw was not at all what we expected. We saw Grandpa lying out like a slab under the Christmas tree. There he was, with the tree strewn across his body, all the bulbs broken all over him. What had happened? I was puzzled… and a little amused. The candle he held was still burning, with Grandpa holding onto it for dear life, trying not to laugh.

Almost Santa-like. How could I forget that big smile he

had on his red cheeked face in his all too familiar, intoxicated stupor. As kids, we laughed, but with Grandpa looking so ridiculous, and his stumbling fall that wrecked the tree, the adults were clearly irritated—Grandpa ruined Christmas for all, in his charade of looking and acting like a total fool.

Even so, somehow, he was still my hero, even though he drank excessively and he treated my grandmother so poorly. That aside, Grandpa was a revered man in our community, and even today people arrive in Markt Schwaben to celebrate Egal's life.

I have fond memories of him, remembering how he treated me, and knowing that he was so greatly respected and admired when he was alive. The people of Markt Schwaben knew grandpa to be a humorous man with great talent. There were talents that emerged out of his era, that live on—this is his legacy. Each year, there is a celebration around poetry, writing and stories being told, that my grandfather inspired in others—and these are shared with hundreds of people that travel to the town to honor the lives and the creative arts. Grandfather's painted renditions still hang in Bavarian living rooms today, at least that is what I am told. That brings a smile to my face. I loved his paintings—and my memories of special times with him!

He taught me great appreciation for the arts, encouraged me to draw and paint—and was *always* very kind to me. That's why it was hard to be mad at him for the harsh and hateful things he did to Grandma. Often times, after school, I would go with my brother to Grandpa's house to watch him paint. Sometimes, he'd take us swimming in the stream, or at a nearby pond. We had so many wonderful times together, outside in nature—and since he was like a little kid himself, he brought us happiness.

My grandfather was born in what is now Austria, and then adopted into a Bavarian household. His own mother could not afford to raise him and his sister. Maybe this is why he was obsessed with getting my grandmother's money. I'm not sure, but the men in my family had a consistent theme in their lives—drinking, money issues, and issues with women having control over money.

I was envious of my brother, because it was clear to me that Grandpa favored his first-born grandson, and the other first boys in the family. After my grandma gave him three redheaded girls, it seemed he never forgave her for refusing him a son. I remember us kids taking turns dancing on my grandpa's big monster feet in his kitchen. I'd wait and wait for my chance, but it didn't always come. When I thought I was next, it appeared that Grandpa had eyes only for my brother. Early in my life, I received the clear message that girls had less value in Bavarian society, and I should wait my turn, or rather—know my place.

But there was an obvious twist to being a girl in the Kufner family; Grandfather would call me "Peterle," which means Peter, but he'd never called me by my birth name, Petra. Having a more masculine nickname made such an impression on me that, for the longest time, I acted like I was a boy. I had lederhosen, shoes and socks fit for boys, wore my hair short, and played soccer, cowboys and Indians. And, God forbid, I be seen fraternizing with dolls. That was beneath me and clearly not up my alley.

Eventually, I figured out the difference between my brother and me, and boys in general, when I was ten, and in the onset of puberty. My body had been developing, but I really didn't make much of it until a soccer ball hit me square in the chest. I remember getting knocked out flat on that soccer field, everyone's eyes on the girl they thought was a boy. My friends hovered over me and said: "Oh, my God, she is a girl! We can't let her play anymore!"

Well, that was the end of playing soccer with the boys.

Although it's quite funny to me today, I remember being so devastated when that happened, like my whole ploy had been foiled. Everything ruined, my female identity displayed for all to see. I got on that orange mountain bike of mine and rode home as fast as I could. Throwing myself on the bed like a wet blanket, I wanted to die, never to be seen again. When my mother came in, I told her what happened and asked her to take me back; "Trade me in for a boy," I demanded. I recall her tight hug and saying to me, "But baby, you are beautiful and should be glad to be a girl."

What I wanted the most was to be treated like my brother, and receive all the favors my brother got from my grandfather. That wasn't going to happen, I know now. It was a male-dominated society and girls really weren't valued as highly as the boys. I often wondered what it would have been like had I been born twenty years later, when most of these silly societal rules and stereotypes had been abolished in the West. The separation caused me pain, knowing I wouldn't be treated as higher class citizens like the boys, but I didn't always let it stop me from athletic activities.

Even though people and life weren't perfect, I had a magical childhood with so many celebrations with a large extended family. When I was four, there was a steep hill by my grandfather's house where dozens of little kids played in the winter. We would walk up and ski down. With grandfather's help, I learned how to ski. I remember him clapping and cheering me on, and so proud of me. Skiing became my passion, and I later had my own instructor/trainer who helped me get into racing with the Mountain Club. Skiing has remained a lifelong pursuit; I still love it.

Grandfather, being the great storyteller, my brother Wolfgang and I grew up with *Grimm Fairy Tales*: like "Hansel and Gretel," "The Frog King," and "Iron Heinrich," and "The Fisherman and His Wife."

How I loved the fairy tales, and when Grandfather Egal recounted these tales, with all his high drama to us after dinner. The one that stood out the most for me was a Hans Christian Anderson Story, "The Little Match Girl." I was so obsessed with this story, that I read it over and over and over and drew many pictures of it. It's the story of a poor girl whose mother and grandmother died, and a wicked father who makes her sell matches for food. She has no coat and no shoes, and has to light the matches to stay warm, so her fingers won't freeze—all the while she looks into other people's windows while they feast on Christmas dinner.

Suddenly she sees a light, and her grandmother and mother appear to her from the sky and take her spirit to heaven. The next day the town's people find her dead in a corner, between two houses, frozen to death. Why did this story fascinate me so? Intuition at such a young cannot be denied. I had a premonition about my grandmother and mother leaving me to fight for myself and that there would be no one in my life to help me survive. I knew somehow that this was going to be my karma, my lot in life as if my story had been pre-written.

Even with my irrevocable, often unsettling awareness and emotion, much about my idyllic Bavarian childhood seemed so perfect—and then suddenly… in a blink of an eye… the story changed!

For this reason, and for some of the things that occurred

later in my family, I will forever love my grandfather—his jokes, his songs, poetry, and his incredible stories and storytelling. It was a sweeter, innocent time in my life. He was so good to us, creating magical moments, but when his mood shifted "in the blink of an eye," he could be a like Jekyl and Hyde.

Over the years, the fun-filled memories that were created by him, played a great role in my healing—which I had to resolve later in my life. Things like my not feeling good enough as the boys, and being keenly aware and sad about his inconsistent treatment of my grandmother. As a result, I became quite the fighter when it came to women's independence, truth, and being respected by men. Yes, he mistreated my grandmother, but I can still see the good in him, and take away the wonderful life lesson of standing always in my truth in relationship to men.

4

Mutter

My Mother, My Heart—
My Family, Myself

Deeply ingrained from Grandpa Egal, my observations and lessons about men would become more important than I knew—because my mother's life would be cut short. Her opportunity to influence me had a time limit, unknown to her, unknown to me. In my wildest imagining, I never suspected that I was running out of time with my mother; my life spent with her had tight restrictions; boundaries: With the mother I loved so dearly? No.

My mother was, in fact, more than a mother. She was my best friend and the one person in my life who saw only the best in me—and loved me unconditionally. I didn't realize it until I became a mother myself, how her love shaped my entire universe and how absolutely fortunate I was to be given so much affection and attention.

She was always very loving, kind and affectionate to both my brother and me. We had extraordinary respect for her kindness and wisdom. Sometimes, we felt a bit of fear when, on a bad day, she'd become irate about things that were happening in the world around us. And we watched her when drama involving relatives got her especially worked up.

My mom and her sister, Irene, grew up quite poor during World War II in Markt Schwaben. The youngest sister, Maggie, was born several years later and came as a surprise to the family.

Her father, my grandfather Egal, was a German soldier in the war in France. When I asked him if he ever had to kill anybody, he said that they used him as a barber and musician. This is where he learned to play the drums, later joining a band. Even though it later became a hobby, he also made some money doing it. He came up with the unique idea of painting pictures of people's homes, then he would frame them. Many people had, and still have, a painting my grandpa did of their home. He was quite successful with that creative venture.

I mentioned before, he had many talents, and he often recited poetry by Karl Valentin, whom he had met during the war and greatly admired. Karl Valentin and Liesl Karlstadt had a long-standing stage partnership, and appealed to all audiences. They worked together (except for a period in the late 1930s and 1940s following Karlstadt's nervous breakdown) until Valentin's death in 1948.

Karl Valentin and Liesl Karlstadt became some of the most famous comedians in German history, and were among the first performers whose voices were recorded. I watched Karl Valentin's comedy with my grandpa on TV often, and remember him and Liesl's comedic style to be quite similar to Charlie Chaplin, and his jokes thought provoking and political.

While in France, my grandpa did not have to fight in the war; his job was to cut hair and play music. My mother would tell me stories about the war, and how only the German farmers were thriving during those times. The German people had to barter for food, and since only the farmers had food they became very wealthy during the war. I don't know if the Nazis took the food from the farmers, but my guess is that is quite likely true.

My mother described the farmers' big fields of potatoes, onions and cabbage; and chickens that lay eggs, and cows that produced milk for butter and cheese. She and her mom had to work in the fields to get food to survive. People in the city had an even harder time getting food, so country folks were fortunate.

There was an incident that my mother mentioned to me several times. It left a huge impression on her. She said that Hitler rode on his horse through our little town in 1943, and all the citizens of Markt Schwaben had to step out in front of their homes saluting Hitler with "Heil Hitler stance." She was so little, and couldn't hold up her arms after standing there for half an hour. When she let her arm fall down, she remembered, suddenly, one of the neighbors pushing her arm back up.

He said to her angrily, "Do you want to get us all killed?"

Even though she spoke to me of tyrannical dominance in her childhood, she never mentioned the concentration camps, and the 12 million that were killed. The fear and intimidation of the SS on the Germans was so tremendous, that people knew if they didn't cooperate they would be shot on the spot.

My brother was required to visit Dachau Concentration

Camp when he was in high school, but my private school in Munich did not have that on the curriculum.

My mother told us stories of how all of the crosses in the schools and churches were taken down, with swastikas put up in their place. She told me that in 1945, when the Americans finally invaded Germany, one of the American soldiers gave her an orange and chewing gum for the first time in her life. She thought he was an angel. Everybody loved the Americans, for they saved the day and liberated Germany from the horror of the Nazis.

My Mother's Family

My Aunt Maggie, the youngest of the three sisters, was approximately eight years younger than Irene. She was trying to get on her feet financially, and when Maggie was in middle school, Irene married my uncle Horst, an elegant and handsome gentleman who was well-established in the textile industry.

Aunt Irene said Horst gave her the foundation for an extraordinary life. I was so fascinated whenever Horst returned from his business travels overseas. The whole family would gather at our house for dinner, and he would tell us stories about his adventures and all the phenomenal things he had seen in places like Hong Kong and Thailand.

As a child, I detected envy for my uncle within my father, and from some other family members, who wished that they could travel and lead different lives. I could not hear enough of his stories of elaborate and elegant dinners in foreign lands, the colorful markets in Hong Kong—and the giant Buddha statues of Thailand. I could have listened to my uncle for hours. I dreamed of going to Thailand and flying all over the world.

Sisters often have squabbles, and my mother would become clearly irritated with my two aunts, who argued over who had better taste and more material possessions. At one point, Maggie stopped talking to Irene for *an entire decade* over ridiculous curtains she was envious of. Their relationship was mended only after Maggie almost died in an accident with a Bavarian-style heating system, a "Kacheloven." It exploded in the house, and she was hospitalized with horrific burns. Irene came to visit her and all was forgiven.

We had a neighbor who had ten children, and they were quite poor. My mother was generous, and she would often give them bags of clothes, and many other things that she thought they needed. One day I remember playing outside when one of the neighbor's girls came out wearing my skirt, and I ran inside the house to complain about wanting it back. My mother sat me down with a very kind look on her face. She explained why she gave the skirt away, and reminded me that I hadn't even noticed it was gone. She taught me the importance of helping the poor—and gave me a subtle reminder of all that I did have.

Another time I recall asking my mom, "Mummy, why are you doing your hair and makeup just to go to the mailbox in front of the house?"

She replied, "Sweetheart, you must always look your best. You never know who you might meet!"

Somehow this stuck with me and I followed her advice, always making myself up, even when I felt like sticking my head in the sand or disappearing from the world.

My mother was able to keep up a façade for everyone around her, making it look as though she was invincible and strong. She was the one person that had the power to bring our family together during challenging times. Everyone came to her for advice and looked up to her as the pillar of strength. I knew a different story.

I saw her physical pain, suffering, despair and her hopelessness as we went about our everyday life. Her toes were crippled by a botched injection in the spine during her polio ordeal. She had a hard time standing and walking for long periods of time, and she had gallstones that caused her terrible pain. However, I knew her emotional pain prevailed over her physical pain, due to her tumultuous marriage to my father.

As a very young child, I worried about her, especially when she would hold and kiss me so tight and tell me the she could never live without me. She would say, "I would rather die than be away from you."

Her attachment to me was more than I could bear—almost suffocating at times. I made it a habit to disappear through my imagination and my dreams—to faraway lands like India and Turkey. I had read *Siddhartha,* by Herman Hesse, which depicts Prince Siddhartha before he becomes the Buddha in India.

My Magical Childhood Dreams

Exploring the world invoked in me a sense of desire to be free to go wherever I wanted to go and be anything I wanted to be. Even then, after my coma as a young child, I knew I had a different destiny to fulfill than to stay in Germany with my family where my life seemed quite minuscule.

I would often close my eyes and find myself flying over mountains, rivers and oceans, and through fluffy white clouds. I imagined rainbows of such bright blue, green, red and yellow—never experienced on earth—and large bodies of water glistening in the sun. I loved getting lost in giant trees and beautiful waterfalls with their fine mist splashing my face in slow motion. I could smell the fragrances of the flowers so sweet that I thought it more delicious than eating my favorite German chocolate cake. Nothing was like it is here on earth. The smell of roses and jasmine were one thousand times more magnified, intoxicating, and the warmth of the sun seemed to heal every cell in my body.

I considered it quite normal to be able to astral travel wherever I wanted to go, wherever my soul or mind took me. I loved my magical world where I was able to fly, and often stayed in my cozy, fluffy white bed dreaming for many hours on end, pretending I was still asleep.

The Aborigines in Australia call the dream world their "awake world," and the awake world the "dream world." I felt like my dream world was my *real world*, and the awake world was the dream. My dreaming took over my life, and my school reports were not very favorable.

Every six months the same report came to the house:

"Petra has a sunny disposition and is kind and considerate to her fellow students. However, she needs to stay focused on the lesson and stop dreaming."

Elementary school was just a blur in my memory, and I could barely get through the lesson of the day. I was always bored out of my mind. I made such an effort to focus on the lesson at hand, but shortly after the teacher would begin reading my eyes grew very tired. The voice of the teacher became a faint sound in the distance, and all I remember is the bell of the school telling us the lesson was over. Most often, I could not recall a single word the teacher said.

How could I give up my magical world of wonder and amazement for lessons in mathematics and history about the Dark Ages and the barbarians?

Not a single cell in my brain was able to stay focused on

school, until later as a teenager when my parents enrolled me in a private high school in Munich. I was fortunate to have a certain German teacher named Mrs. Schulze. She introduced our class to poetry and, for the first time in my life, I found a language that spoke to my heart. This happened through Wolfgang Goethe and the German classics.

The story that influenced me the most was Hermann Hesse's *Siddhartha.* I identified with Siddhartha, the prince who was not allowed to leave the kingdom. The king and queen wanted to protect him, and keep him from the dangers of the world, and never let him out of the kingdom.

In the story, one day, Siddhartha sneaks out to discover that his life was but an illusion. He then decides to become a seeker of truth, leaving the kingdom forever. I felt that I, too, had to leave my home to find the truth about my existence, and learn everything that I could about the world I lived in. Stories like this gave me hope. Perhaps it was the adventurer in me that knew even at a young age, there was a magnificent world out there to be discovered.

Maybe I was escaping the suffering I felt within my family. Even though I might not have known it at the time, dreams helped me cope with the sadness I felt for my mother and father.

It wasn't until much later in my life that I realized that my father was an intuitive and a very kind person, who had to suppress his insights because he felt everything so deeply. It was easier to numb himself with alcohol since there were no tools available for self-improvement, and he lacked communication skills to cope with his intuition.

Fortunately, my mother was not paralyzed from the polio, but she was in great physical pain due to the severe nerve damage caused by the polio virus that she acquired when she was only fourteen years old. She had gone swimming in the nearby lake, and was unable to walk that very same night.

Most of us know that polio was a dreadful virus that swept throughout Europe, and the world, after World War II–it crippled many people. After my mother was released from the hospital eighteen months later, one of her legs had become quite weak and slightly shorter. As mentioned, the faulty spinal injection administered during her treatment at Steinhöring hospital damaged and crippled her toes.

Though my mother was exceedingly beautiful, this only made her feel extremely self-conscious about the way she walked, affecting her self-esteem. She was unsteady when she walked next to me. I could feel her uncertainty, and I'd often let her hold onto me tightly, so she wouldn't trip. I felt bad for her, and sometimes internalized her insecurity.

Flowers For My Mother

It is quite curious to me, thinking back on my childhood, how we remember certain scenes so vividly, and how other things are simply forgotten. There was one incident, in particular, that affected me so deeply that even to this day, I can still feel the emotion that shot through my body like lightning.

My mom had been suffering with gall bladder stones, and was in horrible pain for months. She had gone to the hospital in Munich for surgery. My brother and I stayed with Aunt Maggie.

I recall the smell of iodine that penetrated through my mother's suture that was still lingering after her operation. I can still feel her pain in my body, every detail, as I speak about it: The chamomile tea at her bedside, her pale face, the fear in her eyes, and the gorgeous wildflower bouquet my aunt brought my mother.

Mother was released a few days later and was sitting in bed recovering from the operation, when her sister, Irene, came to visit. She brought the most beautiful bouquet of flowers for her. When my mother saw the flowers, she cried and cried.

I remember exactly what she said that day, "No one ever brings me flowers. I feel like I am already dead!"

That stayed in my head. It hurt to hear her say such things. But it made me keenly aware of her internal suffering.

From that day on, I made it my mission to bring her flowers as often as I could. Determined, I would walk for miles to a stream near our house where Schlüsselblumen grew, with their honeysuckle sweet aroma and their beautiful golden glow. I would pick as many as my arms could carry.

I fondly remember my mother holding me and kissing my face all over when I'd get home with my hand-picked bouquets. The flowers were so delicate that they'd often wilt only a few hours later. It would upset me that they didn't last, as if my mother's happiness depended on them. I cried over the impermanence of things. It was something I'd learn to deal with only later in my life.

"It's the thought that counts, not the permanence of things!" my mother would say in a consoling voice.

Even then, as a small child, I wanted to heal and make everything better for everyone. At times, I felt so helpless and weak to make anything alright within my family, and remember wondering, *will I ever make a difference in this world?*

Being sensitive made it more confusing. I was so skilled at "reading" people I barely knew, yet my mother, and, especially, my father confounded me. Both of them were so empathic like me, albeit in different ways. Mother was more cynical and sarcastic about the world, and Father just didn't know what to do with his deep emotions, so took it out through alcohol and on the family.

When I was five, after Grandfather Egal received a drunk driving citation, my parents were forced to take over my grandfather's successful taxi business. Grandfather spent decades building his little empire, but was forced to retire early. Things seemed to get harder after that with all of the added responsibilities they took on as business owners. When my parents had both worked in Munich with regular incomes, life was a lot simpler.

In my early years, my father would get up each morning and go to work as a 'machinist' for Black and Decker. I would accompany my mother to a nearby town called "Poing" where she was a private secretary at The Science Institute. I adored those drives. I'd stay at their kindergarten facility during the day, where there was a big playground and a wonderful teacher who did so many fun projects with the children.

I will never forget the autumn of 1967, when my mother and I walked the straight line from The Science Institute to the train station. She cried the whole way home, after she said goodbye to all her coworkers and her boss. Her attachment to her work was tremendous; she always said how well she was treated there. I could see how working in her profession made her feel fulfilled, and it made me feel happy when my mother was content.

Life became very difficult for her after she and my father were self-employed with the business. In the beginning, they seemed to be doing okay. After a while, though, I noticed how my father became severely depressed. He wouldn't even get up in the morning. My mother was left to do all of the work, which was obvious to me, because they worked from home.

On the one hand, I didn't think my father could hurt a fly; he'd give his shirt off his back. On the other hand, he was rowdy, boisterous and loud, and sometimes physically violent. I loved my father very much, but I was also very afraid of him. He was unpredictable and I never knew which personality I would meet from moment-to-moment. I guess my mother had married a man much like her father. Everybody in the family tiptoed around my father, including my mother.

Family gatherings revolved around not upsetting him. He would often say the most inappropriate things to my aunts and uncles, about their economic status, the way they raised their kids, or his religious views. Yet, if they ever challenged him, in any way, my dad would create thundering arguments, ordering family to leave the house immediately. Or else.

I often wondered what his 'or else' might mean.

One day, when we got back from a dinner at my Aunt Irene's house, my father was still ranting. He had felt it necessary to give her advice on how to raise her children. He belittled her to no end, claiming that they spoiled their children with material things, and they had become impossible to be around? Irene had had quite enough.

I remember my aunt exclaiming, "Don't you give me advice on how to raise my children. You're raising your children in the Wirtshaus (pub)!"

After that, they didn't speak for an entire year. No phone calls or visits, nothing. It made me realize how difficult it was for the sisters to stay connected, due to my father's crazy and unpredictable behavior.

At times, I witnessed how sensitive my father actually was behind his angry outbursts. When I was twelve years old, Dad came home at night. He had witnessed a horrific accident, where one person was beheaded and four people lost limbs and died. My father said he was the first person on the scene. I noticed the deep despair and helplessness in him, and the way he cried and held on to my mother. I had never seen my father quite like that. It was so curious to me how extremely sensitive he was at the core. He had a hard time letting it go, talking about this incident for months to come.

On another occasion, one of our neighbors was raising rabbits and my father was asked to come to their basement and choose a rabbit for dinner. I witnessed my father run out of that place so fast. He just couldn't handle it. He cried and cried, telling me how all those poor little animals were hanging from the cellar ceiling. He vowed that he'd never eat rabbit as long as he lived. He stuck to his promise.

I found my father puzzling and unpredictable, hard for any child, I'd think, even harder for a sensitive girl like me who couldn't handle violence. Father's angry outbursts were often tempered by random acts of reactionary kindness. I was confused, to say the least. This created carefulness in my steps around him, making it difficult to access my own empathy for my father, as I had for my grandfather. Luckily, later in my life, I was able to muster up some compassion for the man when I realized that the difficulties in his upbringing and life may have caused his erratic behavior.

After I began my studies in psychology at the university in London, I became aware of different types of mental illnesses, and I suspected that my father may have suffered from a mental illness like bipolar disorder, or at least severe paranoia. I am sure he suffered from manic-depressive disorder and PTSD from the bomb shelters he had to spend time in during the war… and he rarely talked about the abuse he had endured from Catholic priests.

I also found out, that during the 1930s in Germany, hunger and poverty were so prevalent that my grandmother tried to drown herself and my father as a baby boy. He was just one-year-old. Looking back, I can see how the trauma was overwhelming for him. It was clear that he didn't have the necessary tools to deal with his own sensitivities and insights about people, or the trauma that had been part of his life from his infancy.

Many mornings, when my mother and I sat having breakfast together, she would be in such despair and confide in me that my father needed to be mentally assessed. She was sure he required treatment. My response, even as a young child, was absolute and always the same. My mother needed to divorce my father and we had to live alone.

I loved my father. But I could also see the damage he was doing to the family.

His incessant drinking and partying became a cancer on my mom's being, along with his laziness. For the life of her, my mother could not wake him up in the mornings to work. My dad was still intoxicated from the night before. By the time I was thirteen years old, the arguing between them got so bad that I thought it would be better if they went separate ways. He could not stand up to her verbally. She was bright and quick in discussion and comments, so his defense was comprised of yelling and screaming and regular threats to walk out on the family.

I did not have much confidence in my father, and realized that our lives would be very peaceful without his emotional outbursts. In comparison to my father, even my grandfather and uncles were calm and grounded role models for me. This made my father's outrageous behavior stand out even more, which was quite unacceptable to the family at large.

I am sure my dad must have felt quite ganged up on. It was common knowledge that my mother was intellectually superior to him. Their communication was channeled primarily through physical affection, but certainly not through verbal or emotional intelligence.

She ran the show, the business, money, the house and our lives. He was a stereotypical playboy who had especially good looks, a few seeds of intuition and a good heart. My mother told me once, "Your father is afraid of the world and I have to protect him."

She felt that was her job. As I grew older, I realized that her protection only enabled undesirable behavior. It was making him angry, codependent and weak. Really, upon reflection—I'm not sure who was the weaker, or who co-dependently needed the other more.

My mother, with her own insecurity and abandonment issues, was afraid that my father would someday leave her. She took away all his responsibilities in the family, as a husband, and in the business. He was like a terrified child, once she reduced him down to a codependent child that needed her.

Apart from their archaic verbal skills, my parents had extraordinary passion that was on display for the whole family to see. It was quite normal for my brother and me to witness my parents exchanging long passionate kisses in the kitchen and my father grabbing her ass and boobs for us all to see. Maybe it wasn't as friendly as I thought back then, but more a statement of his power over her. I'm not sure.

I dreaded the nights when my father was home and we had to sit through an entire dinner with him. My brother would cringe while being reprimanded by my father over and over for not showing enough manners. He'd hold a spoon wrong, make a noise while chewing, or simply not sit up straight. All of these could be triggers—inconsistent and random—that my brother could only guess. My father would use my mannerism as an example to my brother, emphasizing how perfect I was. Even though I'd get a slight feeling of pride about the positive praise, I knew that it was always tinged with pain or revenge—my father, causing emotional pain that separated us as siblings, one from the other, bit by bit.

Later in the evening, my brother would get his aggression out by hitting and teasing me. If he was slapped by my father, all hell would break loose. It was impossible for my brother to please my father, and the abuse that he endured affected the rest of his life. For that I am sorry.

One of my dad's behaviors perturbed me to no end. He'd often joke about how he would have never stayed in Germany if my mother hadn't become pregnant. *Well, maybe you should have done that, Father,* I'd sometimes think to myself, as a knee-jerk reaction. I'd never say it to his face. I did secretly wonder what would have happened had my father followed his original plan to roam the outback of Australia with his friend Max. Max, come to find out, left for Australia without my father and went on to live quite an adventurous life.

My mother was intelligent, tall and beautiful. I loved her thick fire red hair, stunning green eyes, porcelain white skin and freckles. Her sense of style had an air of such feminine sophistication and elegance. I can most definitely say that I felt proud to walk next to her and call her my mother. Whenever we went shopping in the big city of Munich, we could not walk ten feet without cars honking or people staring at us.

I remember her beautiful embroidered leather suits, her red fox hat and her mesmerizing smile. Her sense of humor was sometimes glazed with cynicism and sarcasm. She had a slight hook in her nose that gave a hint of a *witchy* appearance. She would often joke about her nose with us. If she had been born a hundred years earlier, she would have been burnt at the stake. I believed her one hundred percent.

I remember her saying that she wouldn't have survived if she had had polio as a young child just a few years earlier than she did. I didn't really understand it then, how deep her own fear about her condition and her country ran. The subject of the Nazi's was rarely, if ever, mentioned. Later, in my life in London, I would find out that she was referring to the six million "undesirables," handicapped (of which she was one), and gays that were murdered along with so many Jewish people during World War II.

She often spoke about how children made fun of her red hair and how terrible it was for her as a little girl. She also had buck teeth that she had all pulled in her early adulthood. They'd point at her for looking so different from the Aryan model of perfection—blond with blue eyes.

My mother was seven years old when Nazi Germany was overthrown. When I researched the subject as an adult, I often wondered what happened to the tens of thousands of brainwashed children who were so heavily manipulated into the Hitler Youth programs throughout Germany. It must have been quite the mental anguish for many of the children returning to a 'normal' life after the war, when they had to integrate back into society and had to be de-programmed.

How did they feel about speaking Hitler's name? Did they even realize the evil committed by the man they believed was their savior? I realize now how much judgement and poverty my mother experienced at such a young age, how she never completely overcame the effects of her childhood, and a time in history that weighed heavily, taking its toll.

The Theater

My mother loved the theater and Italian/German opera so much so that she and I visited quite a few shows each year.

She would invite me to go with her—and one of my favorite times we spent together. It was easy to pretend I was a grown-up young lady in my long gown and high heel shoes. I loved feeling a part of high society at the intermissions. All the latest fashions of the upper classes were on display; the ladies in their elegant gowns and gentlemen in their crisp tuxedos.

One day, when I was about fourteen, we had tickets to see the play "Faust" by Wolfgang von Goethe. And, it was at my favorite theater, called "Prinzregententheater," in Munich. The theater was built in the Prinzregentenstraße, only forty minutes by car from our hometown. It served as a festival hall for the operas of Richard Wagner.

After the destruction of the "Nationaltheater" during World War II, the Prinzregententheater, named after Luitpold, Prince Regent of Bavaria, became home to the Bavarian State Opera. Even though it also suffered quite a lot of damage during the second war, it was beautifully restored by the time I was a teenager.

I remember the excitement of being with my mom during such a riveting play. We were dressed in our long, black, elegant gowns. I never forgot my mother screaming and holding my hand during one of the scenes in the play. That dramatic play most definitely left an imprint on me.

Wolfgang Goethe's "Faust" begins in heaven. While angels worship the Lord for his creation, Mephistopheles, the devil, complains about the state of affairs in the world. He claims that mankind is corrupt, and revels in the evil and disaster that he is able to cause. Mephistopheles makes a bet with the Lord that he will be able to turn one of his servants, Dr. Faust, over to sin and evil. Well, as it goes, the Lord agrees to the bet, claiming that Faust will remain a loyal follower of the Lord.

Watching this deep message unfold on the theater stage

made me feel like it was a lesson for us all. The theater was packed, and one could hear a needle drop in anticipation of what followed next.

The next scene introduces Faust, while he sits in despair over his life. He has been a scholar and an alchemist, and he feels as though he has come to the end of all knowledge.

Books and chemistry no longer define his life for himself, and he longs to live a life in harmony with nature and with the universe. He summons a spirit to come and be with him, but this only reinforces the fact that he is human and not spirit. He just can't share the spirit's higher knowledge.

In his despair, Faust brews a poison to commit suicide and just as he is about to take the poison, my mother screams so loudly that it echoes throughout the entire theater. She squeezes my hand tightly till it hurts. It feels as if a thousand eyes are on us. Shortly after that scene, a chorus of angels appears on stage announcing Easter day, stopping Faust from completing the act. At that moment, my mother begins to sob uncontrollably and I feel completely overwhelmed and helpless.

I must have read Goethe's "Faust" at least ten times after that. I was fascinated by the reaction my mother had to this scene and how closely she identified with Dr. Faust when he tried to commit suicide. I remember picking up on her despair and deep sadness and I was concerned for her emotional well-being.

The night of this particular play, on the way home from the theater, I recall a car coming towards us on the autobahn. The car was driving the wrong way at eighty miles an hour. Apparently, the person had taken the wrong exit and was confused. We only escaped this collision by one second. My mom pulled to the side of the road to make sure I was okay.

Scared, my heart was beating so fast—I was physically shaking when she took my hand and kissed me.

I remember my mom saying, strangely, "Oh well, sweetheart, at least we would have been already dressed for the funeral."

That was her type of humor—a bit dark and a bit odd. But there was also something very comforting in it for me, reminding me of how Shakespeare claimed that life is just a comedy. She had a good point, albeit a morbid one. To be quite clear—it is very rare when anyone escapes an accident on the autobahn alive. For some reason, we did that night. Today, cars drive even faster than they did back in 1975, and it's even more dangerous.

My mom had a fun way about her—sometimes she would hide behind a door to scare my brother and me, almost causing us to jump out of our skins, from the scary faces and horrific sounds that came out of that woman's mouth. There was a small actress in her blood, I could tell, and I absolutely loved that about her. She was my best friend, confidant and a loving mother.

Another poignant thought always remains about my mother. The untimely loss of my mother made me realize no one worried about me like she did, and when she was gone the world seemed unsafe. When I couldn't turn to her anymore, it changed my life forever.

During family gatherings, after she had a drink or two of champagne, she would frequently say that she would never make it to forty. She followed that with her claim of being afraid to grow old.

I never really thought that she might be onto something. I was about to find out.

5

Off to See the Wizard

It was around noon on Saturday, during July, the hottest month. We all got up late after a very well attended party with relatives and friends in honor of my sixteenth birthday. It was 1977. Even my godmother, Hansi, aka Lady Janine, came from Munich—she was always so sweet, buying me things proper ladies used; beautiful gifts and expensive perfumes.

My father had left the house to go out somewhere and the house had become quiet again. After we cleaned up from the party the night before, my mother and I were quite tired from all the festivities. So, we decided to spend a lazy Saturday afternoon cuddling on the couch together, eating vanilla and chocolate ice cream, and watching TV. One of my favorite movies was on, *The Wizard of Oz*.

We both adored this classic, where Dorothy (played by Judy Garland) slays the wicked witch and, then, struggles to find her way back home. Little did I know that my life would take a similar course to that of Dorothy's. Home, as I knew it, would become a distant memory, a part of my past.

I remember the day so vividly. In my mind, like a movie itself, I must've replayed that afternoon a thousand times, wishing for one more chance to touch my mother, to hug, to kiss her.

After the movie was over, I was excited to meet up with my friends Angela, Petra and Monica. I couldn't wait. We were going out to the local disco to go dancing to further celebrate my birthday. My older brother, Wolfgang, had left with my aunt Maggie and Uncle Juergen. They went to Yugoslavia by car, right after the birthday celebration. Of course, my father, as usual, the *somewhere he went* was the local Bavarian pub to drink and gamble.

After the afternoon and movie time spent with my mother, I ran upstairs to get dressed and do my make-up, so excited to go out with my friends. It had been a magical birthday celebration. And now sixteen, fun with my friends filled me with such excited anticipation.

My mother was downstairs hanging up clothes in the laundry room when I heard her call up to me. "Oh honey, don't go yet, don't go yet! Please wait a little longer!"

At the time, in my teenage frenzy, I didn't think much about my mother's feelings, only that if I stayed home for one minute longer I might die. So, I quickly ran into the laundry room and gave her a quick kiss goodbye. I could not have sped out that door any faster as I made my way to meet my friends, more than ready to get on with my evening disco dancing.

My mother was not a disciplinarian. Instead, she would let us experience life lesson by trying it out—textbook trial and error. She'd let that keen sense of humor lead us in the direction we needed to go, rather than punish us.

For example, the first time my mom smelled cigarettes on my breath, she took me to the nearest store and bought me a pack of cigarettes. I mean—what mother does that? She made me smoke in front of her until I turned green and threw up. This was her way of educating me on the ways of the world.

To this day, I still remember the label and the brand and how it felt to puke it all up. They were filter less Marlboros and tasted like dried grass. I am grateful that I had such a liberal and open-minded parent—her motherly methods worked for me.

After dancing my heart out all evening, to the latest hit songs of the 70s, I came home around midnight. My mom wasn't awake and it was late. I wrote her a note to wake me up at seven o'clock in the morning so that I could go skydiving with some friends. It was another much-anticipated activity I wanted to do, but it all depended on the weather being clear. I had dreamed about skydiving for such a long time, and my excitement for the next day was keeping me in a whirl.

I slipped into my comfy bed about 1:00 a.m. The house was quiet, and my father's black Mercedes wasn't in the driveway. I placed my note on the kitchen table next to a bouquet of colorful flowers. I wrote that I wanted to get woken up at seven.

Soon, I drifted away, dreaming about my life. I'm not sure what time my father finally came home that night, but I awoke to them arguing in the room next to me and pulled the blanket over my head. I plugged my ears with my thumbs until it was quiet again. Their arguing like this was a common occurrence.

"Petra, Petra, Herzi, please wake up!" my mother whispered, as she leaned over me in bed.

Really, I didn't want to open my eyes to talk to my mother.

Not interested in all of the problems she had with my father, because I had grown tired of their arguing. No, I wanted to be a teenager dreaming about my day, celebrations, and skydiving. I wanted to imagine positive and beautiful things that made *me* happy. I sure didn't want to get wrapped up, once more, in the drama and sadness of my parent's marital problems.

Well, at least it could wait until the morning light to talk with her about, right?

At seven o'clock, I was awakened by the "Bzzzz..." of the alarm clock my mom had placed on my bedside table. I heard raindrops falling on the roof and was feeling slightly sad, because that meant skydiving was off for the day. So, I decided to stay in bed for another hour, before going downstairs to join my mother for Sunday morning breakfast. *I was sure to hear the latest on my father's irresponsible ways,* I thought to myself. And that didn't sound like fun.

As I went down the marble stairway, I was suddenly overcome by an eerie feeling. The usual sounds and smells were absent. Things were way too still in the house; only silence. I heard no clattering of dishes or running water from the kitchen, my mother's favorite show on the radio wasn't on, nor was there any scent of fresh brewed coffee in the air. I knew immediately that something was terribly wrong.

I walked past the living room and saw bedding on the couch. I realized that my mother must have slept downstairs, which told me that their argument was a bad one.

With a sense of dread, I cautiously ambled into the kitchen feeling like everything was in slow motion. My eyes immediately spotted my mother. There she was, my beautiful mother, slumped over the chair, her arms hanging down towards the floor. Her neck was leaning against the back of the silver bar of the chair, her head twisted sideways. It was horrible. She was staring straight at me, as white as a ghost with her eyes wide open, her hand in a fist as if she had fought to get out of the chair.

It was then that my senses took hold of her lifeless body, as I shook my mom to wake her up. She didn't move or respond. Immediately, I felt such a sense of alarm and terror. I wanted to scream, but no sound could escape my lips.

Somebody had beaten her for sure. There was much bruising on her neck and left hip. Again, I shook and kissed her to wake her up, but she wasn't breathing. I cried and called out to her, then frantically ran upstairs to get my father. There he was. Up in bed, hung over and groggy as usual. I told him that Mummy was not waking up. He could see the panic in my eyes, and he knew something very serious had happened. He came quickly downstairs to the scene.

My father just stood there and froze. He couldn't, and didn't, do anything. I realized that I was now in charge. I ordered him to get dressed, take her to the living room couch and fetch a doctor. I still don't know how he found the strength to pick her up and carry her lifeless body to the couch in the next room. He was in an absolute state of shock; weak emotionally and physically. Today, I suppose his condition would probably be diagnosed as *neurogenic shock* from a severe emotional disturbance.

After my father went to get the doctor, I called for emergency services. I also rang my grandfather and Aunt Irene. I guess I am one of those people who can rise to doing what has to be done in extreme crisis, though looking back, how at sixteen, I could have acted so rationally, I don't know.

In the last moments of silence, before anyone arrived, I had time alone with my mother, her head on my lap. I noticed her fingers were swollen and, so, took off her rings. There was a sweet, but extremely sickening smell of decomposing flesh emanating from her. It caused me to feel nauseous. My mother's body made all kinds of sounds, which made me hopeful for a moment.

Was she still alive?

I think I knew, at the time, that it might be gases emitting from her body. But I did not want to believe she was dead. How could I? In denial and such pain, I rocked her back and forth like a baby, kissing her forehead. I was shaking. I felt such deep wrenching sadness in my heart. My life felt as if it had just ended—for sure, life as I knew it—had! I prayed to Jesus to not let her die today. Crying, I begged her to stay and not leave me all alone. I could not live without her in this world.

In complete despair, I held my mom's head and whispered in her ear, *everyone loves you, please don't leave me, please don't leave me.* She still didn't respond.

I recall how I carefully examined all of the bruises on her neck more closely and noticed that her nose must've been bleeding at some point. Suddenly overcome with terror, for the first time it dawned on me. *Could my father, in his drunken state, be the reason for her injuries?*

At this horrific notion, I ran upstairs to look inside the clothes hamper. I found something no young woman needs to find. It was a bloody nightgown and pillowcase. Not knowing what to do, I pulled down the attic ladder and hid them in a box in the farthest corner of the attic.

I don't know. It seemed like hours had gone by before my father returned with Dr. Holley, who was the only doctor on duty that Sunday. When he entered the living room and saw my mother's lifeless body on the couch, his face was filled with intense worry. Our eyes met. I knew that my mother was dead. Dr. Holley had known my mother and the rest of the family very well.

Paying close attention to my father, I noticed his panicked behavior and I asked Dr. Holley to give him a sedative. He did.

Our house then became a zoo. The ambulance, my grandfather, my aunt, my uncle and the police all arrived at the house around the same time. Family members were not allowed to come upstairs. The police ordered me to go downstairs and wait with the rest of the family. I didn't know what to tell them and couldn't talk about the bloody nightgown and pillowcase. I just held my aunt's hand instead. You have to remember, I had just turned sixteen.

An hour or so later, my father suddenly appeared. He just stood there, glassy eyed, at the top of the stairs.

Father yelled down to us, "Oh, my God, they think I did it! They think I did it!"

I watched as my grandfather's face became stone-cold. Aunt Irene started to cry, collapsing on the ground. I stood lifeless myself, like a statue.

The police eventually took my father to the second-floor bedroom, calling me to join them. To my dismay, they asked me to show them how I found my mother. This was the darkest day in my life and I was afraid and worried about what would happen next.

I walked back into the kitchen, trembling. The police interviewed me and asked me to show them exactly how my mother's body appeared in the kitchen. I explained to them what I felt... that she must have fainted and fallen, but could not get out of the chair. I never mentioned the bloodstained nightgown and pillow case I was hiding from them. *Had I heard any arguments*, they inquired? *What was my parents' relationship like?*

I told them that they loved each other very much, and that I heard nothing that night. I hid the truth, not knowing what else I could, or should, do.

My father was still held for questioning upstairs when I was asked to leave. I waited with my grandfather, aunt and uncle. A while later, my mother's dead body was carried downstairs in a metal box and put into the ambulance.

I remember feeling like I just wanted them to open that metal box casket, so I could see her, hold and kiss her one more time. But my aunt held me back. I felt such an emptiness within me and knew that my mother was now gone forever. I would never see her again. They carried her body out for good.

The next day, the local newspaper headline read:

"Murder, Suicide or Accident?"

The police interviewed everyone, including neighbors and friends. I remember going to our neighbors asking them to protect my brother and myself. *Please, let the police know that my parents had never argued. Please don't tell them anything.* But they knew the exact nature of the relationship. I am sure they heard my father's yelling plenty of times.

When we received a report from the coroner, explaining the cause of death read:

"Asphyxiation."

And that was that. End of story.

My father was never arrested, charged or tried in the death of my mother.

This is what I believe happened. That night, he came home around 3:00 a.m. They had argued in bed, and he backhanded her on the nose, and maybe gave some blows to her neck. She had a nose bleed, and got up and put the pillow and the bloody nightgown in the hamper. Then she went downstairs, and fainted due to the blow on her nose—falling into the chair, where she hit her jugular vein on the metal bar on the back of the chair, cutting off the oxygen supply to her brain, causing asphyxiation. She passed out and died.

I can never know for sure about the series of events between my father and mother that night—the only thing I knew absolutely for sure back then, is that I would never get to see my mother in the flesh again. *She may have only been able to hold my hand for a short sixteen years, but she has held my heart for a lifetime.*

6

Reflection of Grief

"The most painful goodbyes are the ones that are never said and never explained."

—Bilal Nasir Khan

I was devastated by the loss of my mother and haunted by the way she was taken from me. Several months after my mother's passing, *things* appeared to be going back to *normal* for the family. Birthdays came and went, Christmas, New Years and Easter passed. And the people closest to me continued with their daily life and duties.

How could this be? How could life simply go on as normal? I resented the fact everyone went on as usual, and that l was left in such disarray, sadness and loss... Within me, I had no sense of *normal,* and I desperately needed to talk to someone, anyone, about my mother and how much I loved her—and the grieving pain that wrenched within me. So alone, I anxiously needed to understand the meaning behind all that had happened. And, no one was talking.

My brother, Wolfgang, moved in with my grandfather only two months after the loss of our mother, not long after he and my father had a very disturbing and volatile argument over curfew. My brother's defiance and provocation prompted my father to lose his temper—and my brother ended up with a black eye and quite the beating up of his body from being knocked down the marble stairs.

I wasn't home that day, but I knew things were getting worse between my brother and father. My mother's family had continued to talk to my dad, until after his violent attack on Wolfgang. Then they completely stopped talking to my father, and my brother never returned to my father's house again.

He moved in with Grandfather Egal, who had, by then, cut off all communication with my father as well. He was barely eighteen years old and experiencing his own struggles dealing with our mother's death, and he had simmering anger about our father's violence.

During the time we grew up together, my brother struck me as a sensitive person prone to addiction, and one who had a hard time focusing. He had nervous energy I could never quite understand when I was younger. As a teenager, he was provocative and questioned everything. His personality, and response to life around him, leaned toward the glass being half empty, rather than half full.

Typical of most teenage boys, he clowned around a lot and people loved him. He was one of the most handsome boys in town, and many of the girls had a crush on him. It must've been very difficult for him to be influenced by my father and by my grandfather. Because during all of his growing up years as the only male child in our family, he had stress and pressures put upon him; he endured unfair inflictions from both men, who clearly had their own struggles with alcoholism and other demons.

Me? All Alone

With my brother gone from the house, I was completely vulnerable, alone and abandoned. As outrageous as it sounds, I was now forced to take on the roles of business owner, parent, and the housewife to my father. I felt lost.

With no one to reach out to, and few outlets, I learned early on that I couldn't talk about my spiritual experiences nor the things I saw that I now know were "visions." And, of course, it was impossible to talk about all of the things that were going on in the house. Father wouldn't have it, and it wasn't accepted family practice to talk about *anything* anyway. There was no therapy, no household help, and no relief. I had to figure it out by going inward; relying on myself—and my poor brother was in no position to console me, that's for sure.

I'd spend my time spacing out and daydreaming about all of the places I could escape to from my predicament—dreaming about Africa and safaris, hiking the Himalayas, and I would picture myself sitting at a coffee shop in Paris, watching people walking by. It was clear I had to take care of myself, and to get as far away from Germany as possible, if I wanted to ever heal.

Everything reminded me of my mother, every corner I turned, and every road I walked. People in my small town stared at me in the street with sad eyes, making me feel like they pitied me.

How was I ever going to be happy again, I wondered. It felt like an impossible dream.

While living in the same house, my mother's house, her memory was everywhere. Sometimes when I was alone there,

I´d walk down the staircase, and I'd have visions of my mother standing in her white, bloodstained nightgown.

I'd think: *Why did it have to be me who found the evidence in the clothes hamper?* I relived the scene far too many times in my mind, having to stay in the very place she was murdered. My mother's image would visit in spirit, her nose dripping with blood reaching out to me in desperation with her right hand. I could feel her longing for me and the pain was unbearable.

Gradually, I became afraid to be by myself in the house. I could hear her voice at times. I was constantly reminded of how, when alive, she talked about how she´d return to haunt the house as a ghost when she died one day. How strange it felt that she had said such things. She also said, "Your father will suffer for the rest of his life when I am gone. I will come back to visit to remind him."

When mom mentioned such things to me, I often wondered if she was predicting her own death. I knew she had an intuitive ability to see into things others could not, something like clairvoyance, but her words became too eerie after she died. I couldn't help but think that her soul was trapped somewhere, and that she was still living in the house and trying to reach me, trying to tell me something important I needed to know.

My mother and I were close, and to be with my father without her presence, especially with his unpredictable behavior, and my unanswered questions were extremely challenging.

In too close quarters, my father's weaknesses bared down on me every day. When I needed my father, he was lost in his own emotional wasteland and unable to function. He could barely communicate, and he sure couldn't run the taxi business he was left with, the one my mother and grandfather built.

The whole family knew that my father was somehow responsible for my mother's death, but still, no one questioned why the police didn't convict him of "involuntary manslaughter." Somehow it became the unspeakable, no one would go there.

I knew for some time that I had to get out of my father's house, but as a teenager, I had no idea exactly how I'd do it, but somehow, I would.

One night in the winter, my father made my decision for me. At around 9:00 p.m., I was lying on the couch watching TV, when my father came in complaining about how he just couldn't do it anymore. He'd come to me in his usual drunken state, smelling of cigarettes and that pub stench. He cried like a little boy who'd lost his mama, asking me what he could possibly do to survive this mess. He was clearly the victim in his mind, even though I knew differently. This time, his eyes were particularly blurry, lost, and he didn't make much sense at all.

Before I knew it, he started to hug me and kiss me in a way I knew only lovers do. I had plenty of experience myself, to be honest, with kisses that is, and these were no father-child pecks. These were serious, these were long and these weren't right.

Why was he doing this to me? Was he lonely and needing a woman? *But I'm his daughter!* Had he finally completely lost it? I made an excuse that I had to go to the bathroom and ran upstairs and locked myself in my room to escape the unthinkable.

I never forgot that night; such enormous rage arose in me—and with deep resolution, I made a further promise to myself. *I would never be taken advantage of by any man in anywhere.* My respect for him at the point was completely gone. And I had to work very hard on myself to overcome the doubt, mistrust, and anger toward all men.

Always before, he would take things out on my brother, which was hard enough to watch and accept. As a teenage girl, though, I was helpless to change the disrespectful and violent way he treated my brother. Now I was his target, and I could not be helpless to protect myself. I had to escape from him.

I had put up with his lies, the violence and dysfunction. But this personal violation was the last straw for me. I knew that the only way I could be released from this hell would be to find him a wife, to get him off my back. I'd go on to ask around the neighbor if anyone knew of a suitable partner for him. Perhaps someone would.

Of course, things were never the same, and fell into an even deeper low, after *the incident.* My anxiety and suspicion grew. My father's house was like a prison. From that point on, I slept with a knife under my pillow. Before my father would come home at night, I made it a practice to lock my bedroom door, afraid that he'd come into my room and do the unthinkable.

I was horrified of my father and my trust dissolved overnight. I still took care of him by doing all the household chores and business responsibilities. My brother understood the severity of my situation and asked my aunts to get me out of there. He told me that he would convince them to persuade my father to give me permission to move to England, even though I was under age at only seventeen. There was really no other choice.

It was a hard and lonely time. I always had to save face for the family and play dumb about everything. At times, I'd get some relief. On some evenings I'd get to go out with relatives or my good friend, like Regina, who was already driving and a year older than me. The times with Regina felt soothing and safe. She would often come and take me shopping in her little, baby blue Citroen car, and we would stop at the cemetery and light a candle for my mother, while she'd hold my hand. I needed the comfort and was thankful to have such a good friend to turn to.

I now lived in a different world—a grownup world; a world of concern for everyone in my family—and now, fear for my own safety. The carefree days of teenage innocence and ignorance were gone, and I found it increasingly difficult to relate to my old friends. It was as if they spoke a different language and were of another race, culture and creed. I couldn't listen to any of their problems. All the complaints and problems in their lives seemed so trivial and small, and so irrelevant to the problems that I faced.

My reality had shifted from being a young girl to suddenly being an adult who carried huge and heavy burdens. I could see clearly that time did, indeed, heal the wounds around those I loved, but my wounds were still too deep, still fresh and very painful. Sometimes I would run away to the house of my uncle's youngest brothers—Ewald and Ingrid, who were my distant relatives, but I trusted them with my life. They were saviors for me, and my peers, and loved me unconditionally. And to be honest, I didn't have much else, and few others I could turn to.

Once when I went to visit Wolfgang, a good family friend, lived close by and had become my confidante. I shared with him my dilemma with my father, and asked him to help me find my father a wife, anything to get this monkey off my back. Everyone close to us knew that my father was incapable of running the business by himself and that I definitely needed help with that.

Relief

Much to my relief, Wolfgang soon arranged some dates for my father with women that were widowed or still single in their circle of friends. After meeting several ladies, my father met Francisca. If she could become my stepmother, my plan would work. She was not only a good personality match for him, but I was relieved that she had business savvy, having been a secretary at BMW in Munich. This meant less work for me, and in turn, that meant he also might let me go free.

Franziska's husband had died in a horrific mountain climbing accident in the Alps two years earlier. This absolutely devastated her; you could see it in her sad eyes and in the hopeless way she spoke about her future. She told us that her husband had slipped and fallen down a steep, rocky mountain. She had rushed after him, trying to catch him, but it was too late. She made her way down to him, where he died in her arms. She was trapped on the side of the mountain alone until they were discovered and help could arrive.

To this day, it's hard to imagine how Franziska survived without a scratch on her body, in light of the fact that a helicopter had to airlift them both out. It must have been a case of mind-over-matter—where people get an adrenaline rush of superhuman powers in moments of great danger. As a young woman, I always tried to imagine how she actually did it—made it out alive and all, but it was not something we ever discussed.

It was clear to me, even as young as I was that Franziska was ready for a new relationship. Too young to be single, I always thought she saw my father as quite the catch: In today's world of "singles ads," his would read:

"Handsome, 40-year-old widower. Business owner. Well known and well-respected in the community…"

One day he told me he finally had met someone he liked, and planned to marry her. And one week later I was invited to meet his future wife. My father wanted my approval before he took it any further. It felt quite strange to be my father's chaperone, and to be asked for my stamp of approval just nine months after my mother's passing, but it felt like it had to happen. Attending the wedding in the same Baroque Catholic Church my mother's funeral service was held didn't make it any easier. That's for sure.

"In the struggle for self, on our pathway of life—can I, can others, choose light and compassion when the quiver of rage threatens to rise up from within?" –Petra

I often fantasized what would have happened to my brother and me if my father had actually been charged with involuntary manslaughter. It is so fascinating to me how one decision in life can affect the rest of your life forever. There were times I regretted protecting my father, but as matured and evolved, and became more conscious of my own journey, I realized that the Old Testament "Eye for an Eye" has to change and that we must become more conscious, more aware, more loving if we want our planet to evolve to the next level. Today, as we see parts of the world struggling to hold on to the dark ages of despair and suffering, much of the planet has no choice but to move forward into a more enlightened state.

I had, shortly after my mother died, felt a quiver of rage rising up, but one day while gazing in the mirror, looking at myself, I knew had the power to choose—rage or forgiveness, darkness or light. I became dedicated to a life of forgiveness and compassion, even where my father was concerned.

My Father's New wife

But, it was me, after all, who had devised the plan to get my father someone to take care of him and be his wife in all respects, so I didn't have to risk the unthinkable with him, nor would I have to babysit a grown man whose children were suffering and needed a responsible adult.

Wolfgang, my brother, could not understand how I was able to support my father marrying another woman, or support him in any other way either. I didn't blame my brother for hating my father. I witnessed the way he treated him, the violence and cruelty, and it made me cringe.

As far as the marriage, Wolfgang didn't know that I had done everything I could to arrange this union. It was clear, though, something had to change, and this was my one way out.

Just trying to survive, I had to regain some sense of relief and closure. I did my best to remain pragmatic, to protect our home and all of the assets my mother built with blood, sweat and tears.

Franziska went on to spend twenty-five years with my father. I later learned it was not a happy marriage, which really comes as no surprise. They must have served some kind of function for one another, I suppose. My father died in March of 2009, when I was forty-eight.

That day in March, I got *the call* from Franziska. I booked the next flight to Munich, and I went directly to his house with my friend Otti; not the same house I had grown up in. It was a house my mother had acquired about two miles from town, another amazing property that was in very special place and my father remodeled it and moved there with my stepmother. Before his body was removed, Franziska couldn't get herself to go inside the house where he was lying dead.

We arrived at his house, his body, of course, was no longer there. I called the morgue for viewing but they said it was too late and not allowed. In the living room, my friend Otti and I both felt a strange presence.

Suddenly, the clock stopped. Outside, it began to lightly snow. I remember feeling such a deep sense of relief knowing my father was no longer in his body. We felt an eerie presence in the room, my friend Otti had shivers running down her spine; and I wanted to talk to my father.

We held hands and said a prayer and asked for his soul to be released. Within the tinge of decades of cigarette smoke that had stained the stuccoed walls inside the house, was a feeling of such great despair and loneliness, and the ultimate fear and dread that possessed my father most of his life.

It was such a sad and dismal life he led, and as his daughter, I asked the question based on the many blessings I had been given—*was this man my responsibility to save?* I saw him possessed by the demons that had taken him over, and how he was devoured by sadness and grief.

My stepmother could not deal with the emotional pain, and I could not attend the funeral.

I basically helped her get through the details for the next few months. She still suffers from depression. Twenty-five years of marriage to my father was quite hard on her, but somewhat sadly, she also didn't make an effort to have a relationship with my brother or me. They lived isolated and alone—and Franziska sold the house after my father passed away.

Yes, my father died alone, after drinking his life away. One day I went there and my father started screaming and yelling about things about my brother. I walked out, and my stepmother accompanied me to the car and told me that my father was not a bad man—and I hugged and kissed her goodbye and said: "Oh yeah, ask him how my mother died?

What drove Franziska to finally leave him and move out of the house, was a bizarre happening. At some point she realized that my father was taking her doll collection and ripping their heads off—and that prompted her to get away from him. She had to leave if she ever wanted to save herself and live a normal life. With the help of her friends, in the middle of the night, she ran away, and moved back to her flat.

She told me later that she was afraid of him for many years. He yelled and screamed every night, and hated everyone. *He probably hated himself.* She actually took his shotgun and drowned it in the pond on the property in fear that he would shoot her.

While they were together, I was aware that my father was never attracted to my stepmother, and married her mainly to have a private maid that ran the business. She replaced me, and my mother before me, women assigned to run both private and public life for him.

Franziska was very devastated. Not for the usual reasons, one is devastated at the loss of a husband. Being married to a man such as he was something she couldn't get over. The twenty-five years with him had drastically and unhappily changed her life forever, because of the abuse she suffered. Maybe my mom was right after all. There was something missing in my father and he truly was mentally ill. In a strange sort of way, it was therapeutic for me to be in his house. With him gone, it cleared the air, and I felt I had come full circle, whatever one might call it. People ask, "Are you at peace where your father is concerned?"

My answer, "Yes, I was at peace on the day he died. And today, I'm glad that he was released from his body and his disturbed mind."

I know that my dad was a rowdy guy, but he was also a happy-go-lucky man. I look back realizing I had to create my own life, a better life, coping and reconciling myself to all my father was and all that he had done.

Over the years, I asked myself many questions:

Why did Jesus come to me, and what I am going to do with what I experienced in my near-death experience at nine years old? How did Jesus heal? How was he able to forgive unconditionally?

I asked myself every day how I could become a non-judgmental human, a "real mensch" someone of exceptional and noble character, who could become able to have a heart full of love to heal like Christ.

Jesus said that *we will do greater things than he* and I wanted to heal my father. After I witnessed demon possession in India, I knew it was not my father's fault. At the core, we are all good, at the core we all want the same—joy, tenderness and love, but some of us humans are so beaten, so damaged that we don't know where to even start to be at peace. I wanted not only to forgive, but to become FORGIVENESS.

My Father—A Victim of Circumstance

I now understand that he was a victim of circumstance having survived the trauma of the war. And I'm sure he had no idea how to handle a sophisticated woman like my mother, who was intelligent, complex, articulate and beautiful. He had been such an unhappy man for so long. He tried to find love in other places, outside of himself, because he was shallow and unable to generate it for himself from within.

A few years before he passed away, I would often feel his pain in my heart and I would summon my father energetically to meet me in dream time at the old Baroque Church. I would sit with him and lay my hands on his head to heal him and to love him, so that he too could cross over and know that I loved him.

While I forgive my father for what he did, I can never let go of my mother being taken from me. My father, my mother and myself all experienced such extreme pain. When my mom was taken, and realizing that my dad did the talking, I was sure, my inability to trust was permanent and deeply broken. I became extremely angry with God and the universe.

After many years of struggling with what happened, I had to overcome my own judgement, blame and anger. I had to find my higher consciousness (brain) and struggled extremely hard with myself to become who God intended me to be, and to reach my highest potential.

My mother's death had a profound effect on my life, as it would any young woman. While it's strange to say this: it was also a positive one. Without her death, I would never have become who I am today. Maybe I would have never left Bavaria at all.

My mother's death was, indeed, the birth of my higher consciousness, and began me on a path to become a seeker after truth. This is something I know she would want from me—*and for me.*

7

Leaving, 1978
Walter and Werner
Starry Nights and Wheat Fields

Have you ever heard, "The struggle you're in today is developing the strength you need for tomorrow?" I sure hoped that was true for me, because one thing looked like it was going to work out just as I had hoped and planned.

After finding a woman who could be a wife for my father, and with the family's encouragement, he agreed to sign on the dotted line and allowed me to leave him and the country. I often wondered what would have happened to me if I had not left Germany and remained in the country. I can only guess.

Three weeks before I left for England, I went out to a concert with some friends at a favorite club called "Titanic."

I was surprised and happy when I saw a dear friend, Walter. I remember it like yesterday. He stood there at the top of the stairs near the entrance of the club looking down at me with the same happy expression in his eyes that I had always adored. His gaze always gave me such comfort and joy.

Both of so happy to see one another, he took me by the hand, and we climbed into his Hippie Volkswagon van to drive to my village, outside of the city, near a little stream called "Die Sempt," a secluded, charming place near my grandfather's house.

It was on this clear, starry night in the middle of summer when I lost my virginity to Walter. I was so inexperienced, and he was so sweet and gentle with me. We talked until the early morning about my mom and my need to get out of my father's house. And he shared about his ordeal with testicular cancer that he had recently been diagnosed with. Ultimately, he did survive it.

That special night spent with Walter, truly was the most remarkable and delightful night of my young life. We lazed around in the van, amongst the "chirp" of crickets, the "rib-bitt" of splashing frogs, next to the clean and clear burbling stream; the water doing its own thing, as it steadily trickled downhill beside where we were parked in the van.

The next morning I opened the van's curtains and couldn't believe my eyes! Out of nowhere, there was my Grandfather Edgar "Egal" taking a leisurely stroll down to the stream, since it was near his house. Wearing his Bavarian hat and whistling to himself as he often did, Grandfather passed by our van at the exact moment I opened the curtains to look outside. I was naked and in utter shock when I saw my grandpa's face.

I opened and closed those van curtains so fast, feeling my face turn from white to crimson… or vice versa… in the shock of seeing him right there. I don't think my comedian Grandfather would have ever let me forget this moment, not in my whole lifetime, had he really figured out what we were doing inside that steamy van. I always accepted this as an omen.

The next day was a complete circus; Walter went to my brother and to my father's house to try to influence them to not let me go to London. Walter asked me to marry him, too, but that is another story. A different fate was awaiting me.

Honestly, after I left Munich and went to England, I often wondered why Walter didn't come and fetch me. There were many times I could have used a "Knight in Shining Armor." Little did I know that he was not able to come and find me in my loneliness because his cancer had gotten worse? He always remained a very important figure in my life; he saw me for who I really was beyond body. He served the master for thirty years and then died of throat cancer.

To this day, I remember Walter as a kind, humble and very loving man. He was the one who so respectfully and gently empowered me and allowed me to find myself as a woman, helping to prepare me for the journey ahead.

8

LSD

"I wish there was some hip way of telling you this, baby, but, ah... you're one with and part of an ever-expanding, loving, joyful, glorious, and harmonious universe."

—From the movie *The Trip*

Almost a year had passed since my mother's death. Still very confused, frustrated and searching for answers, it felt like losing my virginity to Walter was one step towards independence. Was I ready to explore the world, or was I just looking for any excuse to fly away, some way to escape so that I could feel something different than the emotional turmoil my mother's death had left me in?

Still, with only a few people I could really talk to and little joy in my life, I was pleased to meet a young man at one of the Rocky Horror Theater shows in Munich. He was in his early twenties and his father was a prominent attorney, and he had also lost his mother. When we met one night over dinner, I could tell he really connected with me—I felt he understood me and my dilemma.

I told him about my experience in my father's house, feeling the presence of my mother's ghost, and how I wished that I had a chance to cross over to talk to her and find out what really happened. He went on to tell me about LSD, the psychedelic drug he often experimented with. As he described the effects, I became intrigued. Werner explained, "It is well-known for changing your psychology, altering thought processes, and giving closed-and open-eye visuals, an altered sense of time—and spiritual experiences.

With my deep need to talk to my mother—it made me wonder if it might help make that possible. I decided to go for it.

After our time together, I went home and started reading numerous books and articles by people who had had experimented with LSD: My world became filled with stories of the British intellectual Aldous Huxley, Italian film director Federico Fellini, Bill Gates, Allen Ginsberg, Steve Jobs, Bill Wilson, the co-founder of Alcoholics Anonymous among others.

I remember when I first picked up on Huxley's life. I felt intrigued and fascinated. He was one of the most important figures in the early history of LSD. He was famous for his novels *Crome Yellow, Antic Hay* and his dystopian novel, *Brave New World.* I loved the way he was able to describe in detail his experiments with psychedelic drugs and it confirmed my notion of wanting to explore it more.

Curious, one evening, I decided to call Werner a few days before my seventeenth birthday. I asked him if he would be open to doing an "LSD trip" with me, and guide me along the way. He agreed immediately. I could feel how passionate he was about this. We planned to meet in Markt Schwaben for my birthday, just a day before the one-year anniversary of my mother's death. I thought *how timely was this?*

I trusted Werner to help me on this journey of discovery. Werner brought his auburn sheep dog, Max, with him and drove down from Munich to my village. He picked me up at the house on that hot summer's day that remains still one of the fondest memories of my life. Together, we traveled to a remote wheat field by the stream "Sempt," near my grandfather's house where Walter and I made love.

The wheat was quite tall, this time of year, and we decided to sit in the middle of the field near a giant oak tree. Nobody could see us as we sat in the middle of the field, two small dots in the landscape. We both took the little, red crystal LSD, not much bigger than a pit. Werner and I sat across from each other, he in his white cotton shirt and khaki shorts and me in my purple summer dress.

At first, I thought it didn't work. I had never taken any psychedelic at all and didn't feel high like I did when smoking marijuana.

"This stuff doesn't work on me!" I said to Werner, inquisitively.

He just smiled and asked me to hold out my palm. Taking some wheat in his hand, he counted out seventeen wheat berries, letting them fall one-by-one into my hand. It was a perfect ritual. On the tenth berry, I suddenly started seeing everything in slow motion. The shafts looked like brilliant rainbow raindrops. When that single berry landed, it made an echo and a sound so pure and lovely that I couldn't wait for the other berries to do their magic.

I started to see colors changing into brilliant rays; glistening golds and silvers danced through the sky. Werner told me he was hearing everything down to the tiniest insect.

After a while, I had to go to the bathroom so squatted in front of the big oak tree. I remember looking up at the tree to find it growing a face much like a happy sun. It started talking to me and smiled in this magical and kind way that gave me a sense of peace. I felt like Alice in Wonderland, in total heaven, with the breeze and cherries filling the trees around me.

The sky opened and an enormous orchestra played Beethoven's 5th with Beethoven, Mozart, Wagner and many of the classical geniuses smiling down and serenading me. At the time, I could feel this tremendous wave of orgasmic joy come over me, something I had not known before, and I thought for a moment I would float away to be with the musical masters of the sky.

Werner will always stand out in my mind as someone who really helped me; he helped me to break past barriers in my mind, and some of the pain I had buried deep inside. During our trip, we witnessed our incarnations from birth to elderly, to death, dozens of times. We were able to talk about what that felt like, as best as we could in the moment.

I was able to see who we really were and how quickly everything in this world transforms itself. Realizing that literally everything, *and* every living thing, cycles through this place, the earth, so quickly, helped me to relieve some of the sadness over my mother´s death. It became clear to me that on a bigger scheme, our lives are so very short—and only for the purpose of our function and transformation. I learned that the soul is in charge of the body and mind, and LSD was a way into recognizing this.

At seventeen, I was finally experiencing something more akin to my soul signature, as a "walk-in." I would learn more about this concept many years from now, directly from Karyn

K. Mitchell, who wrote the book, *Walk-Ins: Soul Exchange.* This would provide me answers to some long-asked questions (discussed in more detail, in the "Walk-In" chapter).

It had been twelve hours and we were exhausted, so Werner and I drove to Munich to Werner's farmhouse, where we had a big breakfast of scrambled eggs and toast. When I left his house he said to me: "If you ever need me, you know where to find me."

Upon reflection, I would have to say my personal relationship with LSD was extraordinary, enlightening and transformational. It gave me a deeper sense of being, about life and death, and confirmed to me that atoms are indeed mostly space and that there is really no death.

Luckily, I did not need to explore this further. I had gotten what I came for. I could move on. As the British philosopher, Alan Watts, said: "Once you get the message, hang up the phone!"

While LSD never became my drug of choice, my experience with Werner pushed me to look into it more. What was this substance and where did it come from? My mind was open; I looked to books for respite in the months before leaving home.

I learned that some psychiatrists believed LSD was especially useful in helping patients "unblock" repressed subconscious thought material, more effectively than through other psychotherapeutic methods, and for treating alcoholism. One study showed that "the root of the therapeutic value of the LSD experience is its potential for producing self-acceptance and self-surrender," by forcing the user to face issues and problems in their individual psyche.

I took LSD in the late 70s to feel something different than what I currently was suffering emotionally, and in hopes of further commune with my mother. But we know LSD got its reputation during the hippie era of the 1960s. It served as a symbol for a whole movement with rock bands like The Beatles, Byrds, Grateful Dead, Pink Floyd, Jimi Hendrix, The Yardbirds, among others.

The "Summer of Love" and the "Woodstock Rock Festival," brought it to national attention. The Woodstock Festival, in Bethel, New York, 1969, was a three-day concert (which rolled into a fourth day) that involved lots of sex, drugs, and rock 'n roll—plus a lot of mud. It has become an icon of the 1960s-hippie counterculture.

As most know, between 1967 and 1969, LSD reached a plateau and became tied to a widespread counterculture, before declining in popularity. After all, change happens. With shifts in people's mindset, the back-to-the land movement, people were tired of the establishment. Just like now, they considered U.S. government a rigged system, which was amplified by the Vietnam War etcetera. Many musicians and popular icons died of drug overdoses; it seemed many musicians just decided to move into new ways of conducting business, which remains true for some today.

In my many hours of sifting through books, I found out that the CIA used LSD for mind control under the program code-named "MKUltra," "a U.S. Government human research operation experimenting in the behavioral human research."

I thought it was very interesting that the CIA set up several brothels in San Francisco under the name: "Operation Midnight Climax." The operation took a few men who would be too embarrassed to talk about the events and dosed them with LSD. The brothels were equipped with one-way mirrors and the sessions were filmed for later viewing and study.

I was shocked to find out that in other experiments people

were given LSD without their knowledge, where they were interrogated under bright lights while numerous doctors took notes. The people were told that their "trips" would be extended indefinitely if they refused to reveal their secrets of their experiences. The people being interrogated were CIA employees, U.S. military personnel, and agents suspected of working for the other side in the Cold War. Long-term illness and several deaths resulted from this. This made me feel quite angry and sick.

After my one-and-only LSD experience, something had shifted for me. Intuitively, I got the message: Take that experience as it was, then leave it alone. I never touched LSD again. I could feel in my heart that it could become dangerous for me and that I would never quite get back to that same place I was blessed with during my first trip.

I knew then that there had to be a way for me to shake out of the old paradigm and the story of my Catholic upbringing in Bavaria. Since I had gotten the go-ahead to study in the U.K. for a year, after all of the pushing and prodding my aunts and Walter had done, there would be new life in store. At least it felt that some people were looking out for me—helping me to prepare my future.

The last day of my life in Munich, I was visiting an old jazz club where some of my friends were waiting for me to say goodbye. I sat facing the door when suddenly a woman walked in with a paper bag in her hand. She scanned the club with her eyes and as soon as she spotted me, walked towards me and handed me the paper bag she was carrying. My friends were all quite surprised and asked me if I knew here. She said, "This is for you—Good luck!" and left the club. I wondered often how she knew I needed the book, *The Diary of Anais Nin*. I carried it with me for many years to come.

9

Arriving in England

The time had finally come, and I was thrilled to have won my father over, and to be going to the U.K. for a year. As mentioned, it took much convincing from family and friends, and some hard bargaining on my part, but my father had finally released me. I told him that if he let me go to England it would be good for everyone. I would most definitely have a better chance in the Munich job market when I returned after becoming fluent in English, and that seemed to please him.

Of course, my father, at that point, wasn't functioning very well. After the dust settled from my mother's death, no one could look him in the eye again. My aunts were very much in favor of me going to England due to my father's erratic behavior, and relieved to not have to worry about me for a while. They never suggested my brother or me to live with them; this way, if I went to England, it got me out of their way too—anyway, that's what I felt.

A few days after my seventeenth birthday, the student exchange package arrived at our house. I was excited to get a chance to make my own decisions, in some part, for the first time in my life. When asked whether or not I wanted to be in a household with children and/or animals, I decided not to choose a family with children. Animals sounded closer to my comfort zone, at that point, and children felt like they would be too much. And me—too much for them.

I remember being a tad hesitant on the day I left home. Would my life change forever? Would I ever return home? Did I even want to?

Even though I had dreamed of adventures far away, I had never flown in an airplane and had not been any further than Austria, Switzerland or Italy which were accessible by car. A Christian organization that placed students in the appropriate exchange student host family placed me with the British couple. My friend, Petra, used this service when she moved to London for a year, so it sounded like a good fit for me, too. However, she left for a different reason: Petra became pregnant by her boyfriend at seventeen and the family wanted to get her out of Bavaria to save face.

In late August of 1978, I arrived on a cloudy day at London Heathrow Airport. I was officially an "Au-pair," what today we call a "Foreign Exchange Student."

In my mind, I was there for one reason and one reason only—to learn the English language and become more marketable. Motivated by wanting and needing to be out of my father's house, I could overcome my nerves; I was ready to go.

That would soon change.

When the host family picked me up from the airport, I could tell right away that they were very conservative people. And, I wasn't. The man of the house, donned a plain gray business suit that hung too big on him, and was seriously out-of-style. His wife was wearing thick, black-framed spectacles with her hair in a tightly wound bun. Her brown pencil skirt, suit jacket and starched white blouse buttoned all the way up to her neck spelled "uptight" to me.

I knew this wasn't going to be easy.

From the airport, we rode together in their baby blue, British-built Ford with a torn interior and rusted body. This was not what I expected, nor what I was used to. My family drove luxury cars and knew the finer things in life, and here I was in the back seat of some strangers' jalopy. I felt like I was in a silent movie being rattled around in the back of that car, wondering when it would stop and the "B" movie would end.

Hadn't I done everything in my power to leave home in a responsible way? And, now, in these few minutes with these strangers, I was ready to head right back.

For me, hearing British English for the first time was awkward and disconcerting. The sound of their speech, the foreign dialect, of course, was very different from my English teacher in high school, and I couldn't make out what anybody was saying, especially these strange people that picked me up from the airport. Of course, I did my best, and tried to make out what was in store for me, doubtfully thinking—perhaps I will adjust in time…

After an hour and a half of chaotic motorway driving, we arrived at my hosts' quaint brick townhouse in the small suburb of Nottingham. The house was a 1,200-square foot box built from brick with narrow hallways, eight-by-eight rooms, single panel metal windows, furnished with drab and lifeless 1950s furniture. I remember my dismay when they showed me "my room." I don't know what I expected, but it sure wasn't a plain cramped cell. I felt trapped already, and I'd just gotten there.

No. Our worlds were just too different. My teenage mind was confused.

This absolutely was not going to work for me. I hate to sound pampered, but living in style was really the only good thing about my life back home. This family's attitude, manner of addressing me, and their simplicity, didn't help things much, right at the get-go. I had come for adventure and stimulation, and I wasn't going to get any of those things with these people.

I was sure I'd get deeply depressed if I stayed, or so I convinced myself. The woman of the house treated me like a maid from the moment I arrived. Right away, Mrs. Heath showed me where to find the ironing board and cleaning supplies, so that I understood my "place" and my responsibilities.

She told me that my job would begin the next morning. Not much more was discussed, no pleasantries, no questions, no endearing gestures… no motherly love.

I thought part of the problem might be that my English wasn't that good yet, and maybe we just didn't understand each other. Like, there was an error in translation or something.

No, that was not it, all she wanted was a servant, not a starry-eyed young woman who needed conversation and affection; not some young girl who didn't know what she was doing. Her tone of voice was snappy and assuming; I felt myself being put down, not lifted up by her response to me, and my sensitive, broken little self couldn't handle it. Why couldn't I be with a different kind of woman, one who could be just a tad more welcoming and respectful towards me.

It wasn't all bad, of course. I was happy to be taking classes at the local university, where I met some friendly people more my age, who were also foreign and fresh off the block. Relieved to get out after a week of ironing and taking care of the house, I was invited to the local pub by some fellow students. We planned our next rendezvous the moment we said "Goodnight" that evening, hoping to see each other soon. I was pleased to have a chance to maybe make some friends.

Arriving at the house 30-minutes after curfew, the "Lady" was clearly upset. She raised her voice at me, exclaiming: "You are unsuitable. We are taking you back!"

I had no idea what this English word meant, "unsuitable," which I now find pretty amusing. Stumped, I looked it up in the dictionary. Apparently, I was "unpassend" in my language. I figured out what she meant and what was happening. I got fired from being an exchange student! I guess they wanted a girl who worked all day for free, stayed in her cell and didn't go out to socialize, and they especially did not one who needed to talk with the family with whom she lived.

I clearly didn't fit their family structure. Stiff, no-nonsense, no nothing is how their take on life felt to me. Oh, well. I was relieved not to have to stay there, but had no idea where I'd go next. Insecurity threatened to rise up, since I had never been so far away from my small township in Bavaria before.

The very next day, I was put on a train back to London, arriving at the Christian center for au pair dropouts, the place they put the miscreants, I suppose. The agency would do the job of finding me another family to house me. I hoped the next one would be better than the first.

During my stay at the center, I was thrilled; it was stimulating to meet all kinds of people from all over the world. Many of them were waiting for a new family placement because the previous one was not a good match. Suddenly, I felt better, knowing I wasn't the only one! There were many stories flying around in the center from girls who had all sorts of experiences, some not so great, some quite humorous. We were able to bond over shared tales of quirky personalities and strange customs, trying to laugh off any sense of being "unsuitable" for the job of being 17- or 18-year old students.

I recall being thrilled to spend time with a couple of Spanish girls that I really enjoyed, along with several young women from Italy. What I didn't do is make any calls home. I wasn't sure how to breach the subject of my initial failure. If I admitted to my father that something had gone wrong, he might force me back home. I couldn't take the chance. This was my opportunity to figure something out on my own and I was up for the challenge.

I settled into the Christian center quite comfortably, only to be placed in a new au-pair position just three days later. A wonderful lady, by the name of Sophie greeted me in the main office for an interview. I remember her being very considerate and kind. She explained that she was a busy psychiatrist and needed somebody to watch after her mother who apparently had the onset of Alzheimer's. This peaked my interest, so I obliged.

Her mother's name was Mrs. Steinberger, and she was an 80-year-old Jewish woman from Austria whose daughter, Sophie, clearly cared. In those days they had no name for "Alzheimer's" so I had no way of knowing what to expect or how to prepare for Mrs. Steinberger and her lapsing memory.

I fondly remember how each morning she would put on her make-up only so that I could wash it back off and put it on again. What a pleasant game we played, me removing the eyebrows she had painted above the original eyebrow line and that bright ruby red lipstick haphazardly placed somewhere on her wrinkled little cheeks. It was quite amusing, our time together. We had a good laugh each morning. For me, this was the best therapy in the world. In no time, I was officially assigned to do Mrs. Steinberger's make-up before she could get her hands on it.

It was just Mrs. Steinberger and myself in her four-bedroom apartment. Her house was a stark contrast to the first home I had stayed, with its high vaulted ceilings and expensive antiques, and a selection of beautiful artifacts from all over the world, to appreciate throughout the space. I had an elegant room with a beautiful red cherry wood closet and inlaid mirrors. This made me feel much more at home, and in my element.

Every day, Mrs. Steinberger would ask to take a walk around the block, which wasn't like any normal walk for a young, athletic girl like me. It would take us at least an hour to shuffle around a very short distance. It was her time to socialize too—she'd make sure to talk to each and every shopkeeper from the footer to the baker, *to the candlestick maker*—and to the grocer and the postal man. She needed me and my help, and clearly in ways she could not have known, I needed her and the comfort of her home.

I felt for the first time I was really living in England, and I relaxed enough to take in the sights and notice the differences. I was amused by how they drive on the left side of the road, their tall brick houses, white toast and orange marmalade. Of course, there was Piccadilly Circus, Leicester Square with the famous Big Ben clock, and the most magnificent cathedrals.

In her condition, Mrs. Steinberger often mistook me for her daughter and called me "Pupperl," an endearing Austrian name for "doll." I was her little doll and I was happy to indulge her in the fantasy. Her flat above the grocery store was so densely packed with lavish antiques that it made it impossible to walk the corridor without bumping into furniture or stacks of old magazines. I was sure she was a hoarder. Or, maybe she just forgot that she had already purchased two of the same china sets before getting a third.

While my time with Mrs. Steinberger was charming, and a vast improvement, I soon figured out I was a little out of my league. I got settled in for a bit, while studying English and English history, psychology and art. The classes were interesting to me, but the occasional intensity of spending so much time with a woman who had dementia started to take its toll. It's a drain on anyone, especially a young inexperienced teen. It's then that her daughter intervened.

Sophie visited several times a week, so we got familiar and comfortable with one another. She was a kind and intelligent woman in her fifties, who was compassionate and a humanitarian. I really liked the way Sophie showed an interest in me. She and I would talk about her family, and that's when my past came up a few times in conversation, and I shared about my mother and father.

Soon into the stay, Sophie realized I was suffering from post-traumatic stress disorder, in shock from my mother's murder, and having had to live with my father and the lie. Being a psychologist, Sophie figured out I was in need of a little more TLC—tender loving care. It was Sophie, who was responsible for me getting moved to a situation that she thought more well-suited for a young lady, where I wouldn't have to be around a woman on the last leg of her life. Sophie was sure that I needed something younger, fresher, and less close to the world of disease and death.

I agreed.

Only two months into my stay with the Steinbergers,

Sophie recommended me to be the dog sitter for the proprietor of the "Old Bull and Bush," a three-year-old pub in Hampstead. The owners supposedly needed a sitter for their beautiful Boarder Collies, and, since it was animals we were talking about, I thought it might work.

I was to walk their dogs twice daily and conduct some light housekeeping at the proprietors' flat. They lived above the pub next to the staff quarters, where many a famous artist or poet had previously lived. The money was good for a teenager like myself and a lot more than the average au-pair made in those days. So, I was delighted to be a dog walker in artsy, colorful Hampstead, where the famous singer Florrie Forde wrote the song "Down At The Old Bull And Bush."

After the pub guests had a few pints for the night, everyone would get out the weathered song sheets and the "Florrie Forde" song, as well as other popular sing-along music. Their festivities made me feel quite at home.

The traditional pub crawl consisted of drinking a lot, singing, and shepherd's pie. I found this so entertaining and humorous, and was amazed that the reserved, stoic British sentiment, after all, was quite loose and rowdy at times. I remember enjoying the old locals that had frequented the pub for decades, and their ploy to meet the pretty young girls from Spain, Italy and France—and how they would get them to sing along in Cockney London dialect, causing all to laugh hysterically.

Every day, morning and night, I walked the two very friendly two-year-old border collies. I'd have to pass by the front of the pub entrance where I enjoyed hearing people singing and laughing. The walks around the famous Golders Hill Park were two to three miles long. I remember how much I enjoyed my time to be by myself in nature. And the dogs, well, I enjoyed their loving, loyal companionship as we walked along together in the fresh air.

The only drawback to this third homestay, was the age of the building and the way it made me feel. My room, sat at the end of a long hallway with at least seven rooms on either side. Each room had a uniquely painted door with names of famous poets or musicians who had frequented the Old Bull and Bush in the olden days.

Immediately on my first walk down the long narrow hallway with dark weathered wooden floor, I could feel a cold breeze that left me with an eerie feeling in my belly. Built in 1660 and over 350 years old, I could tell things had happened there and I was convinced that the "Old Bull and Bush" was, indeed, haunted.

I was horrified when, during the first night there, when the floor started to creak in the middle of the night. This gave me shivers down my spine. What really took a toll on me was the automatic opening and closing of the hallway doors with nobody visible there, and the howling of wolves I recall hearing in the distance. I must admit, I don't think I closed my eyes the first night, or the second night, for that matter.

When I was ready to go to sleep, I recall, reluctantly, finding myself peeking under the bed only to find three crosses. I will never forget that. As a good Catholic girl from Bavaria, this was a bit frightening and made me feel anxious and afraid. Why would anyone ever find three crosses under a bed? Who would have put them there? Isn't that strange, I said to myself. Was somebody trying to tell me something?

Yes, you guessed it. This particular "foreign exchange" didn't last long either. Only two nights. I ran out that day and never came back.

Three homes stay later, I found myself not able to go back

for another try, and decided to stay over at my new boyfriend's house instead. I'd met him through the managers at the Old Bull and Bush.

They were very kind to me and would often give me food to give to the Iranian students that had been cut off financially. I remember cooking for up to thirteen Iranian people at times, and knew that what I brought from the pub in the evening was the only food they'd have all day. In time, Iran and Iranian students would take on significant meaning in my life.

The Shock Of Nazi Germany

"Never do anything against conscience, even if the state demands it."

—Albert Einstein

I must remind you, I was born in 1961, and from age twelve through sixteen, my parents sent me to a private school in Munich. Knowing what I know now, I can't fathom why there was no mention of World War II in the curriculum. There were occasional references to Hitler as a dictator like Stalin, but no one ever spoke of concentration camps to me, at home or in my school. There was no history lesson covering World War II in its entirety.

Nowadays, it is mandatory for students to visit a concentration camp, and everything, including the harsh facts is talked about in text books. I remember my father making reference to some deadbeat people he encountered, and making a statement like, "If Hitler was alive today, this would not be happening."

Once I knew the truth, and was smacked right in the face with it, it became extremely hard to come to terms with comments such as that from my father. My thoughts spun… *Did he feel support for the Hitler regime? Was he in the Hitler Youth? Did he know the truth of it?* I will never know for sure. But I guess that partially explains why I was kept in the dark about Hitler and the Nazi agenda.

My obsession grew for trying to grasp what had happened in Nazi Germany. I had to know why they did what they did—if that is ever humanly possible to comprehend! Probably not.

My school curriculum covered the Celts, Alexander the Great and the Vikings, and other not so important stuff, but Hitler—a taboo subject. It goes without saying that when I arrived in the U.K. as a foreign exchange student, it came as a huge surprise to learn about this revolting and horrific German history I knew literally nothing about. And my country and family were intricately tied to it, yet silent.

I must say, I felt embarrassed on more than one occasion, in class, when the subjects of World War II or Nazis came up. You see, I had no idea that over eleven million human beings were brutally murdered in my own country, only sixteen years before I was born.

Apparently, London had provided a safe haven for many Jews during the war; unfortunately I had no idea what had happened to them. What a shock! I continually wondered—*why didn't anyone tell me the truth?*

When I briefly stayed with sweet old Mrs. Steinberger in the UK as an au pair, I found out her family was originally from Austria. Sophie, her daughter, confided in me that they were grateful to have made it to London after the war, avoiding the holocaust as runaway Jews. To my dismay, I learned for the first time the horrors of the holocaust when Sophie relayed some stories in our short time together. I was revolted and sickened, but appreciative to know the truth.

Like so many others, many of their relatives had been respected doctors and attorneys who were killed in the gas chambers of Auschwitz. Probably a good thing Mrs. Steinberger didn't remember any of this; her dementia, being so severe, might have been a blessing.

My first personal exposure to what really happened in Germany occurred when I walked into a bakery in Golder's Green to buy a loaf of bread. I was kindly greeted by the proprietor, a very thin and tall woman, in her fifties who was standing behind the counter.

"You must be a student, welcome to London! Where are you from, my dear and what would you like?" She inquired with a welcoming and affectionate smile.

"I am a student from Munich, Germany!" I replied in a merry and happy demeanor.

No sooner had I uttered these words, when in seconds, her face turned from rosy cheeked to white as a ghost. She said with an angry and loud voice:

"Leave my Bakery, we don't serve people from Munich here; please leave!"

After this confrontation, I left feeling sad, shocked and surprised. I needed to know all that had happened. Why would I be treated this way?

I was hit with *shockwave* after *shockwave*, as I took it upon myself to read every book I could put my hands on about Hitler and the Nazi's. I refused to speak a word of German for two years. When Mrs. Steinhauser and I watched television, there were still anti-Nazi propaganda movies on Saturday afternoons (never shown in Bavaria). They were a great way for me to practice English and learn more about the ruthless actions of Nazi Germany. I got a glimpse of the *unspeakable* that had taken place, just sixteen years before my birth.

Once my English improved, I was able to read books like *Mein Kampf* by Adolf Hitler, which was banned in Germany until 2016.

How could such a thing happen? Being a mere teenager, along with coping with the death of my own mother, and being a girl who loved people, this consumed me with sadness, and made me sick to my stomach. I vowed *never* to be racially or religiously biased toward anyone, and became ashamed of my heritage and country. The next few months I dedicated myself to learning English fluently; I even tried to change my accent so that no one could tell I was German. I certainly didn't look German with my dark hair and olive complexion, so most people thought I was from either from France, Italy or Spain. I hid my heritage pretty well.

In London, I rented a room from Daniel, who was an artist and publisher—and a beautiful person. I never forget our conversation one night at his fabulous artsy home at Swiss Cottage in London. It was a long weekend, and there were two other students living in the house. After everyone went to bed, he smoked a little weed and somehow the subject of Germany came up.

"You don't seem very German and you don't sound German either!" he exclaimed.

Emotionally, I answered him. "I didn't know anything about the devastation to the Jewish people during World War II, and the Nazi's and what they stood for, until I arrived in England. I feel ashamed to be German, and to have come from a place where people did such horrible things to the Jews!"

He was kind to me, but responded with such sadness in his eyes. "I like you Petra, you have a good heart and you are conscious person, but we lost almost everyone in Auschwitz and I will never set foot in Germany as long as I live!"

Emotionally, I said. "I don't know if I can ever live there again after learning all this. I am so sorry, Daniel that you lost all those people!" I cried and Daniel consoled me.

I didn't blame him then for being so angry. And honestly, I don't know—how does one overcome such horrible atrocities as were committed by the German Nazis? I regretted being kept in the dark, and being so ignorant and naïve.

Today, my brother, Wolfgang, lives in Dachau—not far from the concentration camp that once housed hundreds of thousands of people. I was told by American World War II vets that were in my home town at that time, that the citizens of Munich were told by the American officers to take a tour of the concentration camps as they were evacuating prisoners from Dachau. The German people needed to see with their own eyes what really happened in the concentration camps. They were told such lies by the Nazis. Their propaganda movies painted a rosy picture, and certainly, many of the people wanted to believe in the lies that the government was telling them at that time. The Nazis harnessed the power of mass media manipulation. Obviously, there is much more to Adolf Hitler and Nazi Germany than meets the eye. I share more theories on my website at: www.petranicoll.com

You can see the concentration camp, Dachau from the main road as you ride through town, which has become a tourist attraction. Whenever I visit my brother in Germany, he comments about the concentration camp, and how embarrassed he is when foreigners come into town and want him to drive them there.

Films like "Hitler's Children," clearly demonstrated that during the war, there were some who did not know this was happening right in their own backyards, or at least chose not to know. What is most disturbing is how so many people could not be aware of the suffering that went on right under their noses. Some say they actually believed "It was a retreat for the Jewish people." No! How can people be that insensitive to vibration and feeling of all that is around them?

Today, I'm grateful that there are mandatory trips for students in Munich and surroundings villages to visit concentration camps like Dachau and Auschwitz—to learn of the horror—starvation, experimentation, and the reality of suffering and death of the masses of people—men, women, children—all starved or gassed to death.

How could a man like Adolf Hitler gain such leverage in Germany, with his extreme, radical, evil ideas? … Mass media control? Esoteric magic? Hypnotism of the masses? These are haunting questions for posterity.

Why?

I have no idea why, but for whatever reason I was not supposed to know about the inhumanities of the Nazi's that occurred in my homeland until I got to London. It was a complete jolt to my system! There must have been an enormous shame in my family regarding the war. I presume they wanted to shelter me from the truth, because there was some secret and shame involving my father's family. I wish my mother would have told me more about this.

There were many relatives on my father's side that my brother and I were not permitted to see. And I remember how my mother dreaded to go to my father's parent's house; she thought they were uneducated and primitive people. She always had to psychologically prepare herself to visit them.

I enjoyed seeing my grandparents, but my mother pointed out frequently, how different they were in consciousness and demeanor, but I as a little child didn't understand and just loved them anyway. No one ever mentioned the fact that we had an uncle on my father's side who was an officer during Nazi Germany, who had the same mustache as Hitler. I now have a photo in my possession that shows him standing in front of Dachau concentration camp in 1943, so proud to show his power as he poses for the camera. He looks almost like Hitler. Obviously, my mother shielded my brother and me from this, and ever having anything to do with that part of the family.

My great uncle did fight on behalf of the Jewish people. Imprisoned, and so weak from starvation, he died shortly after the Americans liberated Germany from the Nazi's. The saddest part of all is that his own brother put him there because they were on opposite sides—he had tried to save the Jews.

I remember my father saying to me:

"You should be proud to be a Kufner."

The uncle, who saved Jews from the Nazi's, was a good man. But at the same time, my father was still extremely prejudice toward all foreigners. He didn't want his daughter to associate with children who weren't German born.

Once, at fourteen, I brought a cute Italian boy over to the house, and my father did not let him enter and called him a derogatory name like "Itaker" meaning "Italian guest worker. "It became clear that my father had racial prejudice within him; I was sad that he didn't see beyond heritage, race and color.

I was always inquisitive about my father's background, but he would not tell me much, and all I have today are a few photos from his childhood and youth, and a deeper understanding of the terror my parents experienced as "Children of the War." Every day living life in and out of bomb shelters, obvious starvation, and seeing people die. The war lasted from 1939 to 1945, so you can imagine how much fear, racial prejudice and terror these little children must have experienced during that time, and the post-traumatic stress they carried into their adult lives.

My father became an atheist after being sent to an apprenticeship as a machinist at a Catholic school in Munich.

He told me that the priests did terrible things to the boys, and that he was unable to speak much about it. He did say that one day he saw what they did to his friend and lost control and beat up one of the priests. He never told me the details of what happened to his friend nor him.

I believe he was subject to sexual abuse in the name of Christ, and his innocence and belief in God was broken forever; that explained why he hated the church so much and called the priest's charlatans. The spirit in a human being can be broken. My father's spirit was not intact and he was unable to forgive—and he never wanted anyone to speak about religion in his presence. If we did, he would fly into a rage, screaming, "The church is evil, they are hypocrites and I hate them, all of them!"

My mother would cover our ears and walk us out of the room until he would calm down and regain his senses. Nevertheless, my brother and I still participated in all the Catholic holidays and communions that were celebrated in our little town.

Even as I am writing this story, I feel my father's pain that he must have endured as a young boy. As for me, early on I left the confines of the Catholic Church, to become a seeker of God, greater truths, and knowledge of the universe.

When I was seventeen, and after my mother died, I would often lie on my bed and hold my father's photo in front of me and stare at it for hours in the hope that I could find the reason why he was so angry and closed during my upbringing. I wanted to forgive him, and find a glimpse of goodness in him that would allow me to balance my own rage about his erratic behavior, his inability to communicate positively, his narcissism, and his false ideology of the world. I did not understand. But then again, no one is expected to be whole and healthy after such traumatic experiences, which I came to understand more when I studied psychology in London. From a distance, and with time, I became able to see my father more objectively.

> *"Media manipulation in the U.S. today is more efficient than it was in Nazi Germany, because here we have the pretense we have all the information we want. That misconception prevents people from even looking for the truth."*
>
> —Mark Crispin Miller

10

Mary Magdalene

Whether running away from, or going to someplace better, I couldn't yet say for sure, but either way, I was living in London. Bertrand Russell said, "The world is full of magical things patiently waiting for our wits to grow sharper…" and I suppose that was the stage of development I was in.

It was an extraordinary time for me in London after I left Bavaria and my family. After my first strike out with my host family, I ended up in Hampstead, a much desired suburb of London. I was staying at Mrs. Steinberger's home. It was there where I would meet a woman that would further open me to the world of spirit and to my destiny.

One day, when I was on my way back to the house, just waiting for my bus, a woman about ten years older than me caught my attention. She had an athletic body, and wonderfully animated. And the way she smiled… I thought her interesting to watch. She was standing intently on the other side of the road, watching for her bus. For some reason, I felt compelled to wave at her and thought nothing would come of it. Of course, I was surprised when she walked across the street straight towards me.

In a friendly way, this energetic lady introduced herself as "Ana Maria," in what was very broken English. She claimed that she was from Barcelona, Spain, and that she had to talk to me.

Apparently, I had appeared in her dreams. I thought this a strange first introduction. What did she mean? Ana Maria went on to share that while in a deep depression, she had looked up at the clouds only to see an apparition of me. In her vision, she was told that I had healed her heart in dreamtime. (By definition, "the dreaming" or "the dreamtime" indicates a psychic state in which or during which contact is made with the ancestral spirits, or the Law, or that special period of the beginning.—Mudrooroo, Aboriginal writer.)

Ana Maria was a very tiny, sensitive woman; I assumed this—quite intuitively. She told me she had her heart broken many times when she asked for a miracle, a sign. When she saw me across the street surrounded in a golden light and halo, the same things that appeared in her vision, she thought she had received what she asked for… in me.

Ana Maria said there was more, "You are not who you think you are."

At that point, we were standing under the expansive London sky at a bus stop, so I didn't quite know what to make of Ana Maria. I decided to stick around because she seemed to need me for some reason. In a forward kind of way, she went on to ask me to live with her in Barcelona with her family. Apparently, they would have hotel work for me and I could learn all of the languages I desired. It seemed so important to Ana Maria that I listen to what she had to say, so I did. She was sure that I had a big life ahead of me, and insisted how special I was. "Didn't I know what I was capable of?" she asked.

No. Not really. At that age, who does?

I became a little suspicious, at the time, and didn't quite believe what she was saying. No one had really talked to me this way; it was all new to me. I didn't think much about dreamtime. How could a stranger know these things and so quickly trust me, and invite me to stay with her family?

Regardless, Ana Maria and I became instant friends in a day's time. I decided to bring her back to my apartment to meet Mrs. Steinberger, my exchange host. After introducing Ana Maria, we ran into my antique laden room for a while to chat as if we were schoolgirls off to share secrets in our little clubhouse. I'm sure Mrs. Steinberger, in her forgetful dementia, didn't mind our rudeness.

I remember how funny it was talking to Ana Maria in my Austrian-infused English… and her in a Castilian lisp. How was I going to learn English at this rate?

While we were sitting on the bed of my beautiful bedroom, I felt the urge to share something meaningful with Ana Maria. She was an odd, special woman who was giving me so much affection and, perhaps, significant information. I reached into my jewelry box and found a pendant. It came from France, when Germany occupied the country during WW II. The pendant was a ruby teardrop with a silver chain that I had had since my Grandfather gave it to me on my fifteenth birthday.

I remember holding out my hand and placing the gift in Ana Maria's delicate hand. She put the necklace around her neck. I could tell she was a bit in shock; she couldn't believe it, that I was giving her this. I was touched when this gesture made her cry; then we hugged.

Really, until this day, I don't know why I gave her that family heirloom. My grandfather would have wanted me to keep it, but I didn't put value on things like jewelry. I guess I felt she needed some protection and this was the only real valuable thing I could give her.

This was a tender moment but something seemed a little off about all of the attention I was getting from Ana Maria. At first, I didn't catch it; I was young and naive. Ana Maria was quite affectionate and cuddly. Clearly, now, I think that she was probably hitting on me with the way she looked at me. After all, who immediately asks a woman to go live with them in another country? Years after I met Ana Maria, it came to me that she may have been a lesbian. I really didn't know what was going on exactly. And I wasn't attracted to her physically.

Before we left the room at about 9:00 p.m., Ana Maria told me something I would put in the back of my head for some time. She knelt down on her bare knees in front of me and took my hands. I was quite nervous… What was she going to tell me next?

In a tender voice, Ana Maria exclaimed adamantly: "Don't you know who you are, don't you know who you are?"

Yes, I am Petra a girl from Bavaria, I thought, listening to a crazy woman.

But that's not what she was talking about.

She continued, "Remember? You appeared to me last night in my dream." A silence passed. "You are Mary Magdalene."

Can you imagine my surprise? I thought for sure she was crazy, but didn't want to hurt her feelings. It was the most bizarre moment in my life up until that point, I must say…

Here I was appearing in someone's dream like the second coming of Mary Magdalene from the days of Christ, who claimed that I healed her, that I took her depression away. It was strangely familiar, not surprising and certainly not the last time. Needless to say, this young seventeen-year-old girl from Bavaria just wanted to run as far away from this very uncomfortable situation as possible.

I remember not really believing her at the time. Of course I didn't. But, I have to say—her conviction made it really hard to kick her out of the room. My internal dialogue went something like, "Make it stop God, take her away. I want this gone—and her gone. I cannot hear this, it's a lie! What does she want from me and why?"

Sometime later, I found out from some girls at college, who came from Barcelona like Ana Maria, that Ana Maria was considered what they called a "clairvoyant." Her family was quite known due to their hotel business. Supposedly, Ana-Maria had a reputation as a healer in her hometown.

I didn't cut Ana Maria off. We actually went on to spend some time together, when I decided to get an official reading from her at her apartment.

During the session, I learned about my life's path. I would go on to study many things, and to lose several people along the way. She told me several rather specific things. I remember one more clearly than the others, which I found fairly confusing to my impressionable young mind.

Ana Maria leaned over me to say, "You are going to make a different decision. I wish you were going that way, instead of this way. It's like the revolving doors in life. It's a free will planet and you have a choice."

She knew I would go on to have a long-term relationship with a particular musician and she didn't approve.

Years later...

It wasn't until many years later that I understood the importance of my encounter with Ana Maria. Mary Magdalene would be a theme; it seems, throughout my adult life. While I listened to her that day, I also questioned her, until one day in May of 2013.

I was visiting some friends in Portland, Oregon, where I had a very interesting encounter. My friend, Lori, asked me if I had ever heard of the book *Messenger.* At the time of this discussion, I was fifty-one years old, and had already gone on to teach many workshops and classes, including teaching Reiki to over three thousand students. By then, well, my experiences with the metaphysical had stretched well beyond Ana Maria.

That day, I remember telling Lori, I happened to carry the exact same book in my healing center/bookstore in Roseburg, where I owned a restaurant and juice bar. Lori asked me if I'd met the author before.

She said that the author's name was John, and that he just lived down the street from her house in Portland. Lori thought it a good idea to call him and meet. Apparently, the book had sold 17 million copies and was translated into eighteen languages worldwide. It was a story about a successful businessman, real estate developer, who was running for Congress in the U.S.

He went to see a psychic in Portland to find out if he'd fair in politics. The well-known psychic in Portland, told him that he would be in front crowds of people in the future, but not in politics, that it had something to do with him being alive 2000 years ago, a past life or something.

Upon hearing this, John explained he was just trying to

find out if he could win his election and was startled and curious. He then went to see another reader and hypnotist in his hometown of Portland. For the next six months he was hypnotized on a weekly basis; the sessions were recorded and transcribed and the book, *Divine Guides*, evolved from these sessions.

During hypnosis, John was informed, supposedly, that he was the reincarnation of the apostle Paul. John went on to speak in the book about his experience 2,000 years ago and what really happened to Paul from his perspective.

Lori had met John briefly on the football field while their sons were playing on the same team, so our getting together was pretty simple. John answered the phone when I called and agreed to meet Lori, another of her friends, and me. John suggested a nearby restaurant and told us that his wife was out of town and couldn't make it.

When we arrived, John was already waiting for us in a quiet part of the restaurant in Portland. I was quite curious to hear about his hypnosis sessions and his original encounter with the psychic. Lori and her friend were talking John's head off for two hours. I remember that he just kept looking at me the whole time. I was curious about his energy and the books that he wrote.

Lori and her friend had so many questions that I never got a word in edgewise. It was a lovely evening, and before our departure from the restaurant, John asked me for a business card. A couple of days later, I received a phone call from him asking me to meet him for lunch at the Plaza Hotel. I had to come to Portland from Eugene anyway, so agreed to meet just the two of us. As I anticipated the visit, I recall thinking what a strange and curious energy John had around him and how it made me feel a little bit uncomfortable.

I remember walking into the hotel lobby by a beautiful waterfall. Over lunch, we ended up talking for hours. Well, he did all of the talking, mostly about himself, his history and his journey as an author. It was really fascinating listening to John talk about his journey from real estate developer to running for Congress and then stepping into a completely different role as the reincarnation of the Apostle Paul.

At some point the subject changed, and then John did something odd. He slowly took my hand, refusing to let it go. He asked, "Do you know who you really are?"

I thought to myself… *Well, sir…that is the one question I have been asking myself for decades. So, please tell me.*

I said that I didn't really know, even though my past lives had come up several times over the years. So I decided to ask, "What do you mean, know who I really was?"

John replied in an intense tone, "Well, I wrote about you in my book, *Time Is Now.* He continued, "On page 119, I have a description of you."

He was absolutely convinced that I was the reincarnation of Mary Magdalene. This did not really surprise me, nor was I impressed, as John may have hoped I would be. I had heard this before with Ana Maria, from a psychic in Paris, and by the leader of a secret society meeting I attended in the U.S.

At this point, it was just a matter of what I really believed and was going to do with this information.

As I learned in my yoga practice, I have been always very careful not to let my ego get in the way of my humility. And, if any of this was true, what was I to do with it anyway?

John was very intelligent, somewhat manipulative, well-read and extremely intuitive. My intuition told me that John was not well, nor was he happy in his life and that he, perhaps, was trying to escape his own predicament through me. If I hadn't had the training with my guru by this time in my life, I think that, maybe, I would've fallen for what I felt was John fishing for my attention or energy or something.

I learned from my guru early on that for those who believe this way, we have thousands of incarnations and if we hold on to the past it will haunt us. There are so many of us on this planet that were alive 2,000 years ago, and there are many, many over souls—like Mary Magdalene, Paul or Peter, yes, even Jesus.

(By definition, "Over soul," in the transcendentalism of Ralph Waldo Emerson, "is a spiritual essence or vital force in the universe in which all souls participate and that therefore transcends individual consciousness.")

Many people have past life flashbacks or claim to have memories of their old selves. So, I really couldn't afford to take anything like this too personally. Without being a religious person, I have had so many visions with Jesus, Saint Germaine and many others dear to my heart. We are all connected to the infinite soul of the universe and to multiple incarnations. Lives come and go; visions come and go. It was best to listen to John and allow it to merely confirm what others had said, that, maybe, just maybe—I had a little Mary Magdalene inside of me.

For me, visions had occurred from my childhood onward. Jesus was a big one who'd frequently visit. When I really sat in communion with the spirit of Jesus, the relationship became clearer. In one vision, Jesus told me that I was accurate in my belief that God made man and man made religion and that he would always be by my side. He told me that the human body is one of the greatest gifts. I know that even if I had been Mary Magdalene 2,000 years ago, it was a very difficult life according to Jesus. Often, when he comes to me, I can feel this deep connection with him, and I can only imagine that my love for Jesus in this life is the same as it must have been then.

Today, even my partner, Jerry, tells me constantly that he feels Jesus in the room every time we are together. Many of my Reiki students say they've seen him during their initiations or during meditation. I don't really think of this as special, I believe there are so many people that have a connection to Christ and see him as well. His Soul is ever-present on the planet—I believe this is true especially at this time of awakening we find ourselves in.

I find that, for me, the trick to being human is to be able to grow and evolve, not to be caught by the illusion of "layover" lives. But we haven't always been able to talk about them, share them or tell others our impressions of their reincarnations. Only recently does it seem more and more people are "coming out."

When I was young, I had memories of some incarnations. But it was taboo in the Catholic system to talk about it. So, I just kept them to myself. Ever since the church took out any mention of 'reincarnation' from The Bible during the 4th Century, it's been hush hush. I always felt this was to control the populace. Me? I rarely discussed it with my family. Maybe that's why I tried not to make much of the visions others had of me as an adult.

When I was seventeen, Ana-Maria was convinced I had a big journey ahead of me and she was right. I went against her advice and sometimes wonder how my life would have evolved had I gone to Barcelona with her. Her impression of me would follow me for decades and come up again and again, which I always found fascinating.

Mary Magdalene and Jesus would play integral parts in

my life, as well, as would the esoteric and metaphysical worlds. But I needed to be patient; these things, transcendentalism, take time to assimilate…

11

Madame Blavatsky

Living in England bombarded my already tender emotions, as I got "educated" on my German history and the atrocities that had been hidden from me. Not only was I exposed to the anti-Nazi propaganda, but my personal encounters—like the one with the Jewish lady who refused to serve me at the bakery, my landlord Daniel, who had lost nearly his whole family in Auschwitz, or the postman at Trower, Still and Keeling, who cried on his knees in front of me one day, and begged me to forgive him for bombing Berlin. In all this, I was overwhelmed.

It left me feeling depressed and hopeless about the future of mankind with its incessant greed, thirst for power, wrongdoing and warmongering. Then, I proclaimed myself an atheist. With each act of history, both personal and collective, I increasingly felt like the whole universe had gone crazy.

Was I an alien that had landed along the wrong planet? At this time in my life, I even entertained the idea of taking my own life. Being so sensitive and tuned to the pain and suffering of others, it was becoming increasingly hard for me to handle—this life seemed just too much—I was engulfed in sorrow.

The more I read, the more I realized that our earth's history was ridden with war and grief. Was there ever going to be a time on our planet when humans could live in peace? Was this an impossible task? And I frequently asked… *Why am I so affected by this?*

Then I'd remember my grandfather's words:

"When people have it too good, start fighting, become corrupt, feel entitled and show jealousy toward their own family members, then we need another war to teach us what really counts and what is truly important."

I never quite "got" what he meant. But his words started to come back to me while in London. Was my grandfather saying that the only way to control human greed is when people feel threatened? This didn't make sense in my expansive world view, personally.

Was there no hope? What about the principle of "compassion?"

Even though I was only eighteen, I had become desperate for answers. I couldn't live a life of fear, a life enslaved to systems that I didn't believe in. I grasped for some semblance of order and compassion to surround my life, amidst what appeared to be a world filled with the exact opposite. Was anything like I imagined even possible?

I would dream about a utopian society, about a council of elders who were evolved enough to give sound guidance to this planet. I imagined them sharing their wisdom with the people, leaving out their ideologies and religious views. In contrast, I started to despise the invention of religion, and the wars caused by it.

It felt as if the world was asleep to goodness. Then I learned about the true power of love—love saved me!

Sometimes, I would sit for hours and write in my journal about extra-terrestrial beings that could hear my thoughts. Maybe they could answer the pretty basic questions that were driving me mad,

"Why did God create us if we are so destructive to ourselves?"

"If there is a God, then I want to know His thoughts. I don't want to suffer in my ignorance, my programming, my ancestral predisposition."

"Please God; get me out of my predicament."

I screamed into the universe for answers. I felt so extremely alone!!

My girlfriend, Otti, back in Germany, was also seeking answers about life and death, so I didn't feel so all alone. She had lost her mother, as well, and was looking into things that might provide some answers. She had stumbled upon "Rosicrucianism," a philosophical secret society, said to have been founded in late medieval Germany, and she turned me onto it. This occult sect was filled with esoteric truths about the ancient past, which, concealed from the average man, provided insight into nature, the physical universe and the spiritual realm.

The Rosicrucian's presented the legend of a German doctor and mystic philosopher referred to as Christian Rosemarie, or "Rose-cross," who was born in the year 1378 and was 106 years old when he passed.

After studying in the Middle East under various masters, possibly Sufism, Rosenkreuz was unable to spread the knowledge he had acquired to the prominent European figures. So he gathered a small circle of friends and disciples and founded the Rosicrucian Order.

During Rosenkreuz's lifetime, the "Order" consisted of only eight members, each a doctor and sworn bachelors. Each member undertook an oath to heal the sick without payment, to maintain a secret fellowship, and to find a replacement for himself in this cause before he died. Three generations had supposedly passed between the 1500 to 1600, a time when scientific, philosophical and religious freedom had grown—perhaps the public could now benefit from the Rosicrucian's knowledge.

They were looking for "good men," a secret brotherhood of alchemists and sages who were preparing to transform the arts, sciences, religion, and political and intellectual landscape of Europe from the wars of politics and religion which ravaged the continent.

I was just a young woman, a nobody, with no academic background, but wanted so desperately to be part of the Rosicrucians. But I could not find them.

After much research, I discovered two anonymous manuscripts that were published between 1607 and 1616 in Germany, and later throughout Europe. They were called the "Fama Fraternitatis," and "The Fame of the Brotherhood of Rose-Cross," and the "Confession Fraternitatis,"—"The Confession of the Brotherhood of Rose-Cross." The influence of these documents of mystic-philosopher-doctors had tried to promote a "Universal Reformation of Mankind."

While I was living in London, I was fascinated by the Rosicrucians, and felt that I was finally on the right track for answers. It gave me some sense of hopefulness to learn that the Rosicrucians opposed Roman Catholicism and its preference for dogma over empiricism, similar to the writings by the Protestant reformer Martin Luther.

This group traced their philosophy and science to the

Moors, stating that it had been kept secret for 120 years until the planet was ready. I had so many questions and the more research I did, the more I realized how complex this story really was. This was exactly the information I was looking for.

Was there a way I could connect this esoteric knowledge within my inner self, to evolve to the level of the Rosicrucians, when I had no foundation provided by my family to draw on? I needed to find a teacher and guide. The truth that I was seeking could only come from within my soul consciousness, this I knew without words.

One day at the Golder's Green Library, I stumbled upon a book by Madame Blavatsky, who was the founder of the "Theosophical Society" in 1875. Her writings provided enormous guidance and motivation to search even deeper within myself.

She was born into an aristocratic Russian-German family, and traveled widely around the Russian Empire as a child. "Helena" as she was called, was often sleepwalking, and suffered from hallucinations, was self-educated, and developed an interest in Western esotericism during her teenage years.

This fascinated me, since I, too, was very young when I became intrigued by the occult—supernatural, mystical, or magical beliefs, practices, or phenomena. It was through her writing that the floodgates of insights truly began.

Most of all, I came to understand that I had to find a guru, a teacher or guide, who could instruct me in ancient methods of meditation. I needed someone to help me, to teach me how I could overcome my monkey mind and the power it had over me. She was, without a doubt, the single most influential person on the occult sciences, and her work definitely opened the door to further insights for me. During her lifetime, Blavatsky was a controversial figure, highly respected by her supporters as an enlightened guru, and pronounced as a fraudulent charlatan by her critics.

In the 19th Century, Tibet was a very popular place to travel, for disillusioned Europeans. As an adult, as a telepath and a psychic, she felt it necessary to seek out certain teachers in Tibet. Her theosophical writings influenced the spread of Hindu and Buddhist ideas in the West as well as the development of Western esoteric currents like Ariosophy, Anthroposophy, and the New Age Movement.

She was a world traveler—traveling to Europe, the Americas, and India. Blavatsky inspired me to travel around the world, to seek out and find an ideal teacher. I wasn't sure how I would accomplish this, since I knew my family would never help me reach my goal to expand my human consciousness, where I could strive to reach a level of awareness transcending the mundane. They would call it a crazy idea, and maybe even call me crazy, I was sure.

It didn't matter, Blavatsky's book, *Secret Doctrine,* still fascinated me. In this work, she claimed, she was in telepathic contact with hidden masters, who taught her the occult history of the human race. She continued to influence my desire to find such a master and travel to India. She wrote that during her travels she was led by Buddhist monks through the underbelly of a Tibetan monastery. There, she was shown texts filled with ancient occult principles, and what she claimed was the "mystical secrets of the universe."

I was intrigued by these deep writings. The texts said that man once was pure spirit without a body, but had fallen down to base matter, darkness and chaos. Blavatsky was taught that the most powerful symbol of these esoteric ones was the "swastika." She wrote there were seven stages of evolution and named them "root races." According to her theory, there was one race that should rise again to true spirit, out of the darkness and suffering. This she named "Aryans."

In Tibet, the Swastika was known as the "son of fire and creation," but in Madame Blavatsky's teachings the Swastika was the symbol of the Aryan race. Blavatsky asserted that when she was initiated into certain magical rituals, using esoteric symbols. She had hoped that the human race, once again, would rise into pure spirit.

Helen later gained an international following as the leading theoretician of Theosophy, the esoteric movement that the Society promoted (modern movement and teaching about God and the world based on mystical insight, which follows chiefly Buddhist and Brahmanic theories especially of pantheistic evolution and reincarnation).

Later, in 1875, Blavatsky moved to New York City and co-founded the Theosophical Society, with men by the names of Henry Steel Olcott and William Judge. In 1877 she published *Isis Unveiled*, a book outlining her theosophical worldview. This associated closely with the esoteric doctrines of Hermeticism and Neoplatonism.

Blavatsky described Theosophy as "the synthesis of science, religion and philosophy," proclaiming that it was reviving an "Ancient Wisdom" which underlay all the world's religions.

In 1880, she and Olcott Moved to India, where the Society was allied to Dayananda Saraswati's Arya Samaj, a Hindu reform movement. That same year, while in Ceylon, she and Olcott became the first Euro-Americans to officially convert to Buddhism. Although opposed by the British administration, Theosophy spread rapidly in India and many countries in the world.

Amid ailing health, in 1885 Blavatsky returned to Europe, eventually settling in London, where she established the Blavatsky Lodge and published "The Secret Doctrine," a commentary on what she claimed were ancient Tibetan manuscripts, as well as two further books, *The Key to Theosophy* and *The Voice of the Silence.* She eventually died of influenza in the home of her disciple and successor, Annie Besant.

Trying to make sense of it all, I discovered that it was Blavatsky's work, and her philosophy that influenced the idea of a superior race within Hitler. I have more research on this, which is too lengthy to include within this book; you can visit my website for more information. www.petranicoll.com

12

Are We Made of Stardust?

It was the fall of 1978, and I was enjoying my courses at Hampstead University in London. I had the habit of getting to school early, so that I could watch students from all over the world mingle, before we had to go into the classrooms.

One day, while at school, I remember standing nonchalantly outside. As I was waiting for my English class, I remember watching this group of girls giggling and joking around, huddled around something or somebody. When I finally made out what it was, I saw it was a boy.

Surrounded by this mesmerized feminine clan was a very young gentleman, maybe twenty-five, with black hair and a sleek, sophisticated stance. I admired how he stood with confidence, and the way he was able to capture these women's attention. I wondered what made women behave this way, give all of their energy away to a man?

Close enough to make out their conversation, I could tell they were playing back and forth with the idea of teaching each other something only girls and boys could, and it sure wasn't academics. While I watched this experiment in flirtation, I pretended not to be interested. Quite annoyed with what I thought as child's play from these girls, I remember thinking to myself: "God, give me a break. Who does this guy think he is?"

People might not have thought it, but I didn't really have any girlfriends, and my experience with dating was minimal. Mostly isolated and living in my head and in books, I chose to read rather than socialize. I was an introvert. And reading was deep therapy for me; I was still raw from my mother's death, my father's conduct and myriad of changes to my life. Philosophy and science gave me an interesting kind of comfort and solace I hadn't known before. And the learning within the books was safer than the risk of getting to know people—that was for sure.

While playing the observer, I noticed the young man shift his attention and separate from the group of engaging admirers. As he intently walked towards me, of all people, I could feel my knees shaking, my balance waning. What did he want? Why was he leaving them and coming towards me? Oh, please, no, I thought. Stay over *there*.

When he approached, I could make out his mesmerizing smile. He said to me in a deep and sexy voice: "So what are you going to teach me?"

With a quick retort, I replied, "I have nothing that I can teach you," and nervously put the hood of my cape over my head and walked away.

That night, after my evening classes, three of the same

young Spanish women that surrounded the young man before class insisted that I go dancing with them. They felt sure it would cheer me up. Perhaps they picked up on the fact that I seemed to be alone all the time, maybe a bit too serious and quiet, and that I might need a change of scenery.

The entire time they were working to convince me to go out, they teased me about the incident with the gorgeous guy that afternoon. After much debate and playfulness, I gave in and decided to go along with the joke. That's all it felt like to me. It had nothing of the excitement I'd known, what felt like a lifetime ago on my sixteenth birthday, when I'd gone disco dancing with my friends. That carefree freedom felt a vague memory. *Okay, just for one night,* I thought. I'd try it.

It was actually fun to cram into that tight taxi with all four of us in our disco outfits and high heels, not knowing what to expect. Maybe this was good and I needed to have some fun after all. I wasn't sure, but I was on my way to see what the night might bring.

As we entered the club in Golders Green, I barely had a chance to make out the scene or take off my coat, when I felt this hand grab my jacket and refuse to let go of my shoulder. I looked to the side, *and lo and behold,* there was that same handsome man from Hampstead College. He was dressed in tight black jeans and a leather jacket that had 'Lamborgini' written on the back. He was staring intently at me, as if my mere presence had value.

Without much of an introduction, he exclaimed, "You're here!"

Well, let's just say—it went from there, and turned into an all-night conversation.

I remember the first time our eyes locked and held, and

then, he told me his name. Foad from Iran invited me to take a seat next to him near the bar, and he bought me a drink. Seated a little too close at first, I remember feeling this complete fascination, while wondering if he felt the same.

Foad went on to confide in me the secrets of the Persian meaning behind his mysterious identity. Apparently, Foad means "heart" and his last name being "Farzin" means "Queen of Chess." I thought the way he looked was most revealing—so exotic and handsome, charismatic like a rock star. He was not boring, that was for sure.

We easily talked, non-stop about science and the mysteries of the universe. With much in common, I felt so much hope in finally meeting someone who could share the insights and knowledge that I sought. I recall the girls getting lost somewhere, and the music, dancing and laughing of the club, a mere blur in the background as I focused on this one man. The rest of the world simply melted away, as I centered my attention on him alone.

When the club closed at 2:00 a.m., Foad invited me to his apartment. He wanted to show me his incredible art book collection. When I walked in, I noticed right away the slew of Salvador Dali posters from some of his most famous works. I was an avid Salvador Dali fan at that time, obsessed was more like it, so this was like heaven to me. Dali's surrealism was compelling to me with its obsessive themes of eroticism, death, and decay, which challenged much of the work of Freud that I studied at the time.

In early August of 1978, I was inspired to take more art classes. Art was my world for quite some time, having been brought up with the influence of grandfather Egal, the painter, and often surrounding myself with artists back in Bavaria. Salvador Dali was THE guy. And Foad, well—he wasn't bad either.

I recall being so intrigued by Foad's knowledge of the natural world and art, and our chemistry towards one another, the experience so raw and new to me. It became one of the most memorable nights of my life. It changed my fate forever.

Foad and I had grown very tired from all of the talk and intensity, and decided to simply rest on his bed, doing nothing. I mentioned to him, under my breath, that I felt the presence of my grandmother with us, explaining that she had passed away three years ago. Foad responded compassionately, by holding my hand and stroking my head.

Foad then looked deeply into my eyes, kissing my hand ever so gently. Suddenly, his attic window, vaulted wide open, and an ice-cold wind whipped through the bedroom.

Foad moved closer, leaning in on me, his eyes still gazing deep into mine, when I felt the presence of someone else in the room. This time it wasn't my grandmother in spirit. It was an animal, a bird of prey, with the face of an eagle.

It was then we both completely shape-shifted into animal spirits, human no more. I couldn't make sense of this at the time, except for the fact that I could see and feel ghosts occasionally. *No, but this was different. How could something like this happen?* (Later, this new and unknown experience would be explained to me by a Shaman I would encounter on Orcas Island, in the San Juan Islands in Washington State.)

We had not had any alcohol or drugs, and it was nothing like my one-time LSD experience. This was distinctly spiritual, Foad and I each entered into a spirit world I had never known, nor could I have imagined. We became one with the animal spirits, became the animals. Foad shifted into an eagle, the eagle I had first seen.

If you are not familiar with shapeshifting metamorphosis, it is a strong impetus for growth; it aids us in changing ourselves, our perceptions of the world and our relationship with the world. When we consciously employ positive change in our lives, we can destroy that which no longer serves us, and embrace that which will help us transform in a positive way. When working with animal spirits and energies, it is possible to consciously employ metamorphosis in the form of shapeshifting; not literally or physically changing your form in the way of many movies and fantasy stories, instead it is the act of embracing, emulating or taking into yourself the qualities of an animal in order to experience change and metamorphosis. Shapeshifting can be magically understood as being the ability to change and shift the thought and perceptions we usually inhabit. As a human, we have ways that we perceive the world around us, but for example, with a bat inside our body and mind, the way we perceive the world and ourselves changes radically. Through the processes of inviting the animal energy to become a part of us, we shift and change our own understanding.

Foad rushed and lunged at me for the longest time, hunting me as the eagle. I held my human form until I couldn't do it anymore. I recall being forced to defend my life by transforming myself into the body of a lion. We fought and fought, Foad relentlessly clawing at me with eagle talons, me trying to get away.

We were determined to see who'd win.

I found it odd. It was as if I was hunted, and I was the eagle's prey. My breathing intensified as I ran faster and faster to get away from being captured, when suddenly my consciousness carried me to another realization and to a place of peace.

In this place, I realized my own power and saw myself as

a courageous and wise lion. I remember panting and being aware that my spirit was much more cunning and stronger than the eagle trying to control me. *New awareness from deep within myself revealed that I could kill the eagle with just one powerful swoop of my claw.* In the visionary journey, when he was ready for his final attack, I had pity on him and let him live.

This chase continued for two hours until we both lost all energy and the ability to go on. We collapsed on the bed when it ended, only to wake up the next day in a foggy stupor. In the morning, we just looked at each other.

Foad asked, "What happened last night?"

He knew something strange had come to pass, but couldn't remember what it was exactly. When we tried to compare notes, neither one of us really understood a thing. That night's race, two spirits at odds and power, would set the tone for our five-year relationship.

Anna Maria

Shortly after I met Foad, and I was living in Hampstead, Anna Maria from Barcelona came to visit me at my flat. I told her about the meeting I had with this handsome boy from Iran and how much I liked him. In an instant, her beautiful and childlike face changed from joyful to somber.

Ana Maria told me she deeply wished I wouldn't choose this path; the whole world was at my feet. She begged me to leave this man behind and, instead, she reminded me that she still wanted me to go to Spain with her to learn Spanish and French, and work in the hotel business. According to her vision of me, I could become a successful business woman and speak six languages and live anywhere I wanted.

If I only walked away right now.

I didn't know what to do with her plea. I had known Ana Maria for only a few weeks, and we had some strange encounters. I still wasn't quite sure about her. And here I had only known Foad for a few days, yet felt this great connection and love for him. Something was pulling me towards him that I couldn't seem to control.

After a short moment of silence, Ana Maria said to me: "Unfortunately, you will choose this boy and not your career."

She was right.

13

To Be or Not to Be

Yes, it's true. I didn't take Ana Maria's warning and, instead, chose Foad—a Persian student. He seemed to understand me and, to be honest—he was a walking library. Apart from being a gifted musician, Foad was a science major who had been raised in Tehran within an American educational system. I felt we had so much in common, from art to music—and an attraction that was mostly mental and spiritual.

We spent many weeks together in London. I had been craving intellectual and spiritual understanding, and Foad was one person who gave it to me. To be honest, I felt like I had met my soulmate—had finally found someone who could see my pain, my confusion, teaching me things I could only dream about before we met.

If I had wanted the world, I got it.

Foad was the first person who explained to me how atoms really worked. I remember that conversation while we were sitting in a coffee shop in Piccadilly. The day was gloomy. Foad and I spoke on Einstein's theories. I learned that atoms were about one tenth of a millionth of a millimeter across of a human hair; one of the narrowest things visible to the eye is around a million atoms across. He explained how there are more atoms in one glass of water, than there are glasses of water in all the oceans in the world. An atom isn't just tiny; it's over 99.9% empty space. I was completely and utterly blown away.

Talk about the atom turned me on. Why? Because it included space, it was expansive learning, and it got me out of my simple existence. All the weight of an atom is concentrated in a mind-numbingly tiny object at its center. It's one trillionth of a centimeter across at the nucleus. The rest of the atom is entirely empty apart from a few ghostly objects called electrons that move around at a great distance from the nucleus. An atom is so empty that if the nucleus was the size of a football, the nearest electron would be half a mile away.

That means—even the most solid-looking objects we see are mostly "nothing." If you removed all of the empty space in the atoms that make up a human being, he or she would be a lot smaller than a grain of salt. This new learning was profound to me. All of a sudden, my worries seemed small.

I wrapped my mind around how extraordinary our physical *reality* really is. If you removed all the empty space from the atoms that make up all the humans on the planet, then you could fit all six billion of us inside a single orange.

This discovery was made by Ernest Rutherford, a man I learned had great courage as a scientist; one who was prepared to challenge the establishment. I liked that. So when he announced that the atom was mainly empty, he did it fully aware that his outright claim went against what the scientists of the time were professing.

It was a pivotal and important moment in the history of science. Forced to explain the atom's mysterious emptiness, scientists had to ditch everything they had assumed to be true for two centuries. Out of this came "Quantum Mechanics," a new way of looking at the universe. From that day onward, I'd become even more fascinated by the study of quantum physics.

My most favorite fact that scientists discovered, while investigating the atom, was a law called the "Heisenberg's Uncertainty Principle." In a nutshell, it explains that atoms are in more than one place at the same time until a conscious observer looks at them. Then, they appear stationary because of the person's focus and attention. In a sense, they become "real" by matter of someone's conscious awareness.

Think about this for a moment—if no-one is looking at the atoms that, say, make up your foot, they're spread out across the entire universe. Then, when someone looks at your foot, the atoms instantly merge into the foot-like shape you're so used to. Of course, this is an extreme example. We know that when trillions of atoms bind together to make up everyday objects, like your foot, they stop behaving in a weird spread-out way. No one really knows when and how they switch from one state to the other. But they do.

Even Albert Einstein, the founder of atomic physics, was troubled by the idea that we somehow "invent" the universe every time we look at it. He said, "I like to think that the moon is there even if I am not looking at it."

It seems so random. Where do we draw the line between the strangeness of the atoms and our everyday sensory world? Could it be that we make up the world with our thoughts? I considered this brilliant. If it's true, then we can create new worlds every day; the only reason we feel stuck is because we believe we are stuck.

This enriched my perspective, and gave me a way to more fully understand and accept what had happened in my life—and the nature of relativity. Einstein's general theory of relativity has been one of the most successful developments in twentieth-century physics, providing the foundation for our concepts of space, time and gravity.

This knowledge gave such hope to me, helping me to see that if I could overcome my own limited belief system, I could become anything. I could become everything I wanted to be; freedom was at my door.

I thought about this for many years and became more and more convinced that there was a way to clear old emotional patterns at an atomic level. I knew that if I could overcome my German paradigm, and my family paradigm—break through and create a new reality, I could become anyone and anything I wanted to be. It was simply encased in how I chose to look at a thing, a person, a situation, or a feeling. It was just energy.

I remember many a night staying up reading, in fact "devouring," information about the universe. And, Foad helped feed my rabid curiosity.

We comforted each other, Foad and me. Through books and conversation, through art and music, we could escape into a different world—our world together. I had left my own, and the aftermath of my mother's death; and Foad would go on to deal with the turmoil of a revolution in his home country. For five years, our lives would be filled with art, music and books. Rapidly, our minds expanded and it was exhilarating. But in addition, there was also a lot of conflict and tension that brought us together and kept us together. Eventually, not too far into our relationship, I recognized that

I would not have stayed in the situation with him if there had not been so much trauma and turmoil in his life. His world was crumbling and he needed me.

Foad was a Science Major who had been raised in Tehran in an all American Westernized system with a Father who was a Minister in the Regime of the Shah of Persia Mohammad Rezā Shāh Pahlavī (26 October 1919 – 27 July 1980) who was the ruler of Iran (Shah of Iran) from1941 until his overthrow by the Iranian Revolution on 11 February 1979. His mother was one of the leaders in the Bahá'í Church.

Iranian Revolution

Just a few weeks after meeting Foad, the situation in his birth country became very volatile. All of a sudden, I felt myself being plunged into a situation for which I wasn't at all prepared.

One Monday morning, Foad and his friends were told by British officials that all Persian students (Persia, the ancient kingdom name interchangeable for Iran), must turn their passports into the Iranian Embassy in London. They had only three days to do so.

I remember the terror I saw in his eyes the moment he heard the news. Later, many of Foad's friends would find themselves without places to live or food to eat. The money flow was severed between the two countries. Several of his friends were deported back to Iran, only to be lost in a long war, persecution and imprisonment, and sometimes death.

Foad came from a powerful family with strong ties to the Shah of Iran.

The Shah took the title Shāhanshāh ("Emperor" or "King of Kings") on 26 October 1967. He was the second and the last monarch of the House of Pahlavi of the Iranian monarchy. Mohammad Reza Shah Pahlavi held several other titles, including that of Aryamehr (Light of the Aryans) and Bozorg Arteshtārān (Head of the Persian Warriors).

Mohammad Reza Pahlavi came to power during World War II after an Anglo-Soviet invasion forced the abdication of his father Reza Shah. During Mohammad Reza's reign, the Iranian oil industry was briefly nationalized under the democratically elected Prime Minister Mohammad Mosaddegh before a US-backed coup d'état deposed Mosaddegh and brought back foreign oil firms, and Iran marked the anniversary of 2,500 years of continuous monarchy since the founding of the Persian Empire by Cyrus the Great.

But the Shah was overthrown in 1978 by Ayatollah Khomeini ousting all of the Shah's sympathizers, many of them the elite and well-educated. That included Foad's family. His father and mother, a brother who had been sent to the Red Sea to fight (Foad's father got him out of the country before he would be forced to do the same), and two uncles who were eventually executed, along with thousands of other Persians who suffered or died.

Foad's father had been a minister for the Shah, and his mother was one of the leaders in the Bahá'í Church of Iran.

During our time together, I witnessed Foad's mother be forced into hiding and his father thrown in prison and tortured, only to finally be released six months later, due to Foad's sister Fafar (who had a chain of beauty salons in LA in the U.S), sending $200,000 to Iran for their father's "bail". It was too late; the torture had gotten the best of him; he was mentally and physically damaged by the time they released him.

Foad's student friends were deported only to be lost in the war or executed. Every day, the radio blasted in Farsi (Persian language), announcing the latest tortures and killings. I felt I was living in a war zone and my nervous system, my sensitive nature, was not equipped for this.

I could not imagine staying in London and waiting for Foad to be deported and killed. I could not have continued living if I hadn't tried to save his life by marrying him.

The horrific stories about what so many went through continued to reverberate through the airwaves and our phone calls. Clearly, being on the wrong side of The Iranian Revolution in 1979, like Foad and his family, brought such terrible chaos and pain.

And me—thrust into this real life-threatening drama so suddenly, even experienced from the U.K, was like living in a horrible nightmare that never ended. Somehow, it felt like being on some kind of *survival* automatic pilot in order to carry on amidst the turmoil and uncertainty Foad lived with on a daily basis.

The Shah

The Shah was responsible for the "White Revolution," a series of reforms instigating the hope that Persia would become a modernized world power; a series of economic, social and political reforms with the proclaimed intention of transforming Iran into a global power and modernizing the nation by nationalizing certain industries and granting women suffrage.

Some of the reforms did, indeed, help Iran create a strong standard of living for many of its people, including Foad's family. The country under the Shah's reign welcomed growth and free thinking for some. But those changes, and the intellectuals that made up Foad's family and the Shah's regime, weren't popular with everyone.

The Shah, a secular Muslim himself, Mohammad Reza

gradually lost support from the Shi'a clergy of Iran as well as the working class, particularly due to his strong policy of modernization, secularization, conflict with the traditional class of merchants known as bazaari, recognition of Israel, and corruption issues surrounding himself, his family, and the ruling elite. Various additional controversial policies were enacted, including the banning of the communist Tudeh Party, and a general suppression of political dissent by Iran's intelligence agency, SAVAK. According to official statistics, Iran had as many as 2,200 political prisoners in 1978, a number which multiplied rapidly as a result of the revolution.

Several other factors contributed to strong opposition to the Shah among certain groups within Iran his regime, clashes with Islamists and increased communist activity. The most notable of which were U.S. and UK support for Khomeini n 1979, the year that political unrest had transformed into a revolution which, on January 17, forced the Shah to leave Iran. Soon thereafter, the Iranian monarchy was formally abolished, and Iran was declared an Islamic republic led by Ayatollah Khomeini.

They also didn't like the fact that the Shah recognized Israel as a legitimate state. They believed the Shah was corrupt, along with the ruling elite. Many who tried to speak out were silenced, the Communist party outlawed and sent people to prison for dissenting. It didn't help that the secular government fought so often with the Islamists. Worst of all, the general population felt that Persia had played puppet to The West, America and England.

Soon after, the Iranian monarchy was abolished and Iran was declared an Islamic republic led by Ayatollah Khomeini. Under Khomeini, most were stripped of the liberties afforded them before, including access to excellent academics and an appreciation for the arts.

As the revolution in Iran/Persia went on, so did our life in the U.K.

One thing that had connected me to Foad was our shared love for music and the artistic life. Foad had a rock band in Iran named "Alpha Torre," and was a rock star in his own country during the high-life of the Shah, when many families became very rich. Foad was also a total womanizer—with a classic musician's profile. At the time, it didn't bother me. It's how I met him, after all, surrounded by a bunch of female Spanish exchange students fawning all over him. Instead, the music—it bonded us. I loved it when we attended concerts, from Pink Floyd to Led Zeppelin.

One day Foad had an audition with a friend from Iran. Foad came back visibly irritated from the encounter, and I really didn't understand why until he told me he didn't like the music he was asked to play. I remember Foad saying, "God will insure my hands for a million dollars," because he knew he could play, and play well. He had amazing talent, and on a good day he'd sing Frank Sinatra songs to me for hours. He played such a variety of musical genres as a young Persian, especially Western music, which would later be outlawed in his country.

Foad played Clapton with all of the talent one could ask for. He definitely had the posture and the looks. But when he came back from that audition, he was complaining about the type of music they were playing—it was reggae. At the time, he exclaimed, "Nobody knows about reggae."

He felt it was beneath him and his expertise. In perfect Foad form, he told me, "I'm not going to play that crap, this is not my story. I won't play that music."

Interestingly, just a few months later, we saw that same

band on television. It was the band, "The Police." When Foad figured it out, he was sure to make the point that he would have landed the job if he really wanted to. Talk about pride. Loving Foad came with an excess of pride. I guess he was good for an insecure young woman who was looking for someone to take the reins. I always thought it funny how arrogant Foad had been about The Police audition; the band went on to be quite popular during the 1980's. And, *he* could have been in that band. Sometimes your decisions in life take you down a path that can affect the rest of your life. It's the Yin and Yang energy.

Very soon into our relationship, things went from bad to worse for his family and him. I remember feeling so hopeless that I couldn't help Foad get out of his funk and change his life. He had problems with anxiety and depression and refused to get help. This took a toll on me, but I was determined to help him. Day after day, night after night, I saw how some people became victim to the revolution mentality of loss and persecution, and, then, how others just keep moving forward. Tragedy propels some people forward, and some people choose to give up.

Foad, clearly, was not strong enough and wanted to give up and be a victim.

It must have been such a shock for him going from "well-to-do Iranian world traveler" with cultural capital in his homeland, to becoming a mere refugee in a foreign country. Foad transformed into *a nobody* overnight, and he definitely wore it on his sleeve and let me know it.

Shortly after this time, students were asked to turn in their passports into the Iranian Embassy in London, Foad told me that all of the money sent from Iran to England had been cut off, leaving Iranian students in the UK feeling uneasy and isolated. And I knew, I had this very eerie feeling of threat—if Foad got sent back to Iran like the others, he'd be imprisoned or dead.

Many of our Persian friends were quite trusting and readily turned in their passports; and once their passports were confiscated, they could no longer be protected by the U.K. government. The fate that awaited them in Iran was determined by the religion they followed. Within the next few months, people were tortured and killed by the Komeini Regime, and the situation in Iran became quite hopeless.

My deep urge to save him persisted, but I was *still* only seventeen years old, and how could I influence the situation, except to comfort and encourage him in the ways I knew.

At that point, Foad had become my best friend. He was the only person in the entire universe that I could talk with about Spirit and natural sciences and the world in general. His intelligence always impressed me and I think he kind of liked it. I mean, the guy played chess when he was four years-old, beating grown men. I must say I also couldn't refuse his good looks; he was *really* handsome and charismatic. And *I* was with him.

You must remember that I was just a young girl from Bavaria who before this, had no worldly or political knowledge at all. These few months had begun to open my eyes, but I was still naive and innocent—and the personal wounds from my mother's death remained frayed and raw within.

It didn't make sense to me at all—the country of Iran being turned upside down and inside out—the glaring unfairness of what was being done to Foad's family, and to him, what felt like almost overnight, seemed unbelievable and outrageous.

War, religious fanaticism, fighting, hunger, human suffering. What did all this mean for his family, his country—and what did this mean for me and my relationship with Foad?

All I wanted to do was to heal my personal anguish and love the people I cared for. I was a natural-born healer, and I knew that I could not live in this despair and sadness that Foad was now immersed in. For some reason, I felt it was me who had to fix the situation. It seemed easier to put my attention on serving others who needed me, than to take the easy route and abandon Foad to take care of himself while I took care of myself.

With all passports of Persian/Iranian Students confiscated, I knew I couldn't lose Foad.

14

Foad, Me and Asylum

Escape to Germany! Political asylum was hard to get, but if Foad got married in the Bahá'í faith, he would have a good chance of getting religious asylum.

The Iranian Embassy in London, still needed all of the students in England to turn in their passports, because they were trying to get them all back to Iran. Of course England didn't want them because there was no money to support students who did not have asylum; they wanted to get rid of them. An ongoing eerie feeling nagged at me—if he got sent back he'd be dead!

Looking at the fear in Foad's eyes one day, I thought, *we are running out of time and something has to be done.* Subsequently, I bought two tickets by train to Munich. Leaving at night, we'd make sure it was dark and safer to travel.

Foad still was on a student visa, and I wasn't sure if the train police had information from the Iranian Embassy to check his credential at the border from England to Belgium.

We sat quietly on the train, listening carefully for the immigration officer who was moving slowly down the aisle from car to car, opening the sliding door to check in. It was then I told Foad to hide in the bathroom. I would give him a signal to run to the other end, and then hide in another car that had already been checked, while the officer was preoccupied elsewhere.

My plan worked. Getting Foad out of England was seamless, easy, and we made it through the checkpoint into Belgium and eventually into Germany. Today, it is much friendlier without border checks and Europeans can move around more freely. I don't think Foad would have survived had he been deported back to Iran since he did not want to conform to Islamic religion, and Baha'i's were being hunted and extradited.

The Bahá'í Seal

With his mom in hiding, as a leader in the Bahá'í religion, she smuggled the Bahá'í Seal out of Iran in a box of dried apricots. She put the seal inside one of them, sending it to Foad in Germany.

The tethered cardboard box arrived in Germany at my grandpa's house two months after his mother sent it. Several pounds of dried Persian Apricots wrapped in plastic five times. Foad opened the box with such reverence and love, as he read a ten-page letter addressed to me from his mother which I shall never forget.

In it, she exclaimed her respect and gratitude toward me in how I saved her son's life. I had no way of knowing at that time how much this meant to a mother who loves her son so much—and who knew that if he had been sent back to Iran, he would never have survived.

After carefully opening every single apricot in the box, we finally found the Bahá'í seal that proved that Foad was a born Bahá'í.

When it all started, Foad's father was working for the Shah in a high-ranking position. It was in foreign affairs. He made sure that his son got out of Tehran in the nick of time—he was well aware of all this political unrest before Foad even left Iran. Even though the Shah was a tyrant in his own right, he kept the country safe, and was working toward progress in technology and medicine, and much more.

Ayatollah Khomeini was in exile in Paris, and his extremist group was supplied weapons that came from America and eventually succeeded in overthrowing the last Shah of Iran/Persia.

Many of the government officials within the Shah regime, including Foad's father, would go on to be tortured by Muslim extremists. Many died at the hands of the opposition.

This took a devastating toll on Foad, and, of course, me. By phone, we heard the details of what the Muslims did to him from his sister in the U.S. I'll never forget his response. Foad cried and cried. Soon after, I felt an air of hopelessness around us. And it never quite got better.

Arriving in Germany, Foad and I stayed with my grandfather for a few months, and we married by a judge, not any type of religious ceremony, one day after my eighteenth birthday, against the wishes of my whole family. They were very much against Faod, feeling marrying a Persian was beneath me and our family. He was a foreigner, and my father carried immense racial prejudice. A Persian was lower class in his eyes. Ironically, if my father or family had cared to learn, Foad's family was highly educated, successful, and had an elevated level of social influence. Truthfully, he could be the one looking down at us.

After we married, we spent two months there, then we left and moved back to London. There, we would soon marry within the Bahá'í faith, have a Bahá'í ceremony, which would provide Foad religious asylum.

Iran Facts

In 1980, "the last Shah of Iran" died when in exile. He faced execution if he returned to Iran. President Anwar Sadat gave him asylum in Egypt, where he stayed until his death. Since then, the United States has imposed many sanctions on Iran, trying to influence investments in oil, gas and petrochemicals. The tension has remained ever since.

The Iran hostage crisis in 1981, two years after Foad and I met, only intensified the situation in Iran. Referred by Persians as "Conquest of the American Spy Den," this trouble in diplomacy between Iran and the United States left fifty-two American diplomats and citizens in captivity for 444 days.

What sparked the intense standoff was an Iranian group of students, supporters of the Iranian Revolution, taking over the US Embassy in Tehran.

At the time, I really couldn't fully make sense of what was happening. The hostage crisis was described by the Western media as a web of "vengeance and mutual incomprehension."

To me, I just thought that the level of corruption in the world was bigger than I ever imagined. Many years later, when the movie *Argo* was released, I finally was able to comprehend the level of fear Foad must have experienced. In the film, you can see the fear and terror many experienced at the time. I could understand how Foad must have felt knowing he might be killed and have to go into hiding if he returned, constantly worrying about his family and his own life.

After the Shah died, Iraq invaded Iran and two events led the Iranian government to enter negotiations with the U.S., with Algeria as the middleman. The hostages were formally released into United States custody the day after the signing of the "Algiers Accords," just minutes after the new American president, Ronald Reagan, was sworn into office.

This crisis had weighed heavily on Jimmy Carter's presidency and run for reelection in the 1980 presidential election. In Iran, the crisis strengthened the prestige of the Ayatollah Ruhollah Khomeini and the political power of those who supported theocracy, and opposed any normalization of relations with the West.

This was the beginning of the end of a great nation that died with the Shah.

Numerous governments and multinational entities impose sanctions against Iran. Following the Iranian Revolution of 1979, the United States imposed sanctions against Iran and expanded them in 1995 to include firms dealing with the Iranian government. In 2006, the UN Security Council passed Resolution 1696 and imposed sanctions after Iran refused to suspend its uranium enrichment program. U.S. sanctions initially targeted investments in oil, gas and petrochemicals, exports of refined petroleum products, and business dealings with the Iranian Republican Guard Corps. This encompasses banking and insurance transactions (including with the Central Bank of Iran), shipping, web-hosting services for commercial endeavors, and domain name registration services.

Since 1979, the United States has led international efforts to use sanctions to influence Iran's policies, including Iran's uranium enrichment program, which Western governments fear is intended for developing the capability to produce nuclear weapons. Iran counters that its nuclear program is for civilian purposes, including generating electricity and medical purposes. When nuclear talks between Iran and Western governments were stalled and seen as a failure, they were cited as a reason to enforce stronger economic sanctions on Iran.

I have since read many books on Mohammad, and came to my own realizations that much of the West is regarded as evil by Muslim extremists. The world is split, and I ask myself the question… *will we ever live in a world of peace and harmony?*

I know, that over the centuries, religious fanaticism has caused the strongest divisions between man and country. I dream of a world where religion does not exist, and where conflict is diminished, and instead, a world of higher spiritual insight, compassion for all, *without greed, without hunger*—and where the need for ownership and control over others in the world is considered weak.

15

Initiation into Light and Sound

It was 1983, and I had finished my "A"Levels in English, Art and Psychology. Levels require studying an offered A level subject over a two-year period and sitting for an examination at the end of each year.

I had been living in London for five years, married to a handsome Iranian musician, and working a full-time job on Fleet Street for one of the oldest attorney's offices in London.

Sir Gerald Barstow, one of the partners of the firm Thrower, Still and Keeling took a liking to me, and would come down to my department where I was working as a translator and proofreader and printer. He turned into one of my greatest allies, even in spite of his running after me around the office like a dirty old man. Over the course of our time working together, he would go to battle for me, and this was so affirming.

I watched Sir Gerald Barstow, Sir Gerald or "Jerry" as I

liked to call him, from my basement office window, adjacent to the courtyard parking lot. He was a most fascinating fellow. He'd arrive with his beautiful chocolate brown Rolls Royce around 11:00 a.m. on Monday mornings in his usual elegant style. His driver and secretary would frantically run to get his luggage and shotgun out of the trunk of the car, after his hunting trips. This was a world that was new to me with all of its prestige, intellectual challenge and reward. And, while I wasn't very happy with my life, this job provided some relief.

During my time at the firm, I had convinced him to let me come to work at noon and work till 8:00 p.m. to avoid the outrageous traffic that stretched from where I lived in Hampstead to Piccadilly Circus, wasting three hours in traffic every day.

However, the real reason for the schedule change was that I wanted to be alone; I needed power naps throughout the day.

I felt tired all the time, and didn't understand what was happening to me physically. It wasn't Sir Gerald's weekly advances, the chasing after me around the office, either, that caused my fatigue.

No, I was hearing a constant humming sound in my right ear, and felt pressure in my forehead, and a spinning dizziness. All I could do was to close my eyes and try to flow with it. It was difficult to listen to people on the bus to work and at the office; I had to wear earplugs to block out their voices. So sensitive to sound and vibration, I needed to be by myself several hours a day, to stay present in my body.

It was really quite extraordinary that I had this job. Most people would give anything to work on prestigious Fleet Street Thrower, Still and Keeling. But for me it was torture, even though my work was quite interesting and I was in charge of the Ian Fleming, James Bond files assigned to the firm. There were discrepancies between Hollywood and the Fleming Family, who had written all the James Bond 007 scripts that had to be settled. I proofed and printed everything.

Some evenings, Sir Barstow would come to see me during off hours with an expensive bottle of Cognac, and two glasses. Clearly, he wanted to get me intoxicated so he could get me to ditch my Persian husband and marry him instead.

I always found it funny that Sir Gerald would teach me as he called it "Proper English" or "Oxford English," which is spoken by the upper class in England and is quite different from mainstream British English. He would have me hold my index finger over my upper lip, encouraging me to speak without moving my lip at all, to replicate Oxford English. He'd tell me to never say the word "pardon" when apologizing, but instead to say the word "what" which was the appropriate Aristocratic style of speaking according to Jerry. I found it amusing and silly, and thought he was joking. He seemed quite serious about my potential to fit into the Aristocratic crowd.

He would say, "Petra, I used to be quite handsome and you could become Lady Petra Barstow. We could have many children; you would get your own estate in Whales and have a great life!"

An interesting proposal, but I refused the cognac, the lesson and the proposal—even though my despair and sadness grew stronger with Foad each day. I'd come home at night, and he barely got out of bed by 7:00 p.m. And then he would be up all night playing music after we 'd go out to show or to a concert; I didn't get very much sleep. He never cleaned up our house, and my paychecks paid for everything; our life was completely out of balance and depressing.

I would often watch him sleep in the morning before I

left for work, and knew I had a debt to him. He'd sleep on his back with his hands folded over his heart like a mummy and oh he looked so regal and beautiful.

There is a saying that "The universe will give you only what you can handle." I was almost beyond that, when suddenly, Foad's sister, Fafar, in Huntington Beach, California, invited me to visit and sent me a plane ticket to the United States just in the nick of time.

So in the summer of 1983, I flew to LA, and Fafar, picked me up at LAX in her Ferrari, to spend a few months in California. I shared what was happening to Foad; he didn't work, go to school, or play serious music any longer.

1979 was a very hard time for Iranians in America. The hostage taking in Tehran caused a person in America to strike out at anyone who was from Iran regardless of their religion. People threw eggs and tomatoes on Fifer's house in Huntington Beach; she was also diagnosed with lupus. Things were difficult.

I was distracted and pulled into the drama. It was too much—I didn't need more upheaval in my life. Foad's family in Iran was completely torn apart by the Iranian Revolution. His brother fighting in the Iranian Army, in the Red Sea, and his mother still in hiding, hunted for being a member of the Baha'i faith. On top of all of this, my family in Bavaria continued to fall apart in the silence and mystery of my mother's sudden death.

I was confused, in despair, sad and broken.

Fafar insisted that I leave her "good for nothing" brother and wanted me to stay in the United States but I could not see myself in California. She felt Foad was using me—she gave me enough money, and gold, to get my own apartment upon my return to England. My fairytale village life in Bavaria long gone; I couldn't get it back. My dreams and expectations of England, saving me from my own loss, were shattered.

In 1984, I moved out of my home with Foad, after he applied for rental assistance and food stamps. To my dismay, the British Government came after me for alimony and was ready to garnish my wages. I never figured out why Foad didn't want to work, but he refused to take responsibility for his situation or our relationship, really. He was the smartest man I had met so far, but lacked emotional intelligence. I couldn't get sucked into this void he created.

In need, I asked Sir Barstow to help me resolve this. Jerry subsequently wrote a short letter to the authorities on my behalf. Due to his influence, my issues with Foad were resolved quickly and effortlessly. He offered to send me to college to become an attorney for the firm and work with him.

It pays to know the right people at the right time. Certainly, my life would have been quite different if I had walked through the door that Jerry held wide open, but I didn't. Regardless, my guardian angels were with me.

Haunted by such deep sadness and loneliness, I read books on philosophy and science, hoping for answers, or some wise person's manual for life. I was exhausted and emotionally worn out and felt like running away to a remote island somewhere. I prayed to find a way out, to hide from the world, when I started getting more and more aware of my sensitivity.

My rigid paradigm of fear and guilt from my Catholic upbringing was breaking down. I could not believe that I was on earth simply to get a good education, marry, have kids, grandkids, and then die. I needed to find the reason why I was here. I asked myself… *What am I supposed to do? What is my purpose on earth?*

I left the law firm shortly after my divorce from Foad. I went to work for a real estate office where I met Nile Malka, a very kind girl from Kenya. Around thirty years old, she had emigrated from Kenya with her family due to the unrest and war there.

One day, she came to work at the real estate office in Swiss Cottage, London, with the definite intent to convince me that my life was in grave danger. She wanted to set me up with what she called "mediums", to get help—and I wanted to run. Nile kept insisting that I seek guidance, so I finally agreed.

On a rare snow day in London, I worked my way to Wimbledon by bus. I stood in the heavy snowfall in front of Peter and Beryl Cartnells' house, hesitating to ring the bell. I wanted to run, when a car pulled up beside me and a chubby, endearing elderly couple got out.

Baryl was quite apologetic and wondered if I had been waiting long, as she opened the door. We were greeted with the nervous barking of two little fox terriers, named Rockefeller and Sir Winston.

Their barking distracted me. I followed Baryl into a tiny, room with memorabilia on their walls. Baryl sat down, and asked. "What do you need; why have you come to see us?"

Without thinking, I simply said to her: "Nila Malkan sent me!" And then I added:

"She believes I am in danger. I desperately need to talk to my mother who died a few years ago."

As soon as I spoke, the words shocked me. They just flew out of my mouth; I hadn't thought this before.

She explained how a séance worked, and that she and her husband, Peter, had communication from Hopi Native American Indian chiefs. She told me that the Hopi Elders work through them, to give them information about the "other side," meaning the people that had crossed over and died.

Oh, suddenly, I was so anxious to speak to my mother.

They sat down with me in a prayer circle, where I had to put my hands around the candle and speak certain words that they spoke aloud. After the prayer, Baryl closed her eyes, and she asked me if I knew of an elderly, tall and slender man who had recently died.

My grandfather had just passed away, and I didn't have the money to go to the funeral in Germany, feeling too ashamed to ask for money from my family. My heart ached on the day of my grandfather's funeral—and perhaps now I could finally talk to him.

Stunned that they could access my beloved grandfather, I started crying uncontrollably because I missed him so much. I also felt so guilty for missing his funeral.

Baryl went on to describe him in detail, even able to tell me how he died.

What followed was so amazing for me and I will never forget it as long as I live. She said, "Your grandfather misses you very much. He is so sorry that he did not understand how special you were while he was in his body. You have a big mission ahead of you, and he wants you to know he will always be by your side.

Baryl continued, "He has money in your name tied to property that your father left you and your brother. It is your job to secure this money because of your brother's addiction and habit of lying. You must return to Germany.

My grandfather wished he could have seen me for who I really was when he was alive. He just didn't have the same insights while alive like the ones he now has on the other side, *but now he knew my heart!*

I cannot express how much these words meant to me. Such a gift.

I was amazed that these mediums were able to tell me things in such great detail. Through them, my grandfather also said in the end. "Study law, take what has been offered."

At that point I nearly lost it—my crying, unstoppable.

Baryl stepped outside the room to bring me some tea, and to give me a little break. After I drank the tea she asked, "Do you want to continue?"

"Yes, I want to know about my mother."

She then told me about a soul that was always around me, a little boy who acted like a brother figure, and if I knew anything about him. I was very familiar with this soul, one I had named, Sebastian. She went on to relay to me that my mother had birthed another child. No one knew about this boy; the child must have died or something strange happened.

I found out later that my mother had had an abortion, which was highly illegal in Germany. I guessed that my mother did not want to have another child with my father. Perhaps that is why she often said to me over breakfast:

"Oh, honey, wouldn't you like to have a little brother or sister?"

I would always respond in the same way with a "No thanks, I have enough of my brother!"

I noticed that it made her seem to feel better when responded like this; I didn't understand why at the time. Baryl went on to tell me, "You will be living across the ocean; you will be surrounded by many horses and lead a very wonderful life.

I left this experience feeling greater peace and understanding. Curious, I knew I'd return again.

In actuality, I dreaded the next session. I didn't know what Baryl was going to tell me, afraid that my worst nightmare could perhaps come true.

She called in my mother's spirit. "The first thing she said through Baryl. "I am so sorry to have left you. I never imagined it would be so hard for you."

She added that my father had had an affair when she was alive and that my mother could not bear it. Mother also confirmed my suspicions when she explained that my father felt tremendous guilt for what he had done.

She explained, that it always takes two souls to tango and that I need to stop carrying all the karma for the family on my own shoulders; it was not my responsibility to take on the weight of the whole world. I had to learn to forgive and to love unconditionally.

Growing up, when I watched my parents struggle in their relationship, with their health and within their social lives, I hadn't felt that they were happy. I felt their suffering down to the bone when they were together. It was clear that no amount of material wealth could make them happy and that I had to seek out a different kind of life.

The ongoing pain and suffering I witnessed in my life, the more I wanted to solve this dilemma. I wanted to find knowledge of a different kind. Quite desperate for answers, not even reading the great philosophers like Aristotle, Plato or Socrates was able to help me. I was on my own and had to face up to this fact.

Like they say:

"Despair and pain can lead to great transformation!"

And what a transformation it truly was.

I felt like Neo the main character in the movie *The Matrix* when Morpheus says to him:

"This is your last chance.
After this, there is no turning back.

You take the blue pill—the story ends,
You wake up in your bed and believe whatever you want
to believe.
You take the red pill—you stay in Wonderland
And I'll show you how deep the rabbit-hole goes."

There was no turning back.

Return to Bavaria

I decided to return to Bavaria and *swallow the red pill.* I was already half way down the rabbit hole and there had simply been no turning back. I was just very curious how deep the rabbit-hole really went. Now I realized that I would rather die than not explore the possibility of finding out the truth. I wanted to become an authentic human being, and it was becoming clear that authenticity happens in the guts and bowels of life. With the right tools, I was on the prowl for meaning.

I was learning that being authentic is the grunt-work of the soul, of any deeply human, spiritual path. I couldn't be half here, half there, half-hearted, faking it to look good, and using different strategies to make things easier for myself. That was what I saw everywhere, and the common way, driven by our ego-addicted culture.

It's the human way that lacks wholeheartedness. It takes courage to let the heartbreak—and shatter. I must choose to be broken open, to my soul, to finally learn how to know compassion for self, others, the earth. I decided that it was time to live and love on—fully alive, juiced and ready to serve.

All around me, I had seen, and did see, such waste of life and creativity, due to ego-driven humans. To me, I felt as though I had to download a thousand years of war and human suffering to get to the place of finding myself through my connection to spirit. All my heart aches, combined with my spiritual connections, helping me to understand this better.

I was committed to breaking through the paradigm of my Catholic programing in order to find a higher existence. I could not understand why the world was so ignorant. How is it possible for people to watch the news and see the suffering in war zones, the starvation and natural disasters, while worrying if they had the latest model BMWs or Gucci Bags.

It was time to calm the mind and go inward.

Upon my return to Munich, I called Walter, whom I considered my "soul mate," and asked him if he knew anything about meditation. He had married a most wonderful woman shortly after I left Germany and seemed content. Much to my surprise, he responded by telling me that he was now leading a meditation center in our neighboring village and that he would love to see me.

A few years earlier, Walter's prostate cancer had progressed aggressively. He and his new girlfriend at the time, decided to go on a journey around the world. While in Athens, Greece, were led to a Tarot card reader, who told Walter that he would be led to a spiritual teacher who would help him heal the cancer.

Upon their return back to Bavaria to their home town called Erding, they joined a Hatha Yoga class. The yoga teacher was a disciple of a Sant Sat guru who introduced him to a Sant Thakar Singh, a Sikh guru from India from the lineage of Guru Nanak and who taught the Science of the Soul or "Sant Mat."

When I called Walter, on that auspicious day, the address he gave me over the phone was easy to find from the local train station. It was evening time and quite warm out and I was feeling strangely excited. As I walked through the gate and knocked on the door, there was no answer. At the third knock, I called out Walter's name loudly, when I heard his familiar and soft voice echoing from behind the building. I walked around the corner, just as he was walking toward me and I could not believe my eyes.

He was completely transformed. He had a long beard, and was very thin with sunken eyes and a very kind and wise expression. Six years had passed since I had seen him and since our brief affair. He used to have short hair and a strong body with sparkles in his eyes; very handsome. I was both shocked and happy to see him. We hugged.

Walter opened the door to the meditation room. I stepped inside, feeling slightly nervous and glad. I noticed a picture, and it was of the very man wearing a white turban, that I had been seeing in my dreams for many years.

After visiting for a while, Walter drove me home. Without holding back, I asked him if I could go to India. I felt this pull to meet the master. Walter assured me that was, indeed, a possibility.

My brother had moved out of the house and Rosi, his ex-girlfriend was still living there. When I came home that night, I told her about Walter and Sant Mat and going to India.

We talked, until it was very late at night and fell asleep. It was that night I dreamed the most incredible dream.

Incredible Dream

"Flying through the universe with rose petals floating in midair and an intoxicated scent of roses energizing and filling my lungs.

Suddenly, I find myself perched like a bird, on the edge of a wooden fence looking out across the horizon.

Millions of stars illuminating an indigo blue sky with the moon so big and bright I know I can touch it."

Suddenly, in my dream state, I hear celestial music as though the sound is everywhere around me and inside of me and I feel an energy drawing me to look to the right of the horizon.

A magnificent golden, bright light shines, beckoning me to move toward it and drawing me in.

In an instant, I jump from the wooden fence, perched like a bird and start walking toward this brilliant bright light.

The light becomes warmer, brighter and brighter and suddenly I see a man sitting on a wooden bench.

I recognize him. It is Master, Sant Thakar Singh in his full golden aura shining like a bright star.

I run as fast as I can along a path strewn with big oak trees that create the most magnificent arches on the top, kissing each other's branches. I hear a familiar humming sound in my right ear louder than ever, soothing to me.

I fall on my knees in front of him, his hand touches my face and he looked into my eyes. I feel a sensation much like an electric current from my toes all the way to the top of my head and then suddenly, like a big bang.

My spirit is finally free and I leave my body to fly with the master toward the brightest light I had ever seen.

Together, we fly through universe upon universe until we come to a crystal city with angels flying around and waterfalls flowing like liquid gold."

This vision within my dream was beyond anything I had ever experienced here on earth. It was like a magnificent dance in a place where there was no gravity, no mind, only love. The master removed layers of energy around me, like many dresses falling away, and I wanted to stay with him forever.

He told me that all is well, but that I have to return to my body. Suddenly, I saw Rosi walking toward me. She takes my hand and I am overjoyed to see her there and to know that she, too, had been in this place.

I felt somebody shaking me out of my beautiful journey, calling my name. It was Rosi, my brother's ex-girlfriend calling out to me:

"Wake up, Wake up Petra, Why are you crying?"

I slowly came back from my astral to my physical body. As I opened my eyes, I saw Rosi's face with a worried and deeply concerned expression.

I said:

"Don't worry Rosi!

I am not crying because I am sad,

I am crying because I am so very happy.

We are initiated!"

I then shared my vision with her. We hugged for a long time and shared tears of joy together.

Rosi met Master Sant Thakar Singh a few months later when he came to visit Germany. She would go on to receive the initiation through him directly. We have remained friends until this day.

The word "initiation" means to begin or start. According to Masters of the East, it is the first step on the spiritual path. The process of initiation into "Light and Sound" can be conveyed through a living master, personally, or through an authorized representative. It is achieved through meditation, and the existing master can hand over the baton to a new master, once they have attained a certain level in meditation, qualifying him to take over the mastership of the previous master.

It was on a Sunday, just a few weeks after seeing Rosi, that

I received my rite of passage into Sant Mat from my initiator. She was an elderly woman who appeared wise and kind. She conveyed the teachings on behalf of the master. She was of Russian descent and lived in Munich, one of only three in Germany.

At first, I was told that I had to wait six months for the initiation and that it was necessary to follow a strict lacto-vegetarian diet, and to not consume alcohol or drugs and attend the weekly gatherings in my village. I told Walter that I had already been vegetarian for several years.

Very eager, I couldn't wait that long, and I was anxious to become an initiate. Something about this path made me feel connected and I knew it was time to enter this renewing part of my life. It had been what I was looking for.

Soon after getting the information, Walter called the master in India and told him about me. He was given permission by the master to order the initiation right away.

I truly wanted Walter to teach me, but he was instructed to not be the one who welcomed me into the order. We had been lovers and had shared too much. He and I were connected on a soul level that was so intense; I think the master did not want this to get in the way of our friendship. If we had proceeded suddenly into this very thing I wanted so badly, there was a risk of us connecting again.

During the initiation, my soul was directly re-connected to my higher self in the original form of "Light and Sound." The entire process took about two hours. Some theory regarding life as a soul and the inner spiritual regions was given, followed by two meditation sittings: the meditation of "Light" and the meditation of listening to the holy "Sound Current" within.

It is the master-power that removes the veil in front

of the inner ear and the inner eye, removing the causes or karma for further lives or reincarnations in this world. They say that once this procedure is done, it cannot be cancelled again. In addition the master-power remains with the soul and promises to guide the soul towards self-knowledge and God-realization from the very moment of initiation.

For these rites of passage, I needed to be at least sixteen-years-old (or to have the consent of my parents). I was told that it is always given at no cost and that was the same for me. Like others, I was asked to maintain my family situations, job, religion, customs, and other worldly connections and responsibilities.

As opposed to Vajrayana Buddhism, that requires total isolation from the outside world, Sant Mat believes that it is not necessary to go to some mountain or into seclusion to find God. In fact, the masters have always stressed "man-making," which is to fully maintain one's outer responsibilities while walking the spiritual path. This helped me feel at ease, and make the transition into a way of life that would change my whole way of seeing the world.

That day, after the initiation, I was feeling like the veil had been lifted, and the door to my new world opened. I looked inside and noticed that I felt like I swallowed another piece of the red pill. My body felt alive. The grounds beneath me, and the rabbit hole, were beginning to get a whole lot deeper.

The meditation paved the way for a whole new way of *being*. I knew that if I didn't become real, cooked down to the essence, rather than conditioned to get approval, to look good, the projections from others would continue to seek me out and never let me go. In doing so, I would continue to suffer.

I was finished. No more judgements. Instead, the life of meditation helped me let my authenticity to the work in carrying on a whole-hearted, vulnerable conversation to resolve whatever would arise. It was hard work and uncomfortable, deeply human and often downright miraculous. Intimate. Innate simplicity. Naked. It took courageous work marked by my solid presence.

I cannot explain why meditation was so easy for me, except that I had been a seeker all of my life. Now, sitting to meditate twice a day seemed effortless and quite relaxing. In fact, I often did not want to come back from my blissful state, that I realized through silence and meditation I would be able to reach the "Here and Now" and to come into wholeness like Carl Jung stated when he said:

"I'd rather be whole than good!"

And by whole, he meant real, messy, soulful, deeply human, heartbroken, and soulfully open with compassion flowing first to myself, to the resource, as I became prepared to let it flow widely and wisely, to others.

The masters call it "know thyself as soul," but how?

Through my future experiences of meditation and contemplation in India, I came to realize that I could only live a life real true to myself, my gritty soul. Grit causes friction, makes fire to clear the way for living a revolutionary act. This act is marked by action that the earth and the soul of the world are crying out for. And the cry is going to get louder, more pain-filled, and grievous before enough souls answer wholeheartedly. The awakening of the planet is emerging.

When you get real, it's actually not about you. At some point, it becomes bigger than you.

I knew at this time in my life, I had to become real like "The Velveteen Rabbit," who, in the famous story, is made of velveteen, stuffed and given as a Christmas present to a small boy.

The boy plays with his other new presents and forgets the velveteen rabbit for a time. These presents are modern and mechanical, so he snubs the old-fashioned velveteen rabbit. The wisest and oldest toy in the nursery, the skin horse, which was owned by the boy's uncle, tells the rabbit about toys magically becoming real, due to receiving love from the children.

The rabbit is awed by this idea; however, his chances of achieving this wish are slight.

One night, the boy's Nana gives the rabbit to the boy to sleep with, in place of a lost toy. The rabbit becomes the boy's favorite toy, enjoying picnics with him in the spring. The boy then comes to regard the rabbit as *real.*

Time passes, he goes on to meet some real rabbits and they learn that he cannot hop as they do. Like me in my search for finding what was real, and in what way I was real, when I was a child, he is told that he is not real.

One day, the boy becomes sick with scarlet fever, and the rabbit sits with him as he recovers. The doctor orders that the boy should be taken to the seaside. His room should be disinfected and all his books and toys burnt—including the velveteen rabbit. As you can imagine, the boy must have felt completely helpless.

The rabbit is bundled into a sack and left out in the garden overnight, where he cries and a real tear drops onto the ground, and a marvelous flower appears. A fairy steps out of the flower and comforts the velveteen rabbit, introducing herself as the nursery magic fairy. She says that because he is old and shabby and in fact, real, she will take him away with her and "turn him into real"—for everyone to see.

The fairy takes the rabbit to the forest, where she meets the other rabbits and gives the velveteen rabbit a kiss. The velveteen rabbit changes into a real rabbit, and joins the other rabbits in the forest. The next spring, the rabbit returns to look at the boy, and the boy sees a resemblance to his old velveteen rabbit.

I always loved this story. During this important time in my life, I realized that I had no other choice but to surrender my mind and my ego—like a sacrifice—to the mystery of the master's guidance if I wanted to *live* in this life. This guidance insists on shaping us as a soul-centered contributor. I had to die to the mind, so that I could begin to live fully.

And I was now in it!

My soul had me listening, and Spirit carried me along. I was a goner to the egoistic, mechanistic, competitive ways; the ways that have undone the earth for so many souls who walk the earth, swim her waters, send roots down into her, and those who watch from the skies.

It was clear, that in order to inhabit my own core—my vital knowing center, and a soul-centered way of being, I needed to do the inner excavation through the "Path of the Masters."

Jungian psychology calls it "Shadow Work" and The Shamans call "Underworld Soul Work," including ego-dismemberment work to heal old wounds, and retrieve parts of your soul you had otherwise disowned or split off.

We need these pieces of our souls, as well as aspects of our bodies, and our connection with Spirit, and with the earth, along with the other-than-human-ones and wild, intelligent forms of life, to feel deliciously alive, ready to roll, to serve this crying earth and love them up.

Meditation did this for me.

I would end up spending eleven years meditating eight to twelve hours per day. Learning of meditation that is real work, and asks everything of us; that which turns us inside out. It alters our world completely, but before that happens, we are met with severing old ways, dismemberment, metaphoric death, dreams, visions—both lovely and horrifically heart-pounding and gut-wrenching. Experiencing beauty, raging tears, a broken open heart, blue-shimmering darkness, and warm, comforting light.

I experienced: Death. Rebirth. Love. Hope. A deep sense of connection with it all. And a palpable knowing of what I was here for.

So it's a slow dive, a conscious descent into the depths of your soul, the dark ground of your being and your dreams. The underworld of our psyche.

Diving deep into the darkest corners of our mind is vital work — no way around it — to discover what we've tucked away in the archetypal shadow of our own psyche. Once, and if, we are lucky, we unearth what we had disowned to adapt to the ways of modern Western culture.

And most often, these pieces of our *whole* psyche that we had disowned, for one reason or another, is what make us utterly beautiful, creative, authentic and wildly alive. We move towards an intense realization that we are needed here.

When we become transparent, we stand out—allowing others to "see through" and into us, as our heart and true essence shines. We are clear, direct and kind. Through this, we are not an enigma; we don't leave people scratching their heads wondering who we are or what we've done.

I love watching this process with others. As I share meditations with them, I experience glimmers of myself. For me, my experiences with the masters helped me break free of my past, and to partly remedy the pain and suffering I had experienced.

Moving Into The Life Of Meditation

I was becoming more centered and calmer, moving into a life of a meditation.

When we are congruent, we are holistically aligned, anything is possible. What we think, say, feel in our heart, feel in our body and the actions we take line up to support and reflect each other. We know it in our body, often in our gut, when we keep our attention there.

Being authentic and soul-centered, costs us our ticket to ride from the collective mainstream, to the illusion of safe and secure. It opens the door to our bloody and glistening, whole, broken heart, which reveals to us the honey of this wildly delicious, messy life. This leaves me, you, and those you touch, feeling radically free.

My life had been laced with chaos and unmet emotional needs, and here I was, suddenly willing to be completely exposed. Open. Without choice now. Solid and light.

Authenticity strips away all that is NOT real. Removing all that are not made from love, and have the ability to love. All that is of the enriched soul and inspired spirit remains. There is no living a soul-centered life without being authentic, without mustering the courage to do the excavating in the dark: The Shadow work.

C. G. Jung said: "People will do anything, no matter how absurd, to avoid facing their own souls."

A small inheritance, helped me to move forward with my plans to travel to India, eager to begin this journey of discovery and release with the master.

"Nothing ever goes away until it has taught us what we need to know."

—Pema Chödrön

16

On the Path of the Masters

"Your beliefs become your thoughts,

Your thoughts become your words,

Your words become your actions,

Your actions become your habits,

Your habits become your values,

Your values become your destiny."

—Mahatma Gandhi

India was like a love affair…

I stepped off the plane, the hot humid Indian air hit my face—and I kissed the ground I walked on. I had finally arrived, after flying fourteen hours from Munich.

Since my first vision of the master, I felt enveloped in

a strange hypnotic energy, similar to the energy of being in love—where life is bright and clear. I couldn't stop smiling. I felt like dancing in circles, laughing all the while. I was about to meet my guru in the flesh—and was beyond excited, since I had only seen him in my visions in the astral and causal plane of consciousness.

My heart expanded with immense love—I felt one with every living thing and wanted to hug each and every one, and shout with joy. I had found the master. India felt familiar, as if I had been there a thousand times before. I was finally home and, even, today as I write this, I dream of going back to my beloved India. The food, the smells, the language, the chaos, the heat and even the noise that never stops—I love all of it.

I was twenty-four years old, and going to become a disciple of an Indian guru.

Along with my young friend Sonja, we checked out of customs at the Delhi airport. Master's driver picked us up. Sonja's sister had been living in the ashram for two years, and she was looking forward to seeing her sister and the master.

Within the chaos of India lives a strange simplicity, something that feels so childlike and sweet. With the people, the noise, the assaults on the senses, so dirty and smelly; it is such a completely different world than the West. The traffic is insane and the pollution is unbearable. I recall wondering, *how do people survive here?*

When we arrived at the ashram grounds, a double-story house in the city of New Delhi, we were immediately led to meet the master. My earlier visions had created a picture in my head; the master in his astral radiant form glowing with light all around him, looking godlike, enveloped in a larger-than-life aura.

In person, it hit me—he was human. The master looked

like a regular person, but, then again, I was not ready to recognize the subtleties of his presence.

The smell in the room reminded me of frankincense; the high frequency odor seemed to pulsate from my guru's body. I couldn't get my eyes off him, as he was laughing so heartily. I stared at his eyelashes; they were long as was his hair. I really was like a kid in a candy store. Clearly, he must have thought it hysterical because I kept staring at him.

Then the master looked at me in an inquisitive way and said: "Welcome. You are here again?"

Slightly confused, I replied, "No, it's my first time."

"No, no, you've been here a few times," the master answered in a confident tone.

Past Lifetimes in India

It was then, that I suddenly realized that I had had many lifetimes in India. This was revealed further, many years later, when I participated in past life hypnosis sessions with a close friend and psychiatrist in Roseburg, Oregon, USA—and I was shown that one of my lifetimes was in 13th Century India.

He took me back into several lifetimes: when a monk in Tibet, a dolphin swimming with the speed of light, and in a body of a most joyous being, and as a prince in India.

To meet myself in all these lifetimes, and to see the lessons I had been given was amazing. What stood out the most to me was the lifetime in India, where I witnessed myself standing with a sword hanging from a belt around my hip. The sword, so heavy, it almost pulled me over onto the ground. It was studded with emeralds, rubies and jewels. My surroundings were elegant and beautiful and I was a young boy, no more than eighteen years old, with black hair and very slender build, living in what appeared to be an Indian palace.

I was the observer looking into my past life, feeling all that the boy was feeling. Everything was staged for me to win in that life; I was royalty, rich, but I had no freedom and nothing to fight for. I was bathed by beautiful women, fed the most delicious of foods; even my fights and playtime were staged for me to win.

Everybody had to serve me as they were ordered; I hated my life. The only freedom I had was when I went to the mountain, where my guru lived. We would sit and meditate. He told me stories, taking me into meditation, delving into my soul essence, so that I could feel real freedom.

This past life revealed to me that statues, riches and money never make a person satisfied and truly happy—the only actual freedom there is, is to be liberated from the hindrances and limitations of the mind and the body. I felt like Siddhartha, who escaped his fate as a prince to live a lifestyle of asceticism—characterized by abstinence from worldly pleasures, for the purpose of pursuing spiritual goals, and eventually the Buddha.

With springtime, Westerners also arrived, and there were about thirty-five of us altogether at the ashram. We meditated from three to seven in the morning, before it got too hot and humid, and then again in the evening after sunset. We'd sleep on the second floor under the stars, on a flat rooftop painted white with accents of blue decals. Crows could be heard all day, every day. At first, their sounds irritated me; gradually, their "caw-caw" became wonderfully familiar, rhythmic and meditative, amidst all the traffic noise.

At night it was hard to sit in meditation in the Indian heat, sometimes as high as 108 degrees, and with humidity that left us drenched in our clothes. Mosquito nets were a must, otherwise the mosquitoes devoured us. I learned early on, to meditate all night was better than to lie down and have to get right back up early in the morning.

The master would come out after lunch and we would get on the bus, visiting small villages near Delhi, where he would hold Satsang, a gathering in the presence of truth for his congregation. After the talk, the villagers often served delicious food to everyone attending.

When we were in Delhi, I was given some assignments, like picking people up from the airport and making sure they were settled in properly. Many of the Westerners could not deal with the heat and would get sick right away. Within days, some had acquired horrible dysentery and other bugs that caused enormous physical problems. For me, India was a heaven; I was finally with my guru and completely blissed out, full of joy and happiness. I don't know why I never became ill; perhaps the feeling of such deep happiness had a physiological effect, and kept disease at bay. For one year, I traveled around with the master throughout India. Joy!

Doing My Research on Sant Mat And Masters

Before embarking on my quest to India, I had done my research about Sant Mat and Masters from the East. I learned that Master Thakar Singh was a civil engineer in his younger days and became a disciple to the late Kirpal Singh. Thakar Singh was a Sant Mat Master in the ancient lineage of Contemporary Saints from India who initiated spiritual seekers into meditation on "Inner Light and Inner Sound" also called Surat Shabd Yoga. I found out that all the Sikh names end with "Singh." Derived from Sanskrit—it means lion.

For me, Thakar was my guru, my guide and master, and my learning under him was extremely rewarding. I was truly a seeker, highly attracted to this path, because it didn't involve religion. Religion had left a bad taste in my mouth, especially as I learned about how much it affected my own family and influenced the way I was treated as a woman.

Sant Mat gave me an opportunity to go within myself and explore the esoteric worlds. At this time in my life, I needed this, even if it meant going all the way to the bottom of the rabbit hole.

Thakar's services have been always free of charge and directed at seekers from all religious backgrounds. For me this was really liberating; for once, money wasn't asked for at a spiritual service.

He was born in in the Punjab, in 1929, and initiated by Sant Kirpal Singh in 1965; Thakar began his work as a Sant Mat Guru in 1976. His beloved master had just passed away; now it was his turn to carry the torch.

From a very young age, Kirpal Singh was on a spiritual quest which led him to various Sufis, yogis and mystics. As a matter of choice, he never accepted any of them as a master, continuing to pray only to God to obtain a divine inner manifestation. In 1917 his prayers were answered: During his deep meditations, it is said that he began to see a vision of radiant forms and beings. One of these was a regal character, who he believed was Guru Nanak, founder of the Sikh religion in 1469, who lived in the Punjab near Lahore, the area that is now Pakistan.

In 1924 Kirpal met Hazur Sawan Singh, the famous Saint of Beas, in his ashram on the river in Northern India. It is said he instantly recognized the same "luminous form" that he had seen during the seven previous years, and it was not Guru Nanak but Sawan Singh. After his own formal initiation, he dedicated his life to reaching the highest spiritual awakening he could. Inspired by his master, Kirpal began writing the "Gurmat Siddhant," and "The Philosophy of the Masters," a huge spiritual undertaking made up of two volumes in the Punjabi and Urdu languages. It was finally published under the name of Hazur Sawan Singh in 1935, and later translated into English.

When I arrived in India in 1985, I had read all five volumes, many times, and was now convinced that the path I had chosen was the right one for me. From my previous experience with the Catholic Church, and my father's abuse by the priests, I was in need of much confirmation. Not sure religion was the path for me; I was inspired by the Masters of the East and the teachings of this tradition that would go on to give me extraordinary insight.

During the 1950's, Kirpal Singh traveled for the first time in the West, where hundreds of people were initiated and placed on the path of meditation. He called this "the highest form of contact with the Divine Light and Harmony." Although I never met Kirpal, I had an amazing inner connection with him, as did others in the ashram.

In researching Kirpal and his teachings, I found it fascinating and heartwarming that he could bring people together through the practice of meditation. In 1963, Kirpal was able to reconcile the differences between various religious leaders, including Pope Paul VI and leaders of the Eastern Orthodox Church. While touring to bring compassion and understanding to religious groups, he continued to teach new seekers on the path in the "Way of the Masters of Sant Mat" meditation.

In August of 1972, Kirpal left for his third and last trip to the west. Giving talks and holding meetings, Kirpal was able to instruct more than two thousand new disciples about living a spiritual life. After his master's death, Kirpal felt it necessary to improve himself and prepare for the next steps in his development. He spent five months in a constant state of Samadhi, or "absorption in intense meditation." There, it's said that Kirpal Singh received the message he was waiting for. His master visited him and said: "Return to the world and bring my children back to me."

So Kirpal moved to Delhi, where there were thousands of Punjabi refugees from Pakistan who Kirpal felt were in need of guidance. It was his sacred humanitarian mission to spread the Path of Sant Mat. Throughout India the reputation of Sant Kirpal Singh grew and, in 1957, he was elected the first president of the "World Fellowship of Religions," a leader of the World Conferences. He also was the first non-Christian to be included in "The Order of Saint John of Jerusalem, Knights of Malta," for his deep commitment to humanity. I was moved by his commitment to service.

Translated into fifty languages, Kirpal wrote about spirituality, morals and religious practices and beliefs. I would go on to read dozens of Kirpal's transcribed talks and books. My favorite was the book "Wheel of Karma," due to its insight into karma and its true meaning. His basic teachings revolved around the idea that every human being was capable of making contact with God into "expression Power." This could be found in the Word of the Bible, Naam, Shabd, Om, and Kalma among other works.

Kirpal strongly believed that "the discipline of universal character" was the foundation of every major religion in the world. He touched many lives with the idea that people could benefit from studying Sant Mat meditation in his book "Naam or Word." For me, it made complete sense that people needed to become more introspective and that our society was too outwardly focused and distracted by material things.

This is the path I was committed to when I arrived in India, "The Path of the Masters or Sant Mat, Meditation on the Divine Word" or "Yoga of the Sound Current," also called Surat Shabd Yoga. Sant Thakar Singh, my teacher, described the practice based on what he was taught by Kirpal, his master. It was "a practical form of spirituality which is not connected to any particular religion, sect, or thought."

Sant Thakar Singh

When I met Thakar, I first remember his child-likeness. We had a teacher/disciple relationship that would go on for eleven years. (I stayed as an initiate in India for about a year, and then moved to the Castle Oberbrunn in Bavaria that the initiates of the master bought. After leaving there, I went to the USA with the master, and then eventually was moved to the Lighthouse Center in Oregon, near Roseburg. I was one of the original twelve people to live there. And an interesting bit of history—it used to be the gunslinger, Jesse James's old farm. I did go back to India in 1987 for a short visit and lived in the ashram in Oregon for a year. (I finally left the group in 1994.)

I felt enormous respect for my teacher. When we meditated with the master, he wore white Punjabi suits, which consisted of super wide pants with a drawstring and a long shirt down to the knees. As his students, due to the heat, we wore very light, simple cotton Punjabi suits in different colors.

The first time I put that suit on, I remember thinking: *Why can't we wear these comfortable clothes all the time; nobody cares what we look like.* Unlike in Paris or London, where everything had to be tight and fashionable; this carefree clothing was such a relief.

Although we were told Thakar was born into Sikhism and

wore the traditional garb of the Sikhs, including the turban, we did not experience him in this way. He gave up the traditional practice soon after initiation, but never his traditional clothing, when he committed himself completely to the inner, esoteric practices of his teacher's wisdom.

During the eleven years that I studied Sant Mat, I learned many things. Most importantly for us: learning how to truly surrender, and the significance of self-discipline, not being judgmental of others; self-introspection, patience, tolerance, and, most of all, love.

I remember one auspicious day in Pimpalner, the words of my teacher touched me deeply. We were all sitting outside, underneath the most magnificent starry sky. The master sat there in his robe and spoke to us about the nature of what we call "God."

The meditation and the teachings of Sant Mat taught me that the chief enemy is our own mind, which will never allow our soul to be in control. But instead, our human mind has control over us. The mind does not understand that there are accounts at the end of our lives that we call karma; and that this karma has to be balanced.

If you have a car, and you close your eyes, letting it drive itself, it may hit human beings, drive over flowers, run off the road, or go into the ocean. The car knows nothing about what will happen, where it is going, what it is doing. It has no sense of present or future. Without the soul, the mind is like a car that drives without a driver...People go along blindly.

But when we, as humans, become conscious of our soul essence, it connects everything from our past to the present and future, and we as souls begin to recognize karma. Spiritually-driven, rather than mentally or worldly driven, our soul begins to understand what we are to do and not do;

and what we have done that is not positive, and if there is any possibility to undo the effects of it so that we may not suffer the consequences.

Our lives can be well-regulated by the soul," Master repeatedly told us.

After so many years of meditation, I know now that we can only see what the mind can understand, which is very limited to this physical reality. We are being tricked every day by what we watch on TV, hear and experience in the world and in our lives, but none of that really matters once you experience what is within. This is what I learned from my teacher.

It's like the Native American Indian elders who have spoken to white men about their knowledge of books, intellect, and how that chosen path will not save our planet. Our world is going that intellectual route, due to the primitive nature of so-called leaders.

One of the master's most well-known analogies for the control of the mind over the soul is that of the frog in the dirty drain. The master's tale:

"'If you have a frog that is used to living in a dirty drain,
and you put it in some flowers, it will say,
'What hell have you put me?'
It will not like it.
When it jumps back into the dirty drain, the frog will exclaim,
'What heaven is this? Can something be better than this?'
The frog can only enjoy the dirty drain because its life is in the dirty drain.

I love this story. It taught me how to look for my inner treasures; instead of seeking satisfaction in the material world, I dived deep into the truth of my soul essence.

The master often emphasized the essential requirement of personal experience in all things spiritual; not depending on others but finding reality for oneself. It hasn't benefited mankind to be told that we are soul and belong to God, or that God and the Kingdom of God are within us. Even though it is clearly written in the Bible and other scriptures, in my opinion few believe it. My guru taught me that this is because our mind is designed to believe only in something it actually experiences.

The Nature of Personal Experience

When I think back to these teachings, I realize that they shaped me, molded me into who I am today. I began to seek and find answers into the nature of the universe, God, angels, goddesses, and other entities beyond this world or dimension. It helped me better understand my own psyche, my soul consciousness. The human condition and my personal condition became clearer, the more I listened and learned, and the more I meditated.

The masters say that it is only when a man experiences and sees within for himself, ready at hand, that he can be sure of that thing. Similarly, the main point of initiation is to convince the disciple that there is something worth seeking inside, and that the master's instructions are worth pursuing. If a disciple gets a taste of knowledge without any personal effort, as if it's a free sample, then substantially more will be available in the future with sincere effort on the part of the one who meditates.

I personally experienced this, by going inward, through daily prayer and meditation! God is an essence, is subtle—worldly matter is the opposite, or negation of God. The mind is a subtle matter, so both mind and matter are the enemies of the soul.

The purpose of life is to reunite with God, with whom we have been separated, therefore, life itself, is true suffering, due to this separation. The human form has been especially created to serve this purpose as a vehicle for reuniting with God. It has no other function. It was earned by us after long life spans in other forms. When a person suffers sickness or discomfort, those are reminders of our mortality.

The master taught me that in order to find God, we must first acquire knowledge of who and what we are as souls. Then, we will be able to find something greater. We are not bodies, but souls, and soul is of the same essence as God, i.e., the soul is God, but on a smaller scale. The soul is covered in layers, the primary ones being the body, mind, and intellect. These coverings are not alive; the soul is alive and provides the motive energy which is used to drive the coverings. *We are so identified with these coverings, that we no longer have any idea that we are a soul, and instead identify completely with the body and mind.* This can create suffering.

According to the teachings of the master, God has not provided anything useless. Human beings are functionally complete in terms of their given purpose; they need nothing extra, like worldly education or money.

When we go somewhere, we take only those things with us that we need. When God sent us here, he gave us everything that we need; everything that is useful. Anything unnecessary was left out. The master extends this even to food and drink, and tells stories of people who have subsisted on the inner food alone.

Thakar Singh sometimes quoted Jesus, who said:

"Man does not live by bread alone, but by every word which comes forth from the mouth of God."

According to Masters from the East, this reference has an esoteric meaning. The words which Jesus speaks of is the inner sound current, and the master follows the view expressed in Hinduism, namely that *we are souls passing through a continuous process of phenomenological evolution, moving from one form to the next more complex form, gaining more and more complex consciousness and also more complex desires*—until the soul is lucky enough to find itself incarnated as a human being.

This state of consciousness, such as experienced by a human being is the top of a ladder which continues upward, and a qualitative change between reincarnations is required to go higher. However, the soul can also fall lower if the attention is directed to lower things, like carnal desires, or drug use.

Master said:

> *"This world will go on as it is. Sometimes we laugh; sometimes we cry. Sometimes we are diseased; sometimes we are healthy. Sometimes we are in debt; sometimes we are prosperous. Sometimes we are weak; sometimes we are healthy. Whatever the situation is, there is no remedy for it. There is no help for it. We have to accept it."*
>
> *People do not say:*
>
> *"This is the will of our foolishness."*
>
> *They say:*
>
> *"This is the will of God. Accept it. Suffer."*
>
> *But what is truly the will of God?*
>
> *He says, "Enjoy."*
>
> *"Be ye perfect, even as your Father who is in heaven is perfect."*

Personally, I believe we are to enjoy and strive for a life of perfection. As human beings, we are to come out of the way of suffering. To live in this world is suffering; however, suffering is totally foreign to our soul nature. Rather, life is something we were meant to live and enjoy. That complete, fulfilled enjoyment is not here, however, but with God. I recently saw someone dying, and it served as a reminder that our life truly is with God and not here. My experience with death, so far, has been that most of the people of this world find nothing at the end of this life. They find themselves in nothingness; in hells.

Why is it like that? Because what they have achieved, what they found, be it material wealth or intellectual knowledge, did not really work. It makes me feel very sad that many people die with regrets that their family members are not nearby—they die lonely.

From my life experiences, I have come to believe anyone who thinks this life can be made into something enjoyable forever is being fooled. Mankind grasps at the momentary pleasures only because he knows of nothing better. God is not a silent spectator, watching the world passively; He is fully conscious of the tormented situation here on this earth in which his souls mirror his own self and are suffering.

However, God does not directly intervene in the universe, but makes use of agencies. If there is to be rain, it does not fall from a clear sky. First the clouds gather, and then the rain comes out from them.

If a child is to be born, the mother and father are provided. In the same way, everything in this world works through Spirit and all the higher powers operate in this way, even God. God is One, and has control over vast regions of the universe, both physical and spiritual, and the agencies which handle the management.

The situation is analogous to a king, who has both a prime minister and many generals managing various aspects of his kingdom. No one approaches the king directly, but all interacts with him via his functionaries. In this way he continues to enjoy the total purity, bliss, and ecstasy which is his nature; while the world goes forward in myriad forms. Thus, if God is to interact with mankind, He has to come in the form of a man.

There is no other means available for him to interact directly with us, as the functionaries are controlling the entire region we inhabit. The saints, Jesus, masters and spiritual teachers have been coming to earth since human beings first came into existence.

These functionaries have come in our own time; and they will continue to come as long as there are people who need to be awakened on this earth. The Master Saint has the power to burn these impressions so that they are neutralized; after this, the soul can experience the sound current.

In other words, the master tells us that he can burn our karma from previous lives, and that it is only then that we can hear the inner sound and advance as a soul on the path. He burns our karma from past lives, and the only karma we have to carry is of this life. This is mitigated by meditating a minimum of three hours a day.

Information of interest about sound currents: Sometimes in the news there have been reports about people hearing a mysterious sound that seems to be coming from nowhere. One of these has been called "the Taos Hum." In, *Philosophy of Liberation*, Maharshi Mehi states that not only are there spiritual sounds associated with the heavenly realms, but there are also many vibrations or semi-subtle sounds associated with the gross-material realm. He says one should not falsely assume they are accessing the real inner sound current just by hearing ANY kind of sound that may manifest itself in one's perception during the silence of meditation:

> "There are sounds due to gross vibrations in the material body. To meditate on these gross-material sounds and believe it to be as the full practice of the 'Yoga of Sound' shows a lack of knowledge of Yoga." There are gross-material sounds one can hear in the silence of meditation that do not lead one Above, do not lead to spiritual growth, transformation or enlightenment. Swami Vyasanand: "This is because only the central sound has the power to attract the consciousness to the center and carry the soul to the center of a higher realm. Other illusory material sounds do not have that magnetism to attract the consciousness to the higher realms."

There are inner sounds that one receives instruction from a true master at the time of initiation into Surat Shabd Yoga (Inner Sound Meditation, the Yoga of the Audible Life Stream). These sounds are perceived to come from the right side or center and represent the ascending current. Sounds that appear to be coming from the left side are of the descending current flowing downward into the material creation or multiverse. One is instructed to focus on the "Sounds of the Ascending Current or Audible Life Stream"—certain sounds. There are of course many other sounds one might hear, but one has to focus on certain sound currents. The reason for this is these sounds, if focused upon during meditation practice, will keep pulling the soul's attention up to ever higher and higher levels. These are coming from regions above. Other sounds, though mistaken for the sound current, are interesting, miraculous or even mystical, will not help the Surat-Soul to ascend or make spiritual progress.

"Various sorts of sound currents reverberate in the human system from which the initiate has to pick up the right one and listen to it; otherwise he will go astray and lose his equipoise. The practical guru forewarns his disciple and directs which sound to listen to and which one to discard." (Shiv Brat Lal)

Power of Meditation

Through my eleven years of meditating many hours a day, I experienced the woven tapestry of the master's teachings and the power of meditation. Sant Mat teaches that the appearance of the sound is a function of purity; the purer the vessel, the more easily the sound resounds inside it. Thus, the sound current is a gift which the master can give to those whom he chooses, or perhaps to those he is destined to help from the unending wheel of karma.

What is the wheel of "Karma of Birth and Rebirth?"

A common theme to theories of karma is its principle of causality. One of the earliest associations of karma to causality occurs in the Brihadaranyaka Upanishad of Hinduism.

Now, as a man is like this or like that,
according as he acts and according as he behaves, so will he be;
a man of good acts will become good, a man of bad acts, bad;
he becomes pure by pure deeds, bad by bad deeds;
And here they say that a person consists of desires,
and as is his desire, so is his will;
and as is his will, so is his deed;
and whatever deed he does, that he will reap.

—Brihadaranyaka Upanishad, 7th Century BCE

Beauty of the World

According to the masters, we never get out of the wheel of karma of birth and rebirth, whether we do good deeds or bad deeds. We are always here to reap the rewards. I used to want to leave this earth.

I used to want to leave this planet to be somewhere else. Now, I have fallen in love with this earthly plane, the people, the beauty of the world. It's all about love. It's not about us as individuals. It's about serving others and assisting in raising consciousness. And it begins with us.

In 1986, when I accompanied the master to the United States, he told me something that helped me feel like I had a purpose, a mission, as we all do. He confided in me, that I was one of the people assigned to him to help serve his mission, and that I would be able to reach thousands of people and help them to understand soul essence.

The master also told me that I had to read as many books on religion, science, metaphysics that I could. In doing so, I would be able to reach many people from all walks of life. He said I should always keep the balance of joy in my heart, understanding this third dimensional reality, this earth, is an illusion. I am here, just because I volunteered to serve the mission of the master.

Love is the criterion for a dedicated life as a human being. God is love and love is God, and the way back to God is also through love—just as the master is love personified, sound current is also a conscious current of love. However, the only true form of love from the perspective of life lived in this world—is *called devotion*—love, loyalty, or enthusiasm for the person, activity, or cause.

In my life, it has been true that all other forms of love are either debased through egotism, or are experienced as a form of confusion and delusion, brought on at the level of the mind. I think the nature of romantic love is never sustainable and is doomed to dwindle away. They're real life cases, like the life and love of Ronald and Nancy Reagan, who I believe managed to stay in love for a lifetime; but I wonder what percentage of people can actually achieve this?

Sometimes it happens that someone is interested in us for some reason, and we are also interested in that person for some reason of our own, and then we are friendly to one another. Then we believe in each other because *we each need something from each other.* For example, if I have some food and the other one has some fruit, and he needs food and I need fruit, then we cooperate with each other and become friendly with each other due to the interchange of our selfish motives. So far in my life, I have not really seen unconditional love, even with parents and children. As soon as a child grows up, *it is the human condition to become conditional in our relationships and love.*

We misinterpret this exchange of selfish motives to be love, but it is not. All the worldly relationships and friendships are based on give and take. Fundamentally, no one can love unless they are connected to God, as God is the source of love—and is sometimes described as love itself. Our minds, on the other hand, are totally devoid of love. Any person who is not acting through God, is always selfish.

If anybody claims, "I love somebody," and does not have this love connected with God, then it is not real love. It cannot be. It is impossible.

However, I must include, that the love we have for our children is not mental love. The love we have for our children is an innate arrangement of nature from God. But once the children are grown up, then that special love that was arranged by God is taken away, and again we have only a selfish exchange—and unconditional love evaporates.

17

Hanuman, the Monkey God

Three months had passed since my arrival in India. People came and went at my guru's ashram. It was a revolving door of international visitors, and a perplexing place where I witnessed otherworldly occurrences that changed and enlightened my perspective of the nature of the body, mind and soul.

Each week, the *satsangi's* or students of the master were invited to visit neighboring towns on short trips to witness his satsangs; gatherings where he spoke of good and truth. The villagers, always so excited to see the master, they would kiss his hands and feet, or stand in line to receive "Darshan," a form of receiving spiritual insight experienced by gazing into the master's eyes. It was quite humbling to see the respect and reverence these people had for their guru. To them, he was God-man.

After Satsang, a magnificent feast was served, with sabji, dhaal, lentils and rice, Indian naan bread, roti Jala, eggplant bhaji, cucumber rate and the most delicious desserts—have and mango Lassi. This meal served as Darshan blessing, the end of the ritual we provided. Food was served to all who attended, especially to the poor.

One day, I had the responsibility of picking up people from the airport, and take the new guests' shopping. Most folks coming from the west didn't really know how extremely humid and hot India could get so they would, inevitably, need new clothes. Gisela, the master's secretary from Germany, who knew her way around, would accompany me on shopping, so I wouldn't be cheated by the vendors or get lost. To wheel and deal in the New Delhi markets was such a big job, really, a bit much for me. Gisela was six feet tall, blond and spoke Hindi, so I knew I was in good hands, even though we really stood out in the packed crowds.

During our outings, we would source the finest and lightest cotton material we could find and order fifty Punjabi suits in different colors, many sizes at a time. I found this quite entertaining and exciting; I felt like a viable merchant in India.

The majority of people arriving from foreign countries tended to get sick on the second or third day after arriving. It was dysentery, fever and diarrhea and other virus-related illnesses; an unwelcome *welcome* to their spiritual path. The master would urge them *not* to buy any food from vendors in the city, and to only eat in the ashram, but often, they didn't listen, unable to resist the new culture.

The hustle and bustle of this dramatically different culture was tempting, the noise and excitement, the vibrant colors and aromatic smell of all the delectable spices. At times, it was impossible for me *not* to indulge in some of the delicious foods and drink, from the many vendor carts from which to choose. An initiate, or newcomer, once trekked into the city to get cane sugar juice, but his weakness gave way, and he couldn't stop drinking. Sadly, after the third glass, he fainted with 'sugar shock' and became quite ill.

At the end of summer of 1985, we prepared to leave for Pimpalner—an eight-hour drive away, to visit another ashram, and I was ready. Cabin fever and the Delhi ashram were getting a little too crowded for my taste. I had been there nonstop for eight weeks; being among sick people, and the heat, were getting to me. I welcomed the break.

Each person comes to India for different reasons. Some, to find enlightenment, some came to face their fears, their rage or addictions, but the overriding message was to realize that God dwells within us.

For me, I came to overcome the "monkey mind." to find the truth about my mother and to reach some kind of enlightenment. It is a Buddhist term meaning "unsettled; restless; capricious; whimsical; fanciful; inconstant; confused; indecisive; uncontrollable." Three months into my life of meditation and service, I was making progress, and could tell that my mind was much calmer—and I felt ready to stay for several years.

To reach the Pimpalner ashram, we travelled with the master by bus. Sometimes he would ride the bus with us, and sometimes rode separately with his driver in a little black car. During the journey, we stopped in many villages, where people hadn't seen the master for quite some time. There again, as we journeyed through Maharashtra, Rajasthan and Gujarat.

The most extraordinary dishes were eaten and enjoyed, infused with the most exotic spices.

The base of all food in India is usually rice and Chapati,

the flatbread made from hard "gehun," an Indian wheat that is finely ground. It's then served as a bland background for the spicy dishes, such as sabji, dhaal, served with an array of sauces.

I was fascinated when the food was served on banana leaves; after our meal, they were rolled up and discarded. We ate with our hands, and thank God, for chapatis (thin pancakes of unleavened whole-grain bread) to scoop up the food; this avoided contamination.

We were instructed to be very careful with our hands; it was impolite to eat with our left hand, even if left-handed. The left was considered dirty and used only for wiping yourself after going to the bathroom, no toilet paper needed. For me, I found it amusing to watch a left-handed person trying to scoop food up with Chapatis, using their right hand. No matter, almost all of us would leave our meals with yellow-stained clothes because we were not used to eating without utensils. Curiously, eating with my right became second nature, and forks became awkward; the metal tasted funny in my mouth.

Considered a great honor for the disciples to feed the master's guests, we were asked never to decline any food, ever, even if we were full, so as to not offend. Some of the villages were extremely poor, and had saved money for an entire year to host one visit for the master and his disciples—to produce the most magnificent feast. I wish all of you reading this book could travel and see India and its culture.

Appreciation for India

India has a population of 1.2 billion people. Given the work I was doing with the master, I was able to visit fifteen of the twenty-nine states, including Nepal. This gave me a broad perspective on the various cultures in the region, with all of their vibrant clothing, women's embroidered saris, beautiful gold bangles, earrings and headwear. Being a lover of art and beauty, I was mesmerized by the artistry in their style of authentic dress, especially in my favorite place in all of India—Baroda, the princely state in Gujarat, where Sant Kirpal Singh's ashes were placed at the mansarova.

Driving there, it was an arduous eight-hour journey. With the extreme heat, we constantly searched for a little shade or cold water to splatter on our faces. We'd stop at roadside cafes, similar to those seen in Mexico, and enjoy a cup of spicy chai or ice cold limca, a disgustingly sweet drink made of lemon and sugar. The master would always tell us to drink chai instead of cold drinks, because the cold drinks would make you feel even hotter. Of course, this makes sense now; I've read where a hot drink has an effect on the systemic cooling system, and a cold drink can warm a body, because too much cold causes our blood vessels to tighten. But really—this didn't make sense at the time when all I wanted was cool down.

After many days on the bus, traveling from village to village and city to city, we finally arrived at the ashram in Pimpalner, Marathi. It was a small town in Sakri Taluka, fifteen miles from Taluka where the people worship Hinduism.

Pimpalner has a beautiful dam named "Latipada," which is two kilometers away from the town. I used to go the dam almost every day to cool off from the heat and to get some exercise. I would run near the river "Panzara," and fondly recall its wonderful cooling water as I swam and stretched my body.

Unlike in other parts of India, water is never a problem in Pimpalner. The main occupation is farming, with almost one hundred and fifty small villages around the town. The villagers in the area come to the weekly market on Fridays. There was also a Gram Panchayat, police station and a forest office.

The ashram grounds there felt very isolated and barren, maybe because it was pre-monsoon and really dry when we arrived. Due to our weeklong bus journey, we were all very tired, but I was full of excitement about Pimpalner. I had trained myself to not need to lie down to sleep, and was able to meditate through the night. During my time with the master, I spent a total of two years not sleeping in a bed, and easier than getting up in the middle of the night to meditate.

In Pimpalner, right in the middle of the ten-acre property was a Hindu temple, with a small platform, big enough for a little chair; it is where I would go each night to meditate when everyone else was asleep. I was determined to reach enlightenment and the only way to get there, was to meditate all night long without interference or distraction.

Undoubtedly, I was nodding off into a sleep state some of the time. The master told us that if we sat upright, we would not drop into a deep sleep, and it would help us sustain our connection to the sound and the light. I would sing the mantra to myself and focus on my third eye (the third eye, also known as the inner eye is a mystical and esoteric concept referring to a speculative invisible eye, which provides perception beyond ordinary sight). Or I would plug my ears with earplugs to listen to inner sound; sometimes I would hear the most celestial and beautiful music.

For years, I remember this sensation would infuse every cell of my being with a certain light—it reminded me of the light I saw and felt in my body during my coma, and near-death experience at nine years old. An hour of meditation and bliss, listening to inner sound and light gave my body, such deep rest and relaxation, sleep was not necessary.

Hindu Temple

The Hindu Temple had a Statue of Hanuman inside it, and occasionally, people from neighboring towns would come to worship. It was quite strange to Westerners to see the red paint splattered all over the Hanuman statue in the center of the little temple. The statue looked and felt very violent and ugly to me, and each time I entered, I felt chills running down my spine.

I'd fixate on how cramped and confined the temple was with its little platform around it, where I placed the chair and meditate at night. I could lean my head against the wall of the north side of the temple and that way stay upright all-night long.

The master always told us that disembodied spirits will eventually attack us as we merge with the inner light and sound, because all entities in the universe want what we humans have—*free will!* He said that even angels, gods and goddesses are jealous of humans. And since humans have free will and can control their mind and emotions, he claimed that only one minute of meditation is worth one thousand years of advancement on the other planes of consciousness, enabling those who focused and remained steadfast to fend off malign entities and energies.

He explained that once the sound current inside of us grew stronger (sound current is the esoteric essence of God which is available to all human beings), and the light and our third eye got brighter, entities from many dimensions, astral, causal and super causal would try to distract us from our meditation.

On a particular clear, starry night, I began to understand exactly what the master was talking about. It was getting a little chilly outside, and about two o'clock in the morning, suddenly, a swift wind passed across my face. I thought that, perhaps, the anticipated monsoon season had finally arrived. This had happened for two consecutive nights, with the wind swirling over my head and all around me like a tiny, spinning tornado.

It caused me to feel somewhat dizzy, but I did not dare open my eyes, thinking for sure that this was an entity trying to disturb my meditation. I was afraid, yet determined not to give into the distraction. I decided to shout my mantra to the point that the Mexican girls who also meditated on the temple platform heard me and chimed in.

(It's forbidden to share the Simran, so I will not share it with you here, but there are basically five holy words representing each region of consciousness. The master gave me permission to share the fifth word of the Simran which is "Sat Naam" which means "in the beginning was the word and the word was with God.") This site explains the power of a mantra.

Something was unusual and we all seemed to know it.

The louder the mantra was spoken, the more vigorous the wind became, nearly knocking me off my chair. Before it happened, something unfamiliar started picking at my hair, pulling and yanking. I was horrified. Could I bear what was happening to me? I decided to look.

I opened my eyes; what did I see? An astonishing vision of a real monkey with arms flailing around me—with human facial expressions, laughing and teasing as it paraded about. I jumped up, grabbed my chair, and ran as fast as I could back to my little room in the Western quarters. My heart pounded, and sweat dripped down my back, as I long-jumped straight into my bed. I ripped the blanket over my head, as I kept repeating my mantra out loud. Finally… I fell asleep.

The next morning, I ran up to the master's house near the

kitchen and told Gisela what had happened at the temple. She asked me to wait for a moment and then invited me inside the master's room; I told the story of exactly what and how it happened. I felt weak and a failure; I had not been able to keep my eyes closed, and wasn't strong enough to get rid of this entity.

When I asked Master what this was about, he simply said: "It was Hanuman the Monkey God."

I was fascinated and also a little disturbed.

What did this mean and why did this entity, this Monkey God, appear to me? The Hindu pantheon was pretty new to me and I sure didn't understand why such an entity would be fascinated with my hair.

In those days you couldn't go to your iPhone and google "Hanuman," so I asked around to get the information after my brief talk with my guru. No one in the ashram seemed to want to tell me anything, which was really frustrating to me and made my curiosity peak even more. I was determined to find out everything I could on Hinduism at that point.

I always loved history, but it wasn't until later in life, when I studied the sacred Hindu texts of *The Bhagavat Gita*, *Ramayana* and *Mahabharata*, and was initiated into the Krishna Path, that I truly learned about the meaning of "Hanuman."

I learned that each god in the Hindu religion represents an aspect of our enlightened mind, and it is how the dynamics of soul and ego, of devotion and higher intelligence, of faith and ignorance have come into form so we can understand ourselves. *Hanuman, the great monkey god of the Ramayana is a symbol of the mind that has become disciplined and filled with devotion. Hanuman is the evolved state of our unruly monkey mind that constantly jumps from thought to thought. This mind is fully focused on the presence of the divine self, the lord of life within the heart.*

This is my favorite part of the story of Lord Rama where he asks Hanuman, "How do you look upon me?"

The great monkey gives a three-part answer,

"When I believe I am the body, then I am your faithful servant. When I know I am the soul, I know myself to be a spark of your eternal light. And when I have the vision of truth, you and I, my Lord, are one and the same."

Three states of consciousness are revealed as we flow through our spiritual quest. Many times we identify with the person, the body-mind-ego that we think we are.

At those times we can realize that we are here to do God's work, to serve that higher self in us and in everything. This is the foundation of Karma Yoga, the yoga of service. Eventually we realize we are not as separate from divine intelligence as we thought, and that there is a higher knowing and presence working through us. We sense we are not separate from other beings and that our existence is an expression of the indescribable presence of God in us. This is where Bhakti and Raja Yoga open us further. The most dramatic shift in our perception occurs when all veils lift and we have the vision of truth. Then we know that we are all that exists. We are the Source; we are One and that is called Jnana Yoga.

What allows Hanuman to have this complete vision is faith, also called Shraddha. This faith is the origin of five essential levels of spiritual practice. Hanuman is therefore the manifestation of faith that gives us strength, which transforms our memory and leads us through Samadhi to perfect wisdom.

I believe that true faith is not belief. Faith is not what we think or have been told, nor is it a belief in someone else's belief. It is much more real than that. It is based on the direct experience of *Truth* and therefore more solid than a rock.

Had I known then, that Hanuman was a deity, I would like to have had a conversation with him. I now understood his visit had been an honor. It was so strange to me that no one was allowed to go to the temple after my curious encounter. I missed my little quiet spot on the temple platform… and Hanuman.

A week later, the police and a bus with more than fifty very angry and outraged Indian men arrived at the ashram, wondering what happened to the Hanuman statue that was inside the temple. The entire grounds were dug up by the police, with the help of a slew of Hindu volunteers looking for remnants and evidence that somehow the master made the statue disappear.

I learned quickly that it was a heinous crime in India to remove any deity or statue inside a temple. Luckily, the police never found the lost Hanuman statue or any piece of it. The issue was resolved: the master was asked to buy a new statue and host a ceremony in honor of Hanuman.

I realized much later, after meditating peacefully on the temple platform for the remainder of our stay in Pimpalner that the existing Hanuman statue had an entity attached to it. It was left to the master to get rid of it in order for the initiates to be able to meditate undisturbed.

As a matter of course, we all participated in the Hindu ceremony in honor of Hanuman as requested by the master. When I caught a glimpse of the "new statue," I couldn't help but chuckle under my breath. It was three feet tall, resembling a nutcracker made of wood, very friendly and innocent, and nothing like the one that had played games with me.

Later, during the night of the statue raising ceremony, I cornered my friend, David, from California—and pestered him until he finally told me the truth about the disappearance of the Hanuman statue. I had seen him grinning earlier, and knew there was a secret hidden behind that innocent altar boy look. For sure, he had something to do with this!

He told me that Master had called for him and two other of the strong guys, immediately after I had told him the story about Hanuman bothering me. They were asked to discreetly get rid of the statue.

David said, "We smashed the statue into many pieces and buried it outside the ashram grounds where no one was able to find it again." He also admitted, "I was very nervous when the police came, but luckily it all went well."

Hanuman monkey god was never to be seen again, nor was any of his mischief!

18

Marianna's Suicide

Life and death; neither are simple!

When we lived at the ashram in Pimpalner, I stayed across the courtyard from a woman named, Marianna. She had just arrived from Munich in bad shape, emotionally. At the time, there were about fifty people from the West there, along with roughly thirty Indians.

Our bunkers were in two rows, and built from simple concrete—huts, each with a small room and bathroom.

In the middle of the courtyard was a little garden where we planted potatoes, onions and salad makings. The night Marianna arrived, we had just held a celebration for the villagers to honor the master. Her facial expression fear ridden and disturbed. It was very sad to see her in this state and all I wanted to do was to reach out and help. The whole town had come for a Satsang and a feast. As usual, there was much activity in the langar, the free kitchen, by those preparing the delicious dishes.

Marianna seemed a curiously shy lady. A few days after her arrival, I knocked on her door to bring her a watermelon, and she barely opened the door. When she did, clearly, she was not bathed—and in disarray. She was dripping with sweat from being in the hot room. As I spoke to her, she looked down at the floor, and not at me. Without eye contact, her body contorted, her back hunched, filled me with concern for her. I had this definite sense that she was not well and, so, asked her to come outside with me. She didn't want to leave her room. I reached for her hand and she quickly removed my hand. I felt surprised, disappointed and helpless to welcome her, or to put her at ease.

Knowing she was in trouble, I found out later that the master had written her not one, but three, pleading telegrams to beg her to come to India as quickly as possible. I don't know how she made it to India by herself, except that she was picked up at Mumbai airport by the master's driver. What happened in the interim is a mystery to me, as Marianna could barely function at all.

The master was known to allow people with mental and emotional issues at the ashram, often people with nowhere else to go except to an institution. I could feel his compassion; his heart ached for the people that were discarded by society.

According to what I had learned from the master, such people were "possessed," and in need of some kind of exorcism or extraction. It was not common knowledge among Westerners that arrived at the ashrams in India that Master actually was an exorcist of evil spirits.

Many times, I watched the master drive negative energies out of people. I'd see people speaking in six different languages they never could have known, and a man speaking in a high-pitched voice like a 16-year-old girl. These people were clearly not themselves and it was the master's job to rid them of such harmful things, and get them back to their natural, more peaceful state.

Seeing people levitating and speaking in several languages that seemed otherworldly, or ancient, and emitting strange yet formulaic sounds was not uncommon among people needing his help. One of my best friends, Sonjia, floated right off the floor in front of me. She shook so violently that her body wasn't touching the ground anymore. When the master made a gesture with his hand, Sonjia descended again, where she sat quietly and calmly.

To be frank, while at the ashram, I felt like I was in the exorcist movie half of the time. The kind of things that I witnessed were hair-raising and scary. Marianna's visit was no different.

Marianna arrived on a Wednesday, and right out of the get-go acted really strange. She didn't want to eat with us and stayed in her room all day. The night she hung herself (a few days later) many of us were up on the hill near the master's house meditating. The electricity went out on the entire compound. I felt this was strange but it didn't really interfere with our nightly activities, until James, one of the initiates from Canada, came running into Satsang, us in deep meditation.

James screamed, out of breath, "Oh my god, Master! Marianna hung herself!"

Instantly, two other disciples joined James, ran as fast as they could, and proceeded to cut her down from the rafter. When she fell to the ground, she was dead.

Later, when James told me the story of how he found her, I was stunned that he had the intuition to go into her room in the first place. He said he had heard some strange grunting sounds coming from her room. The second he opened the door, the generator went out. James said he quickly went to fetch a flashlight from his room, which was next to hers. When he returned, in less than a minute, he shined the flashlight into her room, and that's when he saw Marianna dangling there from the wooden beam. She had also slit her wrists with a knife.

Of course, we were all shocked. I was so sorry that I didn't listen to my intuition and try harder to save her—but perhaps that was not within my power or control to do so.

James told us that when he looked at her lifeless body, it was not Marianna's face that he saw, but an evil entity that overwhelmed her body. The entity's intent, James felt, was to take her Life-force.

After James had stormed into Satsang that night, we were all asked to stay there, not to leave until they could figure out exactly what happened. At some point, the master came flying into the gate with his driver, swiftly getting out of the car. By then, Marianna was lying on the ground in the middle of the courtyard. Everyone was asked to go inside, but I couldn't. I stayed to watch the master; I wanted to see what he was going to do. For me, it was too difficult to not to see what was going on, I felt so worried about Marianna.

Suddenly, the master jumped on Marianna's body. I watched him lay on her doing something I didn't understand. Then he took her to the hospital.

A Miracle

To our surprise, that same woman came *walking* back into the ashram the next day. She had slit her wrists, hung herself, and was now breathing. Afterwards, the master had Marianna housed in a room, where myself and three other people would be on 24-hour surveillance for a week. We were not to let her out of sight while we kept her locked in the room.

I will never forget this experience as long as I live. This is when I realized how weak, I was. I realized that all my love, my good intentions, my compassion were not enough to help somebody like Marianna, and that I had much work to do if I wanted to battle the dark force.

I felt like the young Luke Skywalker in "Star Wars," when he gave up trying to lift the plane out of the swamp with his mind—and Yoda told him to JUST DO IT. This was one of the biggest humility lessons I received during the years I stayed with the master.

Maintaining Marianna's status meant conducting oral "Simran"—the chanting of a specific mantra out loud so this entity that possessed Marianna would leave. It was a most difficult task, and quite dangerous and scary at times.

Once, I was sitting on the bed next to Marianna, who was tied to the bed with a rope so the entity couldn't hurt her anymore, causing her to hurt herself. The other initiates in the room sat on the floor with candles burning and a picture of the master.

I was so honored that my guru asked me to help out with this situation. Looking over at her, I suddenly had the impulse to touch her hand and put my arm around her shoulder. She looked so thin, so forlorn, so pale with her bandaged neck and wrists.

All of a sudden, Marianna turned her head my way, the entity screaming from the top of its voice in a vicious male voice. The force and power of the being was so powerful that it was able to lift me off of the bed and throw me against the wall. Horrified, I stood up and ran out of that room as fast as I could and made my way to the master's quarters. Out of breath, I remember telling him that I would never go back to that room again.

The master made arrangements for this beautiful initiate from Turkey to move to Munich and watch over Marianna. She briefly arrived at the ashram to meet Marianna, and get instructions from the master, and then she flew back to Munich with her. I heard that she lived to a ripe old age and that her friend watched over her until the end.

After that, I acquired what we called the gift of "astral smell." I could make out when somebody was possessed by merely sensing, not only the energy, but I could actually smell the entity. Now, every once in a while, when I read the energy of people with disturbances like that, I can smell it from many feet away. For me, it's clear when I sense that hint of blood or formaldehyde— a strong feeling of wanting to help them comes over me—this sensitivity perhaps relates back to my experience with my mother.

This has brought great protection for me and others, because it's not always obvious to the person superimposed; they cannot always help themselves. This was the case with a doctor who was in a business network with me, and so drawn to my energy. Every time I interacted with her, that chemical smell was present, and I knew that problems were lurking in the background, even though she appeared so put together and educated. When I finally decided to disconnect the relationship she became hysterical and almost violent.

"If you can, help others; if you cannot do that, at least do not harm them."

—Dalai Lama

19

Apparition

It had been seven years since my mother's death, and still, I could not let her go, nor could I find peace and rest in my grief. She had died when I was sixteen, and it seemed I should be able to have more closure by this time. I knew I needed help, but could not have predicted how this help would come.

> *"Let us interrogate the great apparition that shines so peacefully around us."*
>
> —Ralph Waldo Emerson

At the age of twenty-four, after my arrival in India as a disciple of the master, like all initiates who arrive in India, I was granted a private interview with the master. My interview, like so many things to me, was most curious, yet so strikingly clear. I asked him about my mother and my family, since that was in the forefront of my concerns.

The master crinkled his nose in the way he was known

to do when telling someone something uncomfortable, and said to me: "She is here; she is with you and inside you! It was a hard, hard situation for three or four lifetimes for your mother, but now it will be better because of you. She couldn't leave you, my dear. Keep meditating my dear heart and talk to her, she will soon receive some help!"

Upon hearing these words, I realized that I was *not* crazy. Since her passing, I had always felt her with me, inside of me. With this message, relief washed over me, and I cried such tears of joy—for many hours.

My mother was with me; my heart knew that she was guiding my journey. New peace prevailed. And with this new knowledge, I felt assured that she too was in good hands. Even though I still didn't fully understand how the master worked on all the levels that he did, I trusted what he relayed to me, and what would come next for my mother and for me.

After many days in silence, pondering this revelation, one night I was sitting in front of the master's house meditating, when I noticed a familiar smell and energy; someone or something touched my lips. It happened just as I was leaving my physical thoughts and body to the astral level of consciousness. I felt calm, as the reassuring fingers on my lips seem to relay, "Be still, I am here." And of course, it startled me as well.

During the Satsang the following night, I wrote a question on a piece of paper. I asked the master if it was possible for entities to manifest in the flesh and touch us. He said it was quite common.

After we talked, the master continued to sit and meditate with the group. He was walking around me in circles until I felt him right next to me. He suddenly grabbed me by the neck, lifted me up slightly from my cross-legged sitting position on the ground, and put his thumb on my third eye. This felt like a hot iron rod pushing straight through my head, making me feel dizzy. He rubbed with great force, and it was excruciatingly painful. Something felt as if it was being pulled out of me from deep down in my spine. When I'd almost given in, I suddenly heard a loud popping sound. I fell down to the ground.

Master lifted me up again and said, "Stay upright now!" This night's experience felt strange and auspicious to me. However, the increased clarity in my meditation was different from other nights—that was for sure.

The next day, I felt such a foreign void, an emptiness I can't even describe to you, something I had not experienced before. I was missing her—my mother—deeply.

That night, while in deep meditation, I experienced journeying to another planet. It was a globe, indigo blue, with millions upon millions of souls sitting and meditating in different formations. Some were squatting, with their ears plugged, similar to how we would sometimes meditate.

I suddenly noticed a being that I couldn't make out at first, floating above the rest of all the souls. While they stayed deep in trance, the body of a woman was floating toward me. As she got closer, I noticed her familiar thick red hair, green eyes and freckles. My mother's sisters were all redheads; I started to understand who might be joining me. The apparition hovered towards me, albeit in a much younger body, with much thicker hair—*my mother.*

This spirit, her spirit, looked at me and I just knew it was my mother because of her eyes, their expression a little sad, but it was clearly my mother's soul within. As soon as I acknowledged it was her, the woman faded out of view.

It was then that she waved goodbye and told me, "It is done now."

For the next few days a strange emptiness prevailed within me; it was as if some part of me was gone. I knew in my heart that the master had taken my mother from my body.

My master continued to tell me to think about my mother whenever I'd go off to meditate. "Keep repeating the Simran and think about your mother," he'd advise. *Think of your mother lovingly, keep repeating the Simran,* was his mantra and advise. I believe that he used this time and those words to help her transition in a more complete way through me and my meditation.

Some people might say that the apparition was a possession or a soul attachment. I knew I was being used as some kind of host but didn't know for what. The master told me later about my mother's past lives, and what this vision might have meant.

He felt she had died of strange circumstances, many times, and that my love for her saved her from many more difficult incarnations to come—had she continued on without my love. Finally, she had been released. And for that I was grateful—and for the greater understanding and serenity I received.

Life Continued in India

The monsoon season had been hitting us hard for two months in Pimpalner. Marianna, the initiate who committed suicide and was brought back to life, was doing well back in Munich accompanied by the woman who looked after her. We heard back at the compound that she had recovered completely, and was now able to live a normal life. My encounter with my mother's spirit and this good news about Marianna brought much needed closure for me.

Everyone was getting tired of the rain; there was mud everywhere. The markets in Pimpalner were selling limited fruits and fresh foods, and our Western crew was anxious to return to the city. For a few weeks we had eaten little, but chapattis and sabji made with onions and potatoes.

I wrote in my diary every day, and contemplated what it would be like to live in India full time. It frightened me to even entertain the thought. But it kept coming up for me to consider. Everything I had witnessed, up to now, was not exactly easy—and what I needed most was to be healed; I wanted to be whole. I wanted it badly, but to accomplish it in simpler ways than I had so far. Meditating around the clock was difficult, and my body ached from it at times.

Many nights I fell over in my chair, losing control, unable to stay awake. I would wake myself up snoring. Other nights were more blissful. I would sit down, and remember leaving my body in meditation, only to wake up the next day fully rested.

One day the master called me into the room where we had a conversation, and he asked me why I wanted to stay in India. I said, "I know that I need help."

He did his famous nose wrinkle and said, "Why do you want to stay in this place Petra, this is a hospital!"

As events would have it, he had me extend my visa just once, allowing me to stay in India for almost nine months. I returned to India a second time the following year, for three months. To fast forward in my life, I was involved with the mission of the master a total of eleven years, one year in the ashram "Lighthouse Center Oregon" in Umpqua, Oregon, USA. Some of those years, I lived in ashrams on the West and East Coasts of the states—and was a disciple who attended regular Sunday Satsangs, a commitment similar to going to church.

During these years that followed, while living in Oregon

ashrams, I observed the phenomenon of entities many times again. My own experience with my mother taught me it was never easy. I had empathy for the people who were suppressed in this way, and felt extreme compassion and understanding, not only for the person but for the entity as well.

The master said that some people are so possessed that if he were to take out the entity abruptly, the person could die. So he had to handle this very carefully. Timing and the style in which this is done were very important.

India sparked a great interest in me to understand human behavior and the ways of spirit. I once had a good friend who was the head of psychology in a county in Oregon. She specialized in schizophrenia and took Reiki classes and retreats with me. This friend told me that she believed schizophrenia to be a form of "spirit possession."

I find it true that in the West, society is not equipped to deal with this, except to give people drugs. To me, that's a shame. When we consider the physical, mental, *and* spiritual, as I saw in India and while living in ashrams, there seems to be a more effective and healthy way to deal with such disturbances of the human mind and soul.

"Sometimes even to live is an act of courage."

—Seneca

20

Welcome to America

"I slept and dreamt that life was joy. I awoke and saw that life was service. I acted and behold, service was joy."

—Rabindranath Tagore

My heart spoke and it could not be quieted. My desire and purpose seemed clear—and this meant I was to *not* stay hidden away from everyday life, the good and bad, but to love people and to serve the world—this resonated as the ongoing theme of my life. Without integrating with real life, somehow a certain joy was lacking.

So, as a young disciple of a Sant Sat Guru, one cannot help but feel somehow privileged to be the chosen one to journey with the master. The decision was made very quickly—and it didn't compare to anything I had ever experienced in my life—all that I knew was that I was so happy; this was my destiny—to journey to America with the master.

From India, I booked a flight to Munich to say goodbye to my family and to Walter. I was to meet the master in Frankfurt right after Christmas, and from there, board a plane to New York.

My trusted friend, Walter, and many other disciples travelled to Frankfurt from the town of Oberbrunn in Bavaria, where some initiates had purchased an old castle that served as a retreat center for initiates of the master. Walter and I went on a long walk in Frankfurt, where he told me that he would always be by my side and that we can still meet on other planes of consciousness—meditations where we experience transformation and are sustained by something greater than ourselves.

Since this was a rushed decision, the day of our travel was soon upon us. There were hundreds of people at the airport in Frankfurt to bid the master farewell. It quite surprised me when he carried my luggage to the check-in counter. I felt so happy, so thankful, so joyful and blessed, in the whirlwind of excitement.

As we boarded the plane, I felt special—*nearly the princess of my childhood dreams.* I had on a beautiful green cape, which I took off and laid over me. It was as warm as a blanket, and without asking or hesitation, the master pulled it over us both. As we settled into our seats, and looking around, I could see this long flight to New York was only half-full. The flight attendant began her duties, bringing us tea and water.

It is difficult to write about this, let alone tell anybody the truth of what really happened to me on the plane. The master said, "You are one of my very special souls and the master couldn't give you much attention in India because of so many people there!"

What exactly did that mean? Was I privileged?

This special attention was extremely challenging. It's an

understatement to say that I was more than confused as the master moved closer and started to French kiss me on the lips; I felt his tongue in my mouth.

With my cape draped over me, he put his hand under my shirt and started kneading my breasts. My heart started beating fast, out of fear of what would happen next… and just about then the unthinkable did happen. He moved his hand under my skirt, and onto the wool tights that covered my legs. His hand moved slowly up my leg and towards my inner thigh. Fear crept up inside of me; I shook from inside out. At that point, I began to pray that he would not go any further. He stopped!

What was he doing? Was this some sort of personal test? Was I being molested? Was the master just a man with desires like any other man? I felt betrayed, downright broken. My spiritual trust in the master had been shaken to the core.

Every cell in my being fought his touch, his scent, his breath. I was disgusted and felt sick to my stomach. I wanted to run and hide; I needed to escape, but could not get out. I could have screamed, but then what? This wasn't a movie playing out in slow motion—this was real life.

What just happened? A mind fuck.

My thoughts went every which way—and cold fear raced as fast as my heart—though I sat there, still as a rock. No words were spoken, and suddenly, he laid his head down on my lap, to take a nap in the open seat. He lay there, like a little child—and I held him. At one point I looked down into his wise old eyes. I could see, to my amazement, the master had transformed into a two-year-old-child, with such love in his eyes. In the most affectionate way, he looked back at me, and said nonchalantly:

"Between you and me, there is no difference!"

Did he mean that he was just human like me, or that I also could become a master someday, or that what had just happened would not change things between us?

What?

By this time, the flight attendants had turned back on the lights and were serving coffee. Breakfast was being served, and I noticed the yellow color in the pancake. We were supposed to abide by lacto vegetarian diet, meaning no animal products, except milk products; I eagerly warned the master not to touch the pancakes.

He looked at me with a certain grin on his face and innocently announced:

"There are no eggs."

This was getting to be quite interesting, with his many conflicting thoughts and actions. Holding up his fork, the master pronged a big bite of pancake, and fed me the first bite. I had no choice but to open my mouth and enjoy the pancake.

This reminds me of a scene in the movie "Matrix" when Neo enters the waiting room at the Oracle's apartment where a bunch of psychic and talented kids were waiting for her to come out. One little boy there was bending a spoon with his mind, and when Neo asked him how he did this the little boy said, "You see, there is no spoon."

I remember the master telling me on the plane that the organization of the master was "a necessary evil." It meant to him that whenever spiritual practice/school/center have to be turned into a corporation or any sort of business practice, it has a tendency to get abused and misused.

And I had realized that my path was quite different from the rest. The master made it quite clear that I was not to live at the ashram tucked away from the world, but that I was to be with people in the world and understand the worldly ways. It seemed I had just had an abrupt lesson in the ways of the world.

I didn't exactly know what that meant at the time, but I do now.

It was an unforgettable plane ride with the master. It created friction within my psyche, and my love for the master was challenged—I was confused and distraught. Clarity gone—the water had been muddied, so to speak. I doubted the master, but never the path he followed of "Science of Light and Sound." I had nowhere to go; I was stuck, so chose to believe that everything was okay, and that he was still my father, my guru, my guide.

Here I was about to arrive in a foreign country, with a famous guru from India, and hundreds of disciples awaiting his arrival at the New York airport. *How do I tell anyone what happened to me on the plane?* (I never spoke about the incident on the plane until ten years later, when my husband asked me directly about what happened.)

Arriving in America

After arriving in New York, and after making our way through customs, about a dozen initiates greeted us, including Joanie. She was a very friendly Jewish Lady with big eyes, kinky long hair and big teeth—and the national representative of his organization, Kirpal Light Satsang, New York.

Joanie ran up to the master with a starry-eyed look, and her hands folded in the traditional Indian greeting position; she bowed to the master, as she said, "Namaste Master, then bowed again."

Master introduced me to Joanie, and handed me over to her saying, "This is Petra from Germany; take good care of her. She will come on the tour with Master, and be living in the U.S."

Traumatized from the events on the plane, I felt so confused. But at the same time, I couldn't see myself going back to Germany. I had nowhere to go, and I wanted to be near the initiates that had become my friends and family. Except for my uncle Ewald in Germany, most of the people in my family didn't understand what was going on with me and thought I had been captured by a cult and severely brainwashed.

In reality, I was desperately seeking like-minded people that could understand me, and the *initiate family* satisfied a huge hunger inside of me to belong somewhere in the world. Granted, from the outside it definitely looked like a cult but then again, what is the definition of a cult?

We know a cult is a sociological classification of a religious movement: literally defined, a cult is a religious or social group with socially deviant or novel beliefs and practices. However, whether any particular group's beliefs and practices are sufficiently deviant or novel is often unclear, thus making a precise definition problematic. As with my response to the master on the plane, I felt I was still grounded—as odd as that might sound, considering the events of my life, and the longing and searching of my heart.

Without missing a beat, I was packed into an initiate's car, and we went directly to Toronto, where the master gave a talk in a hotel. Toronto looked a lot like London, with its brick buildings and beautiful architecture. From there, we traveled from city to city to the West Coast, finally arriving in Seattle, Washington.

Ho' Mana, aka Madeline P.

I will never forget that day. We walked into a house, not sure whose it was, and the master had already arrived. He was sitting in meditation; we quietly snuck into the room and sat down. Half an hour later, breakfast was served.

I was introduced to various people; one girl offered her house for me to stay. After we finished breakfast, I felt somebody's hand on my shoulder, and as I turned around I saw a beautiful tall and distinguished lady, with her hair tied in a bun standing behind me. I immediately stood up to shake her hand when she said, "Hello, my dear, I am Ho'Mana! Where are you staying tonight?"

She invited me to stay at her house, when the celebrations, talks with the master and meditations were over. We got into her light blue Cadillac and drove to Bellevue, Washington where she lived. I felt elated and happy as we arrived at her huge home.

In my whole life, I have never forgotten this night. It sets the stage for many things that would follow in the spiritual and nonphysical realm.

We walked into the kitchen, and she filled two glasses with ice, handing me one. I followed her down a narrow stairwell, where I was amazed to see photos of a man shaking the hands of different presidents, throughout time. Ho'Mana was in the pictures with her husband.

I asked, "Who is the man in the pictures?"

"Oh, that's my husband. He's the head of a Forestry Department of the United States government!"

A bit stunned, but I didn't ask any more questions, as we walked downstairs into a room that had lots of glass cases with different Native American artifacts in them. The artwork caught my eye: baskets and necklaces, and other decorative jewelry made of beads; also beautifully embroidered clothing, and even a Hopi "peace pipe" stood on a special stand in the middle of the room.

I thought… *she must be a collector.*

We walked further into the room, and she said, "Welcome!

This is my meditation room. I usually don't allow people in here, but today I am making an exception. Sit down; make yourself comfortable. I have a lot to tell you.

Ho'Mana and I arrived at her home around 9:00 p.m., and we stayed up talking until early morning. I was exhausted from jet lag, but too excited to sleep.

She poured diet Pepsi, which I thought tasted terrible, over our glasses with the ice. We sat down in comfortable chairs, and looked out the window at her beautifully landscaped backyard, where lights shined on the evergreens, and the falling rain glistened.

Ho' Mana, aka Madeline's story begins with her deciding to visit a Hopi reservation in Arizona, to bring clothing and supplies to the Hopi people.

She shared:

"I always wanted to visit the reservation, not really knowing why I was so drawn to it! One day, I decided to buy a little truck, loaded it up and went to Tucson, Arizona to visit the reservation. When I arrived at the gate, I was greeted by some children who pointed me through the reservation, telling me to drive to the end of the road until I reached a little house on the right, where a man and his woman would be standing in front. I got there, and they greeted me and asked me to come inside, saying:

"We have been waiting a long time for you. You are the woman that doesn't eat meat, and you bring us a message from the master from the East. It is in the prophecy!"

She went on: "There were three place settings, and the man introduced himself as Grandfather David Monongye, a Hopi Native American traditional leader Kikmongwi of Hotevilla. And Son of Yukiuma, keeper of the Fire Clan tablets, who founded Hotevilla Reservation in 1906."

"First settled by the *hostiles,* as he referred to European settlers, a group of Hopi residents were forced out of nearby, Oraibi, AZ, in 1906. Oraibi split, due to ideological differences over European cultural influences of recently arrived settlers, soldiers and missionaries, and influences against which the hostiles were opposed.

Later attempts to reintegrate displaced residents, resulted in another split to the settlement of Bacavi, which later joined with Hotevilla, to create a unified settlement."

"David Monongye is one of four founding Hopis, including Thomas Banyacya, Dan Evehema, and Dan Katchongva. They were appointed to reveal Hopi traditional wisdom and teachings, including the Hopi prophecies for the future, to the general public in 1946—after the use of the first two nuclear weapons on Japan."

"In 1972, Monongye, and three other Hopi elders participated in the United Nations Conference on the Human Environment. Monongye was a co-author of Techqua Ikachi, the traditional Hopi newsletters produced from 1975 to 1986. Monongye inspired Godfrey Reggio's 1982 film, *Koyaanisqatsi: Life Out of Balance.* Monongye was also vocal about problems generated by coal-mining on Hopi land."

Being a young woman from Bavaria, I had no idea about the history of the Native American Indians, or the fact that 50 million Native American Indians lived in the United States for thousands of years—with only 800,000 left in this country by the mid-20th Century.

Tragically, many of them died from the diseases brought to this continent by the Europeans: these included bubonic plague, chicken pox, pneumonic plague, cholera, diphtheria, influenza, measles, scarlet fever, smallpox, typhus, tuberculosis, and whooping cough.

And many were massacred in cold blood, at such places like "The Battle of Wounded Knee." Later, I would watch the movie, *The Trail of Tears,* which made me sick to my stomach, reminding me of Hitler and the Nazis who were evil. But this genocide became but a faint whisper in the wind, and was conveniently swept under the carpet for over 150 years.

Today, the predictions of the ancient medicine people and elders of some of the tribe still stand true, and it is predicted by the Hopi and many other American Indian tribes that the end of this civilization is nearing.

Grandfather David continued to say to Ho'Mana:

"We were told you would come back to us, your name is Ho'Mana which means Light Bearer. You have fought for the Hopi—to help us get the land back… many times."

She shared with me how he stood up and pulled out a piece of very old parchment paper, unrolled it, and laid it on the table in front of her. It was a letter, one-hundred-years-old to the day, written to the president of the United States and signed by Ho'Mana, in her own handwriting. Speechless… she simply cried.

Looking at me, she pointed at the peace pipe in the glass case next to her, and said that that was her peace pipe from a long time ago—and that one of the Hopi made a replica. She continued on, by telling me stories about people in the reservation, and their problems with alcohol *firewater*, drugs and addictions, and how the Indians were systematically exterminated in so many ways.

I wish I could have recorded the whole conversation. Ho'Mana told me that her daughter will publish her story someday. Apparently, Hollywood had knocked on her door for many years, but she never released the story. I wish I could find Ho'Mana. I regret that I didn't return here and I should have responded to her last call to me in 2010 with an immediate visit to Bellevue, Washington.

My introduction to America included history lessons such as these, helping me to gain knowledge and understanding of this country that was so new to me. How could I serve? It began by acknowledging the history that made up this great land.

21

Ashram Marriage

After arriving in the United States, in December, 1986, I enjoyed my brief time traveling with the master, meeting many people and seeing much of this new country. I began to relax when there were no further incidents with the master—as had occurred on the plane flight to the United States.

Traveling south from Seattle, we arrived in California, at Hidden Valley Ranch, to attend a five-day retreat. There, I saw my friend Lori, whom I'd met in Arroyo Grande, CA. She and I had become quite close, and she kept asking me to move to Nevada City, a quaint little village with Victorian homes near the Ananda Center—an ashram of the Yogananda community near Sacramento, where Lori used to live. It was something to consider.

During the retreat, I had a vision with the master's image of floating on a giant swan on a liquid crystal lake that was so magnificent and beautiful that I thought it was heaven. The swan was so big that the master and I were sitting on its back as if it was a sturdy boat. From that vantage point, I looked around and saw angels flying—and mountains were moving and flowing from silver to gold—diamond shaped sparkles with celestial music reverberated from the sky. It was nirvana, and I had left my body to be with the master.

It was remarkable, and I could have stayed in that state of meditation forever if Lori hadn't touched me on the shoulder. She shook me ever so slightly to get me out of meditation to go to lunch with her. I was furious; a meditation experience like this does not come along every day. I explained to her never to touch a person when they are meditating, because you don't know if they are in Samādhi or not. (Samādhi - Sanskrit: Hindi pronunciation: also called samāpatti, in Hinduism, Buddhism, Jainism, Sikhism and yogic schools refer to a state of meditative consciousness. It is a meditative absorption or trance, attained by the practice of dhyāna.)

It was at Hidden Valley Ranch that the master called me in the room again; I was concerned he would try to kiss me, but he never touched me again, which was a strange and mixed emotion for me. On the one hand wishing he would keep me so close to him spiritually, and on the other feeling completely repelled and afraid of his physical actions.

During the retreat, he had a lot of people around him, and everybody attending the retreat received a private interview with the master.

He asked me, "Do you like Jay?

I responded by nodding, "Yes."

He added, "I think it will be good for you to move near Lori. You can go with Jay there, yes?"

"Yes."

It was ironic that Jay, who I had met briefly in India and

then again at Hidden Valley Ranch also had a good friend by the name of Christopher who lived in Nevada City. It was destiny.

Jay had moved from Hawaii, where he and Christopher had been friends for a long time. Christopher had left there also, and moved to the mainland to Nevada City. He kept inviting Jay to join him there, so here we were, "teaming up" to go to the very town where his best friend, and mine, lived.

Jay was eighteen years older than me, and somewhat of a father figure. I felt safe around him, and as we got to know each other more, we talked for hours and hours. Originally, from Baltimore, Maryland, he had grown up with a tycoon father, who he said looked like Richard Nixon.

Jay had gone to "Tucson Acting and Directing School," and had become an accomplished actor. When Jay was in his early twenties, he had married a woman who was the sole heiress to many of the radio and television stations on the east coast. Through these connections, he was handed a golden platter to Hollywood. He looked a lot like Sean Connery and was extremely handsome. He and his new bride were married by two cardinals—and without warning, a year later Jay walked away with the clothes on his back. He bought a motorcycle, ditched Hollywood, and went out to find God.

Nevada City, California

In January of 1987, we moved to Nevada City, California. The master wrote Jay a handwritten note that I will never forget. It read, "My very Dear, Dear Soul, Petra—I have given you to serve each other lovingly!"

I needed to be protected and the master provided—Jay did just that. So, I married Jay a few months later, in April, 1987 in Nevada City. It was an arranged marriage and had I been more empowered, I would never have agreed to marry somebody I wasn't in love with. Maybe I talked myself into being in love with him because I was so afraid to be alone.

On the day of our wedding, Jay's friend Christopher walked through the door, and I almost fainted when I saw Chris for the first time. Here I was in an arranged marriage, to a man eighteen years my senior that I barely knew— and only married because the master said so.

Now, suddenly, I find myself attracted to Chris. I was ashamed of myself. On the path of the masters we were taught to not act on our instincts of attraction and lust. The teachings are all about overcoming lust and desire, and so I kept my conversations with Chris to a bare minimum until years later. I felt such shame, that I forced myself to not even look at him.

We joined meditation groups that met twice a week. The main gathering was always on Sunday morning at 9:00 a.m., with Satsang and meditation, and then a potluck. We went to other people's houses and also hosted at our house. Jay and I rented a little house with a sweet little garden right in the city center, in Nevada City. Since we were not living in an ashram, it was a pretty regular life.

After our marriage, Jay and I had to fly to Southern California to visit his mother. She wanted to meet me in person before agreeing to vouch for my immigration status to stay in the country. And since Jay didn't have any money, he wasn't in the financial position to support me in terms of immigration requirements.

It was a rather strange visit. His two brothers were visiting as well, sitting in the living room, making judgmental remarks about certain characters on TV, while sipping whiskey. And his mother told me that a beautiful young girl like me shouldn't be marrying such an angry man as her son. I couldn't and didn't want to hear those words at the time—it was quite upsetting and told Jay what she said. I suppose he had heard these opinions from them many times before.

His sister, too, who worked for the Hughes Corporation was so infuriated with him that she cut off relations with him completely. I hadn't known until meeting his family that day that he had been married to a woman in San Francisco, and had another son with her.

Overall, Jay was a nice man with some anger issues, but being the "rescue and fix it" woman that I was, I thought I could help him overcome his anger, and at the same time get him really excited about life. But I learned that he preferred to live the life of an old man—he no longer had goals; he liked to meditate, read books and go for walks. That summed up his daily life. Once again, I would be forced to see that I couldn't change other people. Once again, I would be forced to witness that people don't change unless they really want to.

Now, at least I knew more of the truth of who he was. I knew that he had been married twice before. And clearly, he was no longer working as an actor. I would come to recognize and accept that he was a simple man who only wanted to meditate and live a quiet life, and when disturbed in this process would become quite furious and irritable.

22

Birth of John

A child is born... a mother is born...

Mothers often say the birth of their child was the best day of their lives. This was true for me. When I held my baby for the first time on my chest, I felt that amazing connection—such an elevated, united bond. I looked at my baby's hands and feet, and experienced a sensation of simple awe. It is pure magic to have something so perfect grow inside, and then, to finally meet in person—my real, living, perfect baby boy—a human being.

My son, John Michael was born on May 17, 1991. I was thirty years old and ready to be a mother. At the time, my husband Jay and I lived in Roseburg, Oregon, with many of the ashram ladies supporting me during and after the birth. We lived on a 35-acre farm next to the majestic River Forks Park, a place my friends, Karl and Rosie Bauer, German, and initiates of the master, like me, had purchased when they arrived in the States.

Karl was a retired bank director of a German bank. He was in the Guinness Book of World Records as the youngest bank director in the history of Germany. Shortly after our move, Karl asked us to take out the 20-acres of old pear trees and turn them into a biodynamic farm (similar to organic farming, but which includes various esoteric concepts drawn from the ideas of Rudolf Steiner, 1861–1925).

He wanted us to plant a new orchard of Asian pears, and other fruit free of pesticides and other toxic chemical sprays. This time in my life was quite magical, while living in nature and pregnant with my son. We were housed right there on the winding Umpqua River among the pear and apple orchards. The property had an old farm house, a red barn, and numerous small out buildings, surrounded by other farms and expansive fields.

I was truly in the prime of my life, eating mostly organic, raw foods. I felt fantastic and in great shape—swimming and meditating many hours a day—and loving life. All of this distracted me from thinking about my marriage that had some serious flaws. We stayed busy planting gardens and tending to the house, and were heavily involved in the ashram and the people there.

Like so many of the ashram initiates, it was appropriate to have a home birth, and have as little involvement as possible from doctors. I found a wonderful midwife by the name of, Kat. She was spunky, witty and full of energy, and I felt like I was in excellent hands. Kat gave me all the sound advice I needed as a first-time mom, from breathing techniques, to the herbs she wanted me to take during the birth.

Well, the actual birth was a different story. Maybe the herbs were not so effective after all. Everything that could've gone wrong went wrong. After thirty-four hours of pushing and heavy contractions, we discovered that John was posterior. Without a C-section there was no way for me to push him out. Kat told me that both of our lives were in danger. As you can imagine, I was exhausted and ready to do anything to get that baby safely, *and effectively,* out.

Luckily, we had a back-up midwife who had hospital privileges, and she was able to help Kat with the severity of the situation. Her name was Katherine Jensen, a midwife and a pioneer for midwifery in Roseburg—greatly respected by her peers for always standing up for the rights of her female patients to birth their babies naturally, in a home environment. This was reassuring.

Kat called Katherine to meet us at Douglas County Hospital. Something wasn't right. She had seen me and my pain, knowing she'd better act immediately, and when Katherine arrived at the hospital, she reached deep inside of me to break my water. I was able to dilate a little more, but some things were beyond Kathrine's control.

After a little while, Katherine called the doctor on night duty. He was very upset with Katherine for some reason. While in such anguish, I overheard them arguing on the phone.

I was still trying to push my baby out, when Jay reminded me to breathe, and not focus on them—just to focus on me and my body. Of all things, the hospital bed started to collapse and I found myself on the ground. Luckily, I wasn't injured. But I have to tell you, there was a moment when I thought I was dying from the pain and exhaustion. Soon after, the nurses transferred me to another room, where the doctor met us upon his arrival. Let's just say, his demeanor didn't necessarily help me relax. He was clearly irritable, and his bedside manner was questionable.

In my delirium and pain, I was asked to sign a piece of paper. At that moment, I had this strange feeling; I needed some assurance, but also realized that my husband was not going to protect me, or responsibly manage the paperwork.

I could feel his typical disconnectedness and aloofness—which was the very cause of our split. I needed more support. If it hadn't been for the two initiates meditating in the corner on my behalf, and my son's, I'm not sure I would have survived this birthing thing.

After thirty-four hours of labor, and five hours of pushing, they finally gave me an epidural spinal injection that numbed my lower part of my body—and after that, I couldn't feel the pain. I hardly cared anymore if I lived or died; I was physically, mentally, and emotionally, exhausted. The epidural injection was such welcome relief to so much suffering. When the nurses finally wheeled me down the corridor into the operating room, I was completely numb—and feeling beaten down and defeated.

The doctors were scrubbed and ready—but all I cared and thought about was hearing the little cry of my baby, my boy, which finally was heard just a few minutes later. Immediately, Kathryn Jenness, my midwife, snatched the baby out of the surgeon's hands, and laid my son on my chest so that I could feel his heart beating against mine.

I will never forget that moment—I saw my son and kissed his sweet face. He was so beautiful, so perfect, so magical. I felt so much love—all I wanted to do was hold him and never let him go. Kathryn knew the protocol at the hospital well. The doctors wanted to poke and probe John because of the birth stress he had just experienced, but we knew better. I was so relieved when Jay requested to stay with our baby while I rested. He made sure not to let him out of our site, so the doctors couldn't do too many tests and invade our little boy's new life.

At the hospital, Jay initiated John. This made me feel so relieved. And I recall John's response. He just relaxed and fell asleep with a smile on his face, as if he was able to see the light. Jay had opened his third eye by placing his finger on John's little forehead, repeating the mantra so he could be initiated and have his third eye opened, as being the instructions of the master.

I was not a typical patient, even like using a low-light lamp in the hospital room, instead of the usual intrusive overhead lights. And the doctors were surprised that I didn't use the morphine drip after all I'd been through—especially after the C-section. They asked me about my homeopathic remedies—which in itself felt like they respected some of my choices.

After all was said in done, I had no more problems and John was completely healthy. After the fact, it was really the best experience of my life. I loved being pregnant; I loved nursing, loved being a mother—and most of all, loved my baby boy, John.

Life Goes On...

Obviously, my marriage to Jay became more strained and difficult. We weren't attracted to each other physically, even though mentally we actually did quite well. Throughout our marriage, we managed to exhibit love and respect for one another—always and forever grateful that out of this marriage came a great present, my son John.

Our life together was limited to those few things Jay liked, and interestingly, he thought it was my job to go out and fend for the family and make money. Initially, he was very upset that I got pregnant and did not want to abort the child, so disagreeing over that new life and responsibility didn't help us "be on the same page." I must add, later, he realized that John *is and was* his biggest blessing in life.

One day, it was quite amazing when we received a phone call from the master from India asking us to do a children's book. Lori and I were to do most of the illustrations, while Jay was supposed to make corrections on the stories. I had written a couple of children's stories, and with all my avid reading of stories, I was excited to do it. His suggested theme was a compilation of stories about saints and people in history that did wonderful things for children. The book, titled "Good Stories Makes Us Good," was never published and is still sitting on my shelf today.

Looking back, maybe that book project was the master's way to show me that I was a writer. Like many things, I couldn't figure this it out until much later. Jay was very critical of me, and much of what I tried to accomplish, so I gave up writing all together until later in life.

Jay was eighteen years older than me, but behaved more like an old man. Right out of the gate, I was not really used to being with someone that much older. But I think I had to marry a man like my father, and once again I was in charge to earn money and make things happen. I was not yet aware of the repeating patterns in my life, or their fundamental cause.

Move to Oregon

The following winter, we moved to the Ashram Lighthouse Center in Umpqua, Oregon. I'm sorry to say, that agreeing to this marriage, eventually caught up with me—sooner rather than later.

After nearly seven years of marriage, I still could never

quite understand why Jay was so disengaged from life, until I had a vision one day when we were living on the ashram grounds at the Lighthouse Center. Everyone who lived there was required to do a 40-day retreat in a cabin near the main house.

Two people at a time were assigned their retreat. Jay and Lisa were the first. An older gentleman named Don and I were the second team. Upon coming down from the cabin one day to shower, and do some Seva (selfless service) in the office, I found a letter sitting on the keyboard of the computer addressed to me from Jay. I read the letter and cried.

He told me that he had made a big mistake marrying me and that he wanted to dissolve the marriage. I went back to the cabin to meditate and made the decision to return to Germany. Later that evening, I told Jay that it was okay, and that I would plan to leave in the next few days.

He suddenly started crying and I held him in my lap and closed my eyes. At that point I had a clear vision of place in Japan. It was like a compound and there were many people. I was a young girl, maybe fourteen-years-old, wearing a silk yellow kimono. Jay was a Samurai warrior with a stocky body and a pony tail. (The *Samurai* were fearsome warriors whose traditions of honor and discipline live on in the study of jujitsu and Kendo today. The *samurai*, members of a powerful military caste in feudal Japan, began as provincial warriors before rising to power in the 12th century.)

In my vision, I was one of many wives. In that life, it revealed that he was not allowed to show affection, it could make him weak and it could mean death to his whole village if he could not protect the people. He loved me, but wasn't allowed to show any sort affection toward me. I was miserable in that life, and quite frustrated.

I understood him much better. I told him what I had seen in my vision. Many things now made sense to me, why he could not open his heart to me, and why the master always asked if Jay was doing better.

Christopher

Christopher had grown up in a middle-class family in Sacramento, and struggled with the negative effects of dyslexia as a child. He was married to Rose, and our families were friends for a long time. In 1994, Rose left him, with their two girls.

It happened after they had moved to Baja, Mexico, Rose ran away. Today, I know that she thought she could keep him from his addictions—the women and alcohol, but that was not to be. Over the years, Rose and I became quite close and she would always say that Chris had a dark side and that he was able to trick people into thinking he was a very nice person. In reality, he had a drinking problem. With his faults, I still always thought he was a really sweet man.

He was distraught over all of this family upheaval, and came to Oregon for a meeting with the master. There was a retreat going on, and he was having a really hard time. He was getting a divorce.

Even though I knew Chris, since early on, I still could hardly talk to him without stuttering. I was terribly attracted to him, and extremely nervous whenever I was around him. He was strikingly attractive, and looked like the spitting image of Fabio, the Italian fashion model, with his long hair and great body.

I didn't even look Chris in the eye whenever he visited, it was too much. I made every effort to avoid him, not trusting that I could keep my strong feelings towards him hid.

Of course, life has a way of evolving, and seven years after

Jay and I married, with Chris's wife having left him—and all coinciding at the same time. Jay and I wanted out of our marriage, and this opened the door to new possibilities with Chris.

Chis happened to be near, just as I left a meeting with Master and Jay, the three of us together, and the timing seemed oddly coincidental. I had told the master how unhappy I was in my marriage. We had not grown together, nor had we grown to be a couple that was in love. Even so, the master instructed me how to stay married—he told me there was no backing out.

It was gut wrenching and sobering, every cell in my body retaliated against the master's words for me to stay in the marriage. He lectured Jay on the importance of shared duties within the family union and asked me not to leave, but I knew that I could not live in a loveless marriage.

I was ready to explore other ideas and philosophies on my spiritual journey. I felt an inner hunger for more knowledge and for love. My spiritual journey with Sant Thakar Singh had simply come to an end.

While there were many positive and wonderful aspects of the many years spent with the master, they also filled me with confusion about his questionable conduct toward me and others. I had told my husband about the incident on the plane, but he dismissed it as if I was crazy to even question the master.

I had also witnessed people being excommunicated out of the ashram for speaking their truth about his sexual advances, and I knew that if I said anything I would be looked upon, just like those cases. I felt betrayed, confused—and at the same time, frightened to lose the security that I had held onto for so long.

As the master had talked, I had known... *if he tells me*

I have to stay in my marriage, I will have to leave the mission of the master behind. And, well… that's exactly what I was told—"to stay in the marriage."

After the marriage counseling session, I was very angry and disappointed. Jay was detached, and had very little emotional expression or feeling about it either way, which spoke for itself. Our marriage had never been a priority for him; he would rather be alone. It didn't make him wrong or bad, it's just the way it was. To divorce was the inevitable decision between us.

As I walked away, who do I see, but Chris? He saw my distress, and was kind; he listened, after deciding to drive to the nearby town of Oakland for cake and coffee at a popular restaurant called Tolly's. I felt such relief to get away from the ashram environment, and the people there, for a little while.

When we returned from Oakland and drove into the ashram parking lot, I could not get out of the car. My body refused. I didn't want to go back there!

It was then that Christopher looked at me, put his hand on my hand and said, "One of these days, I'm going to have to come and get you!"

Wow, what's happening between us? I thought to myself.

That night I went home and Jay went to the movies. After our seven years together, we rarely did much of anything together, since we lived totally separate lives, and had nothing in common.

I slept in a separate bedroom; we had no connection—emotional or physical. We had a spiritual connection by practicing the same meditation. Chris called that same evening, and told me that he had received a certain car part for our vehicle that Jay had ordered through him. He was in the car business at the time.

I went to bed early and had the most astounding vision after hearing Chris's voice. My heart was so open to him, and wanted to tell him, but I was afraid that it wasn't reciprocal.

I finally drifted into a dream state, and suddenly felt Chris's presence in the room. We touched each other, we hugged, our energies merged. I could even smell the scent of his body—amazingly real, alive, loving and passionate.

I had had dreams with dreams about the future before. I needed to tell Chris how I felt about him, so the next day I called him and said, "Chris, I have to tell you something. I always have loved you since we first met. During all the years I have known you, I have avoided conversations with you because of the feelings I have for you. Last night, I dreamed about you!"

Before I could say anything else his voice over the phone came through loud and clear. "I know what you're going to tell me. I dreamed about you as well."

Then I let my feelings and words flow out, unstoppable. "I was so afraid to tell you. I've been in love with you for so long, and last night, in my dream, you were literally in the room with me. I could feel you; I could even smell the scent of your body—and in it, we hugged and we kissed. I am in love with you! If I die right now, and I leave my body and never tell you how I really feel, I would have to come back and take care of this in another life."

To my surprise, Chris replied, "I feel the same way and I could barely look at you, because of how I felt—all these years."

At home, something had to give. My life was joyless and I had become depressed. I told Jay about Chris as soon as he came home from the movies.

Jay's response was, "Wow, that is really wonderful. I couldn't imagine anyone better for you than Christopher. He's like my brother." That was further evidence that Jay truly didn't love me; he didn't need or want me. If I had someone else in my life, this took the pressure off of him—a relief!

Mt Shasta

Soon afterwards, with this decision made, Chris and I made arrangements to meet and go camping at Mt. Shasta, a beautiful mountain and lake in Northern California. I arrived first. He arrived later, while I was laying in my tent meditating. During this time, I had one of my out of body experiences. I was suddenly transported to the top of Mt. Shasta.

There, St. Germaine appeared to me surrounded with vast rays of light. Then I was taken into the mountain, where I had heard there was a very important portal, connecting to another dimension. *Breathtaking!* This stemmed from my previous learning from Madam Blavatsky and the Theosophical teachings that I found so fascinating.

Our life together had begun. We would end up being together for the next eight years, living in Mexico. (Mexico from 1994-1996, Oregon from 1996-2001).

So, without really recognizing it, I had just gone from the fire into the frying pan. This is when I learned the lesson that you never go from one relationship into another right away. You must take a break and take care of yourself, at least for one year. If I had done that, perhaps there would have been meaningful lessons I would have learned earlier.

Yes, at that point, as promised, I left the master. It was 1994, ten years after my initiation in India. It was clearly time for me to leave.

I decided to move to Mexico with my son—both of

us moving there with Chris—was the best decision. I felt the need to get completely away from the master and the ashram.

I'd had enough of not being enough! Of course, many of those feelings were all in my mind, and probably the residue of my Catholic experience and guilt.

However, a person comes to realize, that living in the ashrams is isolated and separate. They have their place, a monastery lifestyle, which can be very healing for the soul. I had needed that, but after living that way for many years, the disconnect from society had begun to feel very isolated. It felt like there was, "us in the ashram," and then there's "them out there in the world." This forced separateness and limited access to others, and with the outside world, didn't work for me any longer.

For me, at that point, it was extremely difficult to live a life where I felt so lonely—I yearned for connection and expansion—and trusted meaningful relationships.

One day, before leaving for Mexico, while soul searching, I remember going to the library in the little town of Sutherland, Oregon, near Roseburg. It was after I found Krishna Marti's book and VCR, "The Future of Humanity" that I realized that the master is *within.* The master taught me many things, for which I am grateful. And I tried to do what he taught, but I learned that, he too, is just a man.

I would soon come to find out that living in Mexico would immerse me in a new realm of experiences serving people—as a workshop and seminar leader, and a sponsor of many mediums and psychics. It would be there that I would develop my skills as a Shaman, study "Flower of Life" with Drunvalo Melcicedek and study to become a Reiki Master Teacher—once again, on the fast track to learning everything that I could.

The truth lies within—the guru is within; the master is within—God is within.

"Inspiration and motivation may come from others, but true inspiration comes from within."

—Catherine Pulsifer

22

My Transcendental Journey—Time had Come to Leave the Master

Marital love seemed to be everywhere, yet it kept escaping me. I had made choices that weren't right for me, but I didn't see the patterns in my life that influenced my decisions until much later. I was walking in circles!

Everything came further to a head concerning my ashram life in Roseburg, when my best friend, Lori's husband, read her journal that she had left on the kitchen table, after she returned home from a retreat with the master at Hidden Valley Ranch. Her husband learned that she had been kissed and fondled by her spiritual teacher for ten days straight. He had done this to her for several hours a day, and she had detailed documentation in her journal about how she felt during these moments.

I interviewed her, almost thirty years later, and she gave me the original letters to read that the master wrote to her husband, in defense of his actions, when confronted by him. What didn't make sense to me was, how even to this day, she defends the sexual aggressions of the master and his conduct.

Besides all of that, I had had enough of Satsang's discourse about this earth being the valley of death, filled with possessed people—and with our responsibility as followers to be in continual battle fighting the dark force. Their belief that incarnation was all about suffering and sacrifice, instead of seeking joy and having fun, had grown old and worn out, after my eleven-year commitment to the Sant Mat.

I was yearning for a normal life, whatever "normal" meant at the time. I knew I wanted to get back to Christmas's and Easter celebrations, and to honor the events and traditions that I had appreciated in my life as a child.

I realized that I was unable to reproduce the culture I took for granted as a child. And I suddenly felt sad for my little boy, John, that I was so far away from family and my Bavarian traditions. I knew in my heart that if I wanted to be happy, it was up to me, and me alone, to make choices that created it. I couldn't simply sit still and wait for happiness and contentment to show up on my doorstep; I had to take an active part in helping it to become a reality in my life, and in my son's life.

Without a doubt, I knew I had a purpose for being here on this earth, even though that purpose seemed to evade me. One thing was for sure; I knew my son gave me purpose as a mother, and beyond that, I would discover what else the universe might unfold for us.

When Albert Einstein was asked by Rabbi Herbert Goldstein: "Do you believe in God?" His response was:

"Only if every individual strives for truth, can humanity attain a happier future. Strange is our situation here on earth. Each of us comes for a short visit, not knowing why, yet sometimes seeming to divine a purpose. From the standpoint of daily life, however, there is one thing we do know: that man is here for the sake of other men, above all for those upon whose smiles well-being our own happiness depends."

Seeking the Divine—and Purpose

When I initially found Sant Mat, the whole thing seemed like a great idea and in my case, I believe it was divinely guided. I learned more than I could have imagined, and I grew to understand more about myself and my place in the world.

I got initiated, learned to meditate for days on end—experienced the spiritual by immersing myself in meditations that took me beyond my physical body, but into my soul. I discovered that my soul, unending and infinite, would not die. There was magnificent and glorious life independent of my body.

I met the master within, becoming good friends, allowing him to personally escort me through the inner regions in his radiant or astral form, where after some years a person becomes all knowing, and more powerful as we become a "saint" and arrive at Sach Khand or heaven—there, to live an immortal life and reside forever.

I know our purpose, mine and yours! Seek to grow in spiritual knowledge, learn to nurture and love ourselves, the very essence of our soul, which in turn empowers us to nurture and love others. We then spend the rest of our lives here on earth guiding other souls on the path to Sach Khand or heaven. And once we believe this is possible, which I do, if you attend gatherings, read the books and listen to the stories of others who have achieved this, you are pretty much hooked.

At that point, you will do whatever it takes to get initiated, and commence to become a disciple, all the time understanding that it's going to be hard work—there's nothing easy about it. It involves a commitment to regular meditation. You and I are sure to succeed with the grace of the master, and the grace of God.

So it goes as an initiate: The life of meditation is tough, so is the stillness and sitting. The continuous repeating of the five holy names, the mantra takes dedication—and when nothing is happening, or at least not evident to us, it can be discouraging. Years go by. Decades go by. We may eventually accept that what we ask is not going to happen, but by now are believers. So we decide to do seva, we serve others, do volunteer work, instead. All the time, other initiates have become part of our social circle, and our friends.

This journey convinces us, 100 percent, that this path is the truth and the only real way to God. Logically, it makes total sense. We come to accept that if we have failed to make progress, it's because we have personally failed to live up to the high standards demanded by the masters. We continue to work on becoming better ourselves. But we know the master will come and save us at the time of death. This, then, becomes the fallback position. The master is every disciple's insurance policy.

When a broker offers you life insurance, you want to laugh in his face, because really, he is selling death insurance. We feel we already have the best life insurance policy in the universe. All disciples have this feeling of superiority over others, and it is unavoidable, because they are convinced that they are part of the chosen few that will be saved in this world.

What the disciples of Sant Mat cannot see is that all religions are the same. The Muslims believe that Mohamed will liberate their souls, and that they are special because they are believers of the Koran. The Christians believe that only through Christ can they make it safely to heaven. The reason the Sant Mat followers believe so strongly, is because the books and satsangs explain that the only path is through a *living master* and there have been past masters, but they cannot help you now.

It makes perfect sense, and that is the point. Once you believe this is the only real path, there is no way a person can ever leave. After all, where will they go? Who else can save them if all other religions are false.

Sant Mat sees those who turn their back on the master as unfortunate people, who will never have results in meditation. They consider the choice to turn away from the master as "really bad" because the master is God's living representative on earth.

Just because an individual might not personally have results doesn't have much impact on them, because they know they are on the right path—that of following the master. The Sant Mat disciples' belief, and all beliefs, appear to be the absolute truth to those who believe them. *They are not considered opinions, but spiritual truth.*

That is why the disciple of any religion cannot avoid being dogmatic. And aren't we all a little dogmatic at times?

Human beings are very good at taking a belief, accepting it, and making it appear to be the absolute truth.

If you think about it, the atheist or agnostic who does not believe in God does exactly the same thing. He or she takes a belief and makes it appear to be the truth. An honest person who is agnostic can only say "I don't know." He is neither a believer nor a nonbeliever and takes no sides—that is consistent with the definition of an agnostic. Because all sides of doctrine are filled with beliefs, and with regard to religious beliefs you never get 100 percent proof, at least not on this earth.

The attraction of Sant Mat is that a person can do the "experiment" and get to Sach Khand, the highest region. If one arrives, you can finally say "I know" rather than "I believe."

And on the flip side of the discussion, of course, there is still the question of delusion. Perhaps each one of us is just deluded, and have not arrived anywhere. Or maybe a person gets a mental shift and realizes the journey is not literal, and that Sach Khand, or heaven, is not a place so nobody arrives. There will never be any objective proof.

Your inner experiences are just that—yours! They are intimate, a precious secret, and cannot effectively be completely shared with anyone. Enlightenment is a personal experience. It cannot be handed on a silver platter for someone else to examine. And not being able to exactly define precisely what it is, it makes it become even more impossible to prove to others—because it is not of the material and physical world—rather it is spiritual. The two, physical and spiritual, are separate worlds and cannot fully meet. Neither is any more real than the other.

Anything subjective is, by its very nature, impossible to prove objectively. There is the domain of "objective things" and the domain of "subjective things." They are separate worlds, with some things too abstract and difficult to envision to the earthly mind. I have found it is impossible to talk someone out of their faith, whether it be Islam, Catholicism and Christianity, or Judaism. Neither one of them is any more real than the other. They are different. When you are dying—the daily objective becomes irrelevant and the subjective after life becomes all important.

Any 'spiritual' journey is subjective, and this is why the objective person tends to doubt, needing and asking for proof. Tangible proof cannot be given when it comes to faith. I could not prove to my German, logical and objective thinking, family that I had a near-death experience, or seen Jesus, or been in a place we refer to as heaven. Had I shared that personal experience, I would have been exposed to much ridicule and interrogation. It was more comfortable to avoid scorn from them, so I chose to live erroneously within their objectivity—which for me, after nine years old, wasn't my true experience or reality—so in itself, my life with family felt false, like walking within a dream.

A quote from Teilhard de Chardin says, "We are not human beings having a spiritual experience. We are spiritual beings having a human experience.

When a Sant Mat or Rhadha Soami follower leaves "the path," it simply means he or she has changed their focus from subjective to objective. On an objective level, Sant Mat appears to be nonsense. However, to me it made perfect sense at the time, because I was not concerned with the objective world. I need something more, and my experiences were real to me—and quite frankly the objective world view has not much hope in it. The pain and harshness of the objective, tangible world was especially true for me at seventeen years old. I needed something so much more. I could not define it, but my soul longed for "something more."

It is easy for people to remain objective when their world is organized and safe, and going as they wish. Take away any of their creature comforts, have a diagnosis of an incurable disease, or like me, have your mother or other loved-one killed, and immediately prayer and a yearning for something more enters the scene. Objectivity, and our human selves are tested under such circumstances. I have seen this a thousand times with people who become sick or lose their wealth. From one instant to the next, in desperate times people turn to faith and prayer.

Be Careful the Path

I recently read a disturbing article about some of the ISIS tactics to recruit young people from the West into their army strong holds. I realized that it is exactly the same recruiting style that the SS used for the hundreds of thousands of Hitler youth, and many other world groups who prey on the vulnerabilities of others. They are notorious for programming people for their own deranged purposes. How many young people get involved and then realize that it was a mistake, but can't get out? Maybe you know someone who told their family that their decision to follow was because of some ultimate truth, but now can't or won't quit. That would mean to admit they are wrong. Pride!

Like me, most young people want to follow a path, want to feel special, prove themselves with initiations, want to find a purpose. The capitalist idea of acquiring wealth as the primary goal of their existence is long gone. If we don't have consistent beliefs and common goals in our world—what are we to become? Is it really possible for humans to ever come together as a race under one God? If only that could be… if so, that seems far into the future. There is a saying:

"Be careful what you wish for, you might get it!"

I had to make the decision to change, and make new choices in my life. I am in awe of how quickly the universe responds to our dreams and desires, as long as we are on a clear and right path.

It was Chris, Jay's longtime friend, that was there for me on that auspicious day Jay and I met with the master. I am not sure I would have had the strength to leave Jay, and leave Oregon by myself.

I knew that my decision to follow Chris would separate me from "the family" I had known so far in the United States, leaving me quite isolated and alone, but in reality, except for my son, I was always alone anyway.

For the sake of my own seeking, and my own sanity, I had to journey forward into what I believed to be *the truth*. I wanted to find joy again, I wanted to have fun, I wanted to live a so-called normal life. I wasn't seeking material things, I just wanted to live, to love, and to give my son hope and happiness in his life. I knew I would not be a good mother to him if I was unhappy all the time.

For many years, I had been exploring and attracted to science and metaphysics, reading and meditating, that I had to give up many of the everyday things people take for granted in life. But now, my disappointment in all types of religion was better understood. I recalled the master's words he spoke on the plane flight to the United States—they still reverberated—he said, "The organization of the master was a necessary evil!" At the time, he was disappointed in his management and his leaders, who were still lead by their ego rather than spirit.

When I found Sant Mat, it met my needs, and seemed the answer to everything I had been seeking, and yet, there were the master's sexual indiscretions that I could not understand no matter how many excuses I made for him or how many people were telling me that it was a treatment of sorts. *Yeah, it was a treatment alright.*

I will always remember my love of the community of people, the meditation, the vegetarian healthy lifestyle, the mantra, the gatherings, the music, the beauty and simplicity of the ashram grounds. What I did not love were the rules to only read the masters books, not to study other healthy lifestyle techniques, and not to listen to any other music, except the approved Indian classical. And partying and having fun was out—and I was such a young woman at the time!

Thakar Singh passed away in 2003. I finally reconciled with what happened to me with him on the flight to the United States from Germany. That in itself, was a journey of insight and forgiveness.

"You cannot create experience. You must undergo it. – Albert Camus

I have learned since then, that even as the guru or Godman walks among us, we must not allow our psyche to run amok. We cannot seek to find the godhead in another human. I understood, after reminders once and again, that turning the guru into a supreme being with no faults, and one with no darkness, and assuming he was absolute perfection—was just not true!

We must question everything, and everyone. We must follow our innate instincts, trust our intuition, and not be led by the powers within people that control us and manipulate us. I had seen my guru before I met him in the physical realm, and in that vision, he looked so perfect—with light and love beaming at me.

When I saw him in the flesh, I could not believe it was the same person. I think when we fall in love, it is similar, we look at a person with such unwavering love and trust—seeing only what we want to see—beauty and perfection.

Jiddu Krishnamurti

During this period of wavering about continuing to live in the ashram, I was reintroduced to Jiddu Krishnamurti. He was born in British India, and was a speaker and writer on matters that concern humankind. In his early life he was groomed to be the new world teacher, but later rejected this position and withdrew from the organization behind it. When that happened, I was able to relate to him more than any other teacher in my life.

What was so fascinating was that my early attraction to the occult through Madame Blavatsky and Annie Besant was my connection to Krishnamurti, who in early adolescence, had a chance encounter with prominent occultist and theosophist, Charles Webster Leadbeater on the grounds of the Theosophical Society headquarters at Adyari in Madras, India.

He was subsequently raised under the tutelage of Annie Besant and Leadbeater, leaders of the society at the time, who believed him to be a "vehicle" for an expected world teacher. As a young man, he disavowed this idea, and dissolved the "Order of the Star of the East," an East Indian organization that had been established out of the Theosophical Society, with the intention of preparing the world for the arrival of a Messianic entity.

He said he had no allegiance to any nationality, caste, religion, or philosophy, and spent the rest of his life travelling the world, speaking to large and small groups and individuals. My *favorite books, among them: The First and Last Freedom, The Only Revolution,* and *Future of Humanity.* His last public talk was in Madras, India, in January 1986, a month before his death at his home in Ojai, California.

Today, through non-profit foundations in India, Great Britain and the United States, supporters of Krishnamurti still carry on his words and his work.

A Gift

I believe that everything is a gift. As you know by now, I've had the most exciting life anyone can dream of, filled with great joy and sometimes great sorrow. I have been taught by a San Sat Guru, found great love in my life, had the most amazing son, have extended family that loves me, and close friends who are still in my life since childhood.

I've seen many lands, and explored many ideas and creations. Now I live in paradise where I am allowed to write—and I know very well that nothing is by chance.

We have to become good receivers of love, relationships, and blessings. We also have to know deep inside us that we deserve to be loved, and that we also deserve outrageous prosperity if that comes to us in life.

Something deep inside of me tells me that I will end up in India at the end of my life. Perhaps that will be the ultimate gift.

Meditation

Krishnamurti said it very well:

> "You must take a plunge into the water, not knowing how to swim"!

> "Meditation is one of the most extraordinary things, and if you do not know what it is, you are like the blind man in a world of bright color, shadows and moving light. It is not an intellectual affair, but when the heart enters into the mind, the mind has quite a different quality; it is really, then, limitless, not only in its capacity to think, to act efficiently, but also in its sense of living in a vast space where you are part of everything."

"Meditation is the movement of love. It isn't the love of

the one or of the many. It is like water that anyone can drink out of any jar, whether golden or earthenware; it is inexhaustible. And a peculiar thing takes place, which no drug or self-hypnosis can bring about; it is as though the mind enters into itself, beginning at the surface and penetrating ever more deeply, until depth and height have lost their meaning and every form of measurement ceases. In this state, there is complete peace, not contentment which has come about through gratification, but a peace that has order, beauty and intensity. It can all be destroyed, as you can destroy a flower, and yet because of its very vulnerability it is indestructible. This meditation cannot be learned from another. You must begin without knowing anything about it, and move from innocence to innocence."

"The soil in which the meditative mind can begin is the soil of everyday life, the strife, the pain and the fleeting joy. It must begin there, and bring order, and from there move endlessly. But if you are concerned only with making order, then that very order will bring about its own limitation, and the mind will be its prisoner. In all this movement you must somehow begin from the other end, from the other shore, and not always be concerned with this shore or how to cross the river. You must take a plunge into the water, not knowing how to swim. And the beauty of meditation is that you never know where you are, where you are going, what the end is."

Leaving The Master

It was a series of heart-wrenching events, some I've shared, that brought me to the realization that after eleven years of studying Sant Mat with my guru and meditating many, many hours every single day, I accepted it was time for me to finally leave my life in Oregon.

The little magical child inside me was dying, and I knew it. I was getting more and more serious, and feeling sad, depressed most of the time. I knew there was more. I wanted to live a glorious life and believed the master wholeheartedly, when he said that *true glory is only to be found within* us through meditation and not outside of us. I knew this was true—I had to explore this physical world, in all of its wonder and beauty, to enhance the use of the gifts that were within me.

I wanted to see and experience as much as possible. It was time to bring an end to this journey with the masters, the ashram and their people. I wanted to grow beyond, and serve others outside the limited borders of the ashram.

And how did I remember the bad times? Well, when an important intimate relationship goes sour, it's tough to adjust, but eventually there's a realization that you're better off after the splitting-up.

I knew I was definitely not in the right place. My heart, my soul needed answers—freedom to choose. I realized that I was conflicted about my life, and lifestyle, on the path of the masters. I needed to be free to seek a different life. I was so tired of being confined to one system, a series of protocols and rules—those things that restricted my authentic self, and did not let my inner child shine.

I was ready to follow my dreams…

"Dreams are illustrations… from the book your soul is writing about you."

— Marsha Norman

23

MEXICO

"It is in your moments of decision that your destiny is shaped."

—Tony Robbins

The decision had been made, and the day had come. On a warm summer day in 1994, Jay, put me and three-year-old, John, on a bus to Sacramento, where we were to meet-up with Christopher, his good friend, and the person with whom I wanted to start a new life.

Jay had expressed it before, and now that the day was here, he was excited that Chris and I had connected so well. It lets him off the hook; he could pursue his meditative life, and be free from being a husband and a father. He had reminded me often that he was not cut out for being a family man and that I would be better off with somebody like Christopher.

Upon arriving in Sacramento we acquired an extra vehicle to drive down south, towards Mexico. Christopher owned an unfinished adobe home in Baja, near Tijuana, that needed to be completed. The drive was treacherous to Rosarito Beach, a little ocean town along the Baja Peninsula, right between Tijuana and Ensenada. The traffic was crazy! The chaos of traffic, and people everywhere, caused us much confusion, almost getting lost several times. The hot and humid weather added to our discomfort.

When we finally made it through the noisy city, we drove along the majestic beaches of the Baja. I, then, calmed down, realizing that things were going to work out for John and me.

We approached Chris's adobe home at the Santa Monica Plaza, a gated community right on the ocean with fifty homes or so, most of them converted mobile homes, surrounded by decking and plants. It looked peaceful and nice.

Chris unlocked the gate to his garden that was slightly overgrown with yucca plants. We walked a few yards further to the front door, where a big Buddha statue greeted us in the foyer. The coolness of the adobe house swept over us the moment we stepped inside.

The sun was setting, and the cool breeze refreshed us as we sat on the couch watching the sun set into the horizon. I recall the fresh ocean air blowing on my face, the French doors wide-open. Chris suddenly jumped up from the couch, startling me, to unroll a red Persian carpet tucked back against the wall.

I got up to help him. I was so exhausted and relieved to be out of the car, but I sensed he was slightly irritated after the stressful drive. I picked up on his stress level. I wondered… *Did he feel he had made a mistake bringing us down to Mexico?*

Chris was my hero, and Baja would prove to be a great move for us, but this first day, I hoped that I had not jumped from the frying pan into the fire.

Chris hadn't been to his house since his wife and kids left

him many months earlier. The electricity and water had been turned off and the furniture was covered in white sheets to protect them.

Things were in disarray, as I took it all in. I didn't realize that there was no railing on some stairs behind me. After unrolling the carpet I stepped back and accidentally fell down into the basement below. I heard a loud thump, felt the pain, and realized I had fallen. I was not able to breathe. I closed my eyes and listened to my body to find out what was wrong. The drop was a whopping twenty feet to the basement landing where I found myself, with my back on the sharp edges of the stairs.

Chris's steps could be heard running down to the basement. John was wailing from the top of his lungs, and Chris told him to stay upstairs—*so scary for a little boy to see his mother fall.* Before I knew it, Chris was holding my hand. There I was lying on the stairs, hardly knowing what had just happened to me.

In my stupor, I quietly begged Chris, "Let me go to the light, let me go to the light!"

What I meant and what Chris heard were two different things. I just wanted to heal myself and go within. He thought I was dying and ready to meet my maker.

In his panicked state, Chris screamed something at me like, "No, no, keep your eyes open. Don't go to sleep. Don't die!"

To clarify, I let him know I just needed to meditate, be by myself, to relax and close my eyes. Chris took my son and ran to the neighbor's house to get flashlights, and to ask them to watch my upset little boy. He called the ambulance. Chris really didn't know what was wrong and how badly I was hurt, and, frankly, neither did I.

About a half-a-hour later, I was taken to the Rosarito Beach Hospital in the funkiest ambulance I had ever seen in my life. I remember the trip well. The stretcher was made of plywood and every time the car hit a bump on the rough, rocky road, I felt like I was being stabbed again and again in my lungs and I could not breathe. When we arrived at the hospital, I was released without x-rays, assuming it was my ribs. I was told to stay in bed, and after several days, I did not improve at all; still, in excruciating pain.

I didn't completely know what was wrong with me, and it upset me when Christopher left me alone on the second day after our arrival in Mexico—in this condition, and all alone with my baby boy, John. He had become clingy and unable to separate from me. He was in a new place and without his father for the first time in his life.

Chris was obligated to visit with his children, or he would lose the battle for his visitation days with his two daughters, that were ages four and ten. At that moment, feeling abandoned and alone, I was so sad for John. I know he needed me, but I couldn't move, was suffering a great deal, and my face showed it. John needed to be nursed, but I was helpless. Truth be told, I was devastated that Chris had left me in that state with my three-year old child and my trust in him was highly challenged. I couldn't completely settle into the relationship, and remembered what the master had said about romantic relationships and how fickle we humans really are—one day we say we love someone and the next day they do something we don't approve of, and we immediately withdraw our love. I didn't want to be that person.

I understood on a mental level, why Chris had to fulfill his obligation, but on an emotional level, I was injured and broken, and needed him to be there with me. That day alone, was the longest day I spent in Mexico during the two years we were there.

The day after Chris returned, something strange happened. Chris and John were down at the beach playing, and I was alone, resting, when I heard a loud knock on the door. A male voice called loudly in a Spanish accent,

"Christopher, Christopher, it's Miguel!"

My broken ribs prevented me from being able to speak loudly. So I was trying to figure out how to make myself heard or seen. I remember scooting out of bed, and somehow shuffling my body along the floor when Miguel finally saw me in the hallway and opened the door. Luckily, he helped me get to the living room couch and introduced himself as Dr. Miguel Lanzagorta, child psychologist.

He was a doctor working next-door at the Dansbach Clinic, an alternative Cancer Clinic at Santa Monica Plaza, our neighborhood.

As soon as Miguel sat down with me, he immediately put his hands on my chest and started praying in Spanish. That's when he told me that he was a healer and a doctor, and that he just returned from the Yucatán with Don Miguel, a famous healer. He was sure I needed to get help right away.

I was surprised by his sense of urgency. That's when I knew that something was very wrong with me. He looked at me, with such deep concern and sadness in his eyes.

I told him, "Chris and John are down at the beach." Miguel acted quickly.

He jumped up, exclaiming, "I'll run to the beach right now and tell Christopher, so that I can take you to Madre Sarita's house right away. She is the grandmother of Don Miguel. She will be able to help you heal. You're very sick!"

Apparently, Chris and Miguel had met four years earlier

and had grown very close. This was during the time Chris's ex-wife, Rose, gave birth to their daughter, Alexandria, at the clinic.

When Miguel returned with Chris and John, I overheard Miguel explain to Chris how severe my situation really was. He insisted they take me immediately across the border to Madre's house. As you can imagine, with all that pain and bumpy roads, I dreaded the long drive into Chula Vista from Rosarito beach—not to mention the hour-long wait at the Tijuana border.

Hadn't we just come that way? Every little bump in the road would hurt me. John was very emotional and sad by it all, I could tell. This was not going to be easy for him or me.

When we finally arrived at the home of Madre Sarita, everyone there was already expecting us. Apparently, Miguel had called Madre and explained the situation. Chris carried me into their living room, which was set up as some sort of waiting room with pictures of saints from different religions, and healers from all kinds of traditions.

I was quite nervous, and at the same time hopeful that I could get some help. Since the hospital didn't even take x-rays, I thought, *maybe more is wrong with me than I think.*

We were in the waiting room for about ten minutes. "Coco," the translator, called us into the room with her broken English and gentle voice. I was afraid and tentative. *Where are we and what were they going to do to me?*

I had spent many years with the master, during which he told initiates to *never* see "healers"—and, God forbid, we receive any kind of "hands-on healing."

So, here I was, in the room of one of the most famous Mexican healers getting ready for psychic healing and psychic surgery. And it was against everything I believed in at this point.

I remember "Madre" as a sweet and beautiful lady in her eighties, with the kindest eyes I had ever seen. They reminded me of my mother's affection—making me feel safe and protected. The first thing she did was ask us to place our hands around a candle with the picture of Mother Mary on it.

She prayed aloud in Spanish, her voice soft and gentle. The more she recited the prayer, the more relaxed I became—and the more trusting. After the incantation, I saw Madre tell Chris and John to leave the room. What followed next would change my life forever.

With a kind smile, Madre asked me, "Why are you so afraid to come see me? My assistant, Coco, and me, do not bite."

I asked, "How do you know I'm afraid?"

She said, "We knew you were coming. Your spiritual teacher with the white turban had already been here… he told us!"

In that instance, my anxiety left my body.

And in my new-found sense of calm I said, "You must understand that on my eleven-year path with the master, any kind of healing, pranayama (control of our breathing) and laying on of hands, were all forbidden. It was a very strict and monastic path. Not many people were able to handle the rigorous discipline."

Right then, I believed with all my heart that by going to see "a healer," like Madre Sarita, that was not only forbidden by the master, but one of the greatest violations against the teachings of the masters, and here I was. Much was unknown, and I was quite frightened."

This was all so surreal to me, but, then again, wasn't totally unheard of. Seeing visions and exorcisms by the master prepared me for what she had to say, and what came next.

At the beginning of my treatment with her, I felt like this was one extremely bizarre, yet exciting and fascinating experience. I watched Madre pick up an uncooked egg out of a white bowl. She then rolled the egg all over my body in a sort of circular motion. This made me so relaxed that I almost fell asleep. I felt safe.

I found out later, that this method had been used for ages, apparently taking physical, astral and causal impressions of the body. After the exercise, Madre preceded to crack the egg into a medium sized water glass. To my surprise, the egg yolk sank to the bottom of the glass like a metal coin or rock would do. This sinking represented the physical body, while the floating egg white trapped in the water represented the astral and causal body.

The next step in the ritual was to determine the degree of damage done to my body by reading the way the egg appeared in the glass. She made it clear that she was able to see what was broken by the way it floated, congealed or separated.

Madre explained, "I can see the pancreas, the broken ribs, and your kidneys are bruised. Ah, here is the spiritual body!"

And, it was in this moment that I decided to study shamanism.

She said that my decade-long meditation practice, for so many hours a day, had caused me to disconnect from truly living. She knew I was sad. Madre's words touched something deep inside of me so poignantly, that I thought about running out of the room.

Here I was—listening to a wise old healer woman who tells me that the very thing I had been devoting my life to, was causing my extreme sadness.

She then performed, what I later found out was considered psychic surgery on me. Madre placed both hands on my belly, and I could literally feel her hands going inside of my body. It felt as though a warm energy like a heating sphere had entered into my system. It felt as if things were moving around near where my C-section incision was from several years before.

Madre asked me to lie on my stomach, reaching into my spine, giving me this floating sensation. I remember thinking to myself, "Oh, my God, I feel her hand inside of me. I better breath, I better breath."

Coco translated the whole time. Madre's diagnosis, "Oh, there is a little scoliosis. Let's go fix that and some old scar tissue that is still on your back! Let's take care of that."

I could feel the warm energy moving around in my spine, up and down several times, as if somebody was walking around my body. I found this to be most curious. In fact, for years as a child, I had had scoliosis and my mother would take me twice weekly to therapy to improve the curvature of my spine. They made me do all these horrible exercises. Twenty-five years later, I was being told that this healer can fix my scoliosis. I was speechless!

The translations kept on coming until Madre suddenly stopped, then said, "You know you aren't really here for broken ribs. You are here because of your lungs."

I recall asking why she thought that. "What did that mean?" I was confused, and so surprised when I heard those words spoken, yet something about the words rang true.

"You have such a deep, deep sadness inside of you, which has to do with your mother. This has infected your lungs. You were very close to dying," Madre explained.

She told me that my guru basically arranged this accident, so that I would come to see her, and that after this treatment I would never be sick again. Madre then handed me a tall, slender bottle with a picture of a lizard on it. It had the instructions for the medicine to be taken three times a day for two weeks. She gave me three cotton balls that I was instructed to spit into during the night and bury in the morning. This was Shamanism at its best.

In the extraordinary way she had about her, Madre concluded, "Esta noche va a tener un sueño, y en el sueño se borrarán los pulmones." Translated: "Tonight you will have a dream, and in the dream your lungs will be cleared."

It made sense, because I was born prematurely and weighed barely five pounds. My lungs were always the most challenging part of my body with a history of whooping cough and croup.

I believe, and now know, with every fiber of my being, that all physical issues or diseases, inherently have an emotional component attached to them. My experience with Madre opened me to this concept. And my unexpected occurrence with hands-on healing work was so powerful, with Madre that it would go on to shape my life.

After my treatment, I rested on her massage bed, covered by a white warm blanket. She then spoke to me about the future of our planet as she sipped hot tea. We sat for another hour, Madre spelling out her visions she had of what was to come:

"There is much sorrow ahead of us… At the turn of the century there will be a very tall statue, building or buildings in New York that will fall. When they fall, it will be the beginning of much unrest and war, World War III. Everything will change after that."

Of course, I didn't know that she was talking about then. Of course it was the Twin Towers, but this was seven years before Nine-Eleven terrorist tragedy in 2001. As you can imagine, I remember exactly where I was when I was told the Twin Towers had collapsed, leaving thousands dead.

I immediately thought back to Madre's predictions; shivers went down my spine. I realized that since this had come true, then perhaps some of the other information Madre gave me that day, may also be true. To be honest, at the time, I dismissed some of her words that had been translated to me—their meaning being so far from my known reality, I could not take it all in.

Her visions outlined major catastrophes:

"Many tsunamis and earthquakes will come. The entire coast of California will be gone. There are many UFO ships on standby to evacuate people. These ships are hidden from sight in a fourth dimensional field not visible to the human eye. You and your partner should move inland Mexico and get ready for this. Many helpers are needed, and right now you cannot see who Christopher is. He is a very special spirit and you cannot see this right now."

At the end of my session, she gave instructions for Coco to explain how I was supposed to take the medicine in the tall, slender glass bottle, saying that my lungs would be clear in a short time. She said I needed to take long walks on the beach and breathe in the ocean air.

After Jay found out about my accident, he wrote a letter to everyone in the ashram that I had left him and that God punished me for leaving by sending me down the stairs. Amazing, how people can twist their realities to feel less guilt.

24

Homesick for Oregon

For the first two years in Mexico things were very good with Chris. He and I were in love, and he was very sweet to me, although there were some signs that should have given me a hint of what was to follow. However, I was so smitten that I just didn't want to look at the reality of what might be around the corner.

After meeting Madre, Miguel and Coco, and as we got settled in our life in Mexico, I sponsored many psychics, mediums and healers at our house in Mexico. We had a woman who was a remote viewer who worked for the CIA, and we met, Frank, who worked for the FBI, who spoke about the alien coverup and "MKUltra." And Gary, who worked with "Golden Light Frequency," and taught "Emotional Processing," which I eventually incorporated in my Reiki classes. He still comes to visit in Oregon. Not to mention, Ann, from Sidney, Australia who channeled Saint Francis of Assisi, and gave me a very important message. Drunvalo Melchizedek, the author of four books, including, *The Ancient Secrets of the Flower of Life.* "The Flower of Life" system taught me so much about the history of our planet.

I made sure I booked lots of different teachers and groups, otherwise I would have gone crazy with feelings of isolation. Especially with John now in a Mexican kindergarten, where he also learned Spanish, it left me without much to do in our home at Rosarito Beach.

Two years after arriving in Mexico, I became so homesick for my friends in Oregon, that in 1996, we decided to return to the U.S. after our house sold.

Chris finished work on the house, and we finally sold it. When we arrived in Oregon, we struggled financially. Some of the money and proceeds from the house in Baja had to go back to his father, and even though Chris's wealthy ex-girlfriend, Susie, gave us a large sum of money as a down payment for our river house, we were really roughing it and living in a mobile home while building and remodeling a house on the Umpqua River in Roseburg.

We were in the process of opening Sulawesi Juice Works and Kiva Center for the Healing Arts, a dream that Chris and I had (for me minus the restaurant). Because here I was, running a restaurant, coffee shop, bakery, healing center and gift shop—I was overwhelmed!

We had one other partner, but he was having his own difficulties and couldn't contribute much. We seriously underestimated the cost to open the door to our new business. The building had to be jacked up and was almost condemned, but Chris was able to save it and it still stands there today due to his wonderful building talent. We were living from day-to-day, struggling to keep the doors open.

We were living in Idlewyld, just east of Roseburg, with

friends K.J. and Param, and their three boys. They helped us out, letting us house-sit their lake house on 120 acres in the forest, while they stayed in Sisters, Oregon for the winter. Their boys were on the ski team.

It gave us a great opportunity to work on the building in Roseburg, and get the store ready and not have to pay rent. When we opened, we immediately felt great support from the community of Roseburg, with so many people in town happy to have an alternative, healthy place to eat. The metaphysical gift shop was a hit also, and we sold a lot of books, cards and candles and gifts.

Our friend, Gary, a spiritual teacher from California, had just arrived the night before, to do some readings at the lake house. I sponsored him often, and have arranged many retreats and readings for him over the past two decades.

It's always amazing how a day can go from the ordinary, to being a day you remember for the rest of your life. Three weeks after we opened, was just such a day. The restaurant and things were going well, and I was making carrot juice and baking muffins to prepare for the day.

I remember the morning well. The phone rang, just as I had bit down on a carrot and broke my front tooth. It was Gary calling to tell me that Chris had gone for a walk and had fallen off of a cliff, and that the ambulance had taken him to the hospital. My heart almost stopped. In shock, I felt I was coming to an end.

Gary rushed into town to pick me up, and we drove to the hospital where the doctors told us that Christopher had broken his back and shattered his heel into many pieces. Surgery was impossible!

After a few days, Chris received a big check from, Susie, his ex-girlfriend—and she sent him to Breitenbush Hot

Springs for recuperation. At the time, the surgeon told Chris something very uncanny. He said! "If I do surgery on this foot you will take a long time to heal. You're better off to go home and heal yourself, because these sorts of surgeries take many years, and we never know if you will be able to walk again."

Hobbling around on crutches for many months, with Breitenbush funded by Susie, he began to feel a lot better.

While he was there, he had an amazing experience. He ran into a person who introduced him to Alphabiotics (an alternative medical practice that claims that most disease is caused by stress and a lack of "life energy"). This really saved his life and he became a practitioner of alphabiotics, and helped many people.

Chris was multi-talented, a gifted carpenter, and could have been productive doing many things, but sometime after this, his binge drinking got out of hand. He was often intoxicated, and became quite verbally abusive.

I woke him up at 3:00 a.m., to tell him I could no longer help him. During the night, I had an experience lying next to him where I saw that a demon had possessed him, and that this was a demon that only the master could deal with. I told him what I had seen, and convinced him that it would be best if he went to India, right away, to get some treatment and help.

I told him that I loved him and that I would always be by his side, but I could no longer assist in his healing. He cried in my lap for hours and told me that no-one ever loved him like I did. We had a wonderful day the next day, it's funny how the universe works.

At first, I thought he was going to India for six months to see the master, receive help, then he would come back and we could pick up our relationship where we left off, but that was not to be.

Instead, Christopher decided that if he left, he would never come back and that was hard to handle. I could wrap my mind around six months, but *forever?* That was hard to grasp and triggered every fear imaginable inside of me.

He said that it was not fair on John and me, for him to leave for six months. What he really was saying was that he wanted to exit and not be responsible for anyone—and that this was his ticket out.

I felt my heart ripped out of my body. I felt such sadness, such grief, and had a very difficult time letting him go. But the universe has different things in store for us, and there is always another plan to heal us as we go forward. My co-dependence was highly challenged since I could not imagine my life without him; my heart broke. I felt abandoned, alone, misunderstood and so very, very sad. I could barely function.

A few days later, my friends in town arranged a breakfast gathering at my favorite place on the river at the Steamboat Inn Lodge. I was under the weather that day and didn't really feel up to it, but forced myself anyway after receiving phone calls from my friends.

After getting to the lodge, Paul walked in, a wonderful carpenter, talented winemaker and musician. I had seen him at our music parties at the river house and had been previously introduced to him. Paul sat next to me and noticed how sad I was, and that I had the sniffles. He just rubbed my back for a while and said to me, "Don't worry, everything will be fine." He didn't know what was going on in my life, but he could see I was not okay.

The Universe Provides

That morning over breakfast, I told my friends about my childhood in Bavaria mushroom hunting with my grandpa and brother Wolfi. It was mushroom season in Oregon and Paul promised to take John and I out to the forest to his secret spot for the best Chanterelles.

The following Sunday he came to the house to pick us up. I just thought it was a friendly gesture and Chris, well, he had known Paul from all the parties we had over the years. Paul, John and I never did find a single Chanterelle mushroom that day, but something happened that was very strange.

I went to bed that night and had a very vivid dream, more like a vision. I was in a cave somewhere with many Native American drawings etched into the rock; Paul was there and we were Native American Indians together. We spoke a different language and we had a lot of love for each other.

Could it have been a look into our past life together?

We were very closely connected within the dream. The next day Paul called me on the phone and asked to meet me. He sounded slightly urgent on the telephone so I agreed to meet with him that same afternoon.

When he arrived, he told me about his strange dream and about a cave and drawings that looked like ancient Native American hieroglyphics. I don't quite know how to explain it, other than that the universe made sure that my heart would not break, by giving me a heart connection with Paul—so that I could let Chris go.

Of course, no sooner did Chris realize that somebody else could love me, he changed his plan and asked to marry me. I declined, and asked him not to drink for an entire year, then we would talk more…

When I told Paul about this, he made me swear on my mother's grave that I would never marry Chris, or he would never speak to me as long as he lived. He did not trust Chris, and thought I was gullible and innocent. *He was of course right.*

Then Chris asked me never to see Paul again and I agreed. Shortly after, John and I left to see my family in Germany.

When we returned from Germany, Chris had totally disappeared and all his belongings were gone from the house. I didn't know why he left, because everything was wonderful between us when he took us to the airport, but little did I know that Chris led a double life.

Chris went to India after having an affair and getting a girl pregnant. Paul was disappointed that I fell for Chris's tricks, and did not see me again. I grew stronger, and I learned that the universe always had a plan to protect and keep me emotionally, mentally and physically safe.

I received a phone call from my neighbor, Julia, and she told me that I should sit down, and in that moment, I knew that what she was going to tell me was not good news. I hadn't heard anything about Chris for quite some time now, except that he did really well in India, and that he worked with many people with alphabiotics. I also heard he had moved to Thailand, and met a woman from Munich, who was in the healing arts.

The last time we spoke on the phone was when he called me from Seattle airport on New Year's Eve at 12:30 a.m. as he departed to India to see the master. He told me that I was the love of his life, and told me goodbye.

Julia began to tell me why she had called. She said that Chris had come back from Thailand to put his house on the market. He had been driving 85 miles-per-hour down Little River Rd. on a very rainy night—and he had slipped and run into a tree exactly a mile from our old house. She told me that he died in the arms of one of our friends who is a fire department volunteer.

Tears streamed down my face, I knew it was best for him

to be released from his body, because no matter how hard he tried, he could not overcome his addiction and fight his demons. I felt so sad, such despair, grief and sorrow. After calling his older brother, I couldn't get myself to call his mom to inform her of the news that her son had died. No mother in the world should have to face that dreadful news.

I know it ripped her heart out, and for me, we had so much unfinished business. I had to say "Goodbye," and be with him so I called his brother to give me permission for an open casket. My good friend Andy drove me to Roseburg to the house and it was quite eerie and strange to be there again.

After his brother flew in from Southern California and arranged the viewing it helped me a great deal. I stayed with Chris for many hours. I cut his hair and put roses and pictures of his girls (who had not seen him for a long time) in his hands. I kissed him. I finally got to say good-bye.

Madre did not give me this prediction, that I would lose someone I had loved so dearly. Chris died in the car crash in 2002, six years after we returned from Mexico.

His ex-wife, Rose, was still a friend, and she called me a week after the memorial service and asked what happened. Chris's brothers did not tell her he had passed away and the death certificate said he was single with no children nor ex-wife. I urged them to fly out immediately from Florida and make the older daughter, Kendra the executor of the estate. We beat the brother's application to be executor by one day.

I did my best to help the girls have some closure to their father's untimely death, and also made certain that Rose received her back child support out of the house proceeds. It was the honorable thing to do.

Unfortunately, Rose died five years later of cervical cancer. I am terribly sad for the girls, losing both their parents. I'm grateful that we are still connected today.

I must add that abandonment was my biggest lesson in life. I had to learn to overcome the fear of abandonment which was woven throughout my life, from the time I was two years old. I have finally conquered it and know today that, too, is an illusion.

And for now, it's important to remember that there is no villain in the story, certainly not Chris—every person does the best they can with what they have. My journey is that of compassion and love, and not judgement.

New Awareness

It wasn't until I started writing this book that I realized who exactly Madre Sarita was. One night I woke up at four in the morning, and something told me to do a Google search on "Madre Sarita." Come to find out Madre was the Grandmother of Don Miguel Ruiz, the famous author of the self-help/spiritual book, *The Four Agreements*.

Ever since meeting Madre Sarita, I wondered when I would be led back to Mexico. One day, I would love to talk to Don Miguel Ruiz about his grandmother and the things she divulged. Miguel's books have influenced millions of people. I had been turned on to his teachings when I owned my healing center and bookstore, using his information in many of my classes.

Apparently, Don Miguel learned his craft when he was asked to translate his grandmother's prayers, lectures and workshops from Spanish into English. He learned the content of her teachings in both languages.

Miguel Jr. came to understand the power of faith. He saw first-hand how she manifested her intent to heal people, both physically and spiritually. Don Miguel Jr.'s apprenticeship lasted ten years. When he reached his mid-twenties, his father intensified his training. At the apex of this power journey Don Miguel said to his eldest son,

"Find your way out. Go home and master death by becoming alive."

Don Miguel Jr. is married and has two young children. And so, as a Nagual (a human being who has the power to transform spiritually into animal form), he begins once again to pass along the wisdom and the tools of his family's traditions in helping others to achieve their own personal freedom and optimal physical and spiritual health.

Ready to share everything he has learned; Miguel Jr. has taken the lessons of his father and grandmother and discovered his own personal freedom. Being able to apply his teachings to the world around him, gave Miguel Jr. a new understanding of the lessons his father and grandmother had passed on to him, once again giving him the desire to pass on his beliefs, helping others achieve their own personal freedom.

25

Walk-in

"I am who I am and I am who I was, and I am who I will always be!"

—Emrys

It was a paradigm shift for me—and it may be for you, the reader of my story, however, it is one to be considered...

I stared at the sun dancing off the shallow riffles in the Umpqua River that flowed at the edge of our property... and remembering back, I was mesmerized, once again, by the series of mystical events that had occurred in my life.

An unanswered question: Why didn't I open my eyes that day at the hospital when my mother and aunt walked into my room? I wondered why—but I didn't know. I couldn't understand it. And my actual memory of the two weeks I spent so sick at Steinhoering was limited. Decades later, I wanted to figure out what had happened to me when I slipped out of consciousness at nine years old.

I often wondered why I couldn't remember a single meal, conversation, or any visits after the first one from my mom and aunt. Had I just blocked out the memory of the events that took place because my body, or mind, or spirit, just couldn't handle it?

All these years later, I know we are all connected to the infinite soul of the universe. I believe we have multiple incarnations. Lives come and go; visions come and go.

I could never shake the feeling, when I returned home from the hospital, how I felt so disconnected from my father and my brother, but not from my mother. It took me more than thirty years to determine what had transpired when I was sent through a vortex of some sort in my near-death experience, and had experienced that altered state at nine years old.

> *"When you find yourself surrounded by sane people excited about your idea and lending support, you realize, perhaps, you are not as crazy as you think you are."*
>
> —Paresh Shah

In 1996, some of my questions were about to be answered. My Reiki teacher, Karyn from Chicago, came to teach a class at my property in Oregon.

This happened around the time that Christopher and I had settled back in to our home Oregon, after leaving Mexico. The restaurant and healing center were going strong, and we had purchased a mystical piece of land on Little River, near Roseburg, OR. The great grace of a native shaman helped us raise the sweat lodge with traditional branches of willow. I remember the first time I saw this beautiful property with its majestic and ancient redwood trees seated on the edge of the tranquil riverbank. I was convinced this was the place where great healing would take place, helping me continue my own healing and spiritual work for others.

It was late summer and the weather was ideal for building and conducting sacred ritual. Karyn, performed a sacred fire ceremony and an "attunement," this being the way one is initiated into Reiki energy healing—and during Reiki attunement the flood gates of Reiki energy are opened. It is done to open up the crown, heart and palm chakras to allow the universal energy of Reiki to flow, allowing each person to explore and expand inborn healing energies.

I was excited to participate in the class, along with nine of my Reiki students. I was surprised to see a vision of an old, Tibetan master appear just after Karyn kissed me on the forehead as a part of the initiation.

She kissed me on the forehead a second time and said to me:

"Welcome! It's so nice to see you again."

While I didn't know exactly what she was talking about, it became clear that it wasn't Karyn who was doing the talking. It was a message from the ancient teacher, I witnessed.

That same evening, after everyone had gone to sleep, Karyn joined me on a walk along the riverside. It's then she asked me a very important question that would change my life.

"Have you ever read my book, *Walk-Ins*?"

Answering, I said, "No, I didn't know you had written anything other than Reiki manuals."

Karyn explained that her profession in Chicago as a Naturopathic physician led her to the field of hypnosis. She had gone on to hypnotize hundreds of people who suffered near-death experiences. She then documented their stories, and the characteristics of walk-ins, later writing her book: *Walk-Ins: Soul Exchange.* I wasn't sure why Karyn was mentioning all of this to me, but I was soon to find out.

Karyn egged me on: "Petra you have to read it because I am really sure that you are a walk-in!"

"Have you ever been in a coma?" She asked.

Frankly, I was a little stunned. How did she know?

I hadn't told her much about my earlier life. I hadn't told many people at all. Knowing this might be important, I spent some time sharing my story with her. As my story progressed, I felt this wave of energy come over me, a kind of "knowing," as if I was meant to talk about more than just my hospitalization. I remember saying to Karyn:

"Love is what we are born with. Fear is what we learn. The spiritual journey is the unlearning of fear and prejudices, and the acceptance of love back in our hearts. Love is the essential reality and our purpose on earth. To be consciously aware of it, to experience passion in ourselves and others, is the substance of life. Meaning does not lie in things!"

Karyn seemed to accept all that I was saying, as if it were a natural part of the walk-in conversation. We continued to talk, moving along the river's trail.

She went on to ask me if I had any memory after I was released from the hospital. I told her, "No."

I shared with her that I felt as if somebody had downloaded new memory into my head after I left the hospital as a young girl, feeling a certain disconnect as if it was not really my house, my family—and the German language was suddenly so difficult for me. It had bothered me at the time that I couldn't seem to get emotionally attached to the people around me, except to my mother, but even my mother was upset by how independent I had become at such a young age.

I recalled to Karen how I had wanted to get away, and I often spoke of leaving Bavaria when I was old enough and traveling to faraway lands. My mother would often cry and hold me so tight and tell me that she would die if I ever left her which made me feel very guilty for having those thoughts in the first place.

After my stay at Steinhoering Hospital, I had a hard time being present in "the now." I was always somewhere else—daydreaming and flying out of my body and hearing that strange humming sound in my right ear. Voices and scenes in present time would somehow grow distant and I was then enveloped in this cocoon of love, warmth, light and sound which made me feel so happy and blissful, similar to what I experienced in the hospital. Karyn found this to be quite relevant.

My mother would frequently mention to me how attached she was to her mother and her family when she was a girl, and how she never even wanted to go on vacation or a summer camp—and pointed out how different I was from her. She couldn't understand why little Petra constantly talked about moving someplace else, why our small Bavarian village just wasn't enough.

I told Karyn that the greatest challenge for me after my near-death experience was watching how judgmental humans can be, especially my family. Afterwards, I seemed to have become acutely aware of people's behavior, feeling nauseous when I was not authentically kind to someone, or judged them somehow. It bothered me to no end. It was physically painful for me as a young girl when my family would sit around and talk about other people's shortcomings, and gossip.

Rather for me, compassion and empathy came naturally. I wanted to help those in need or lacking, and not talk behind their backs. I'd even get into trouble at school for my extreme sensitivity and obsession with fairness. I had always been sensitive but my reaction to things became more intense and I sometimes couldn't believe I behaved this way. I explained how I so badly wanted to show compassion to all living beings. It was disturbing, and I just couldn't understand why humans had to suffer so much.

Karyn listened intently as I told her how I had felt like a foreigner in my own country, intolerant of the racial prejudice, even the rivalry within my own family. With each tale I shared, it was clear to Karyn that I met her walk-in criteria. By the end of our outing, she had me intrigued. I was excited by the fact that this "walk-in" explanation might explain all the changes I had undergone since blacking out under the coffee table when so young, so long ago. I needed to know more.

Shortly after the Reiki course ended, I picked up a copy of Karyn's book. In it, she explains how two individual souls have agreed to switch places, one in spirit, one in the flesh. She claimed that the embodied soul in this partnership is the one who has gone as far as it can in its development and is ready to move on, beyond this world. In turn, the soul that decides to take its place chooses to serve on this earth in a different capacity than in their previous life as a part of their own growth.

The more I read, the more I understood.

Whether I was a walk-in or not, or whether I completely agreed with this abstract, I learned that a walk-in doesn't necessarily recognize or relate closely to the people around him or her after the soul switch. He or she may have lapses of memory from the other occupant and her recent experience here on earth. As a walk-in, individuals don't usually recognize the reason they came—or why they changed places.

For me, growing up, I had felt for so many years that I

was a stranger in a strange land. I just didn't know my purpose there, in Bavaria, and was a little puzzled by it. I felt this longing not only to know about my fate, but also the greater meaning of life, way beyond my small township.

Why do these switches occur? Or do they?

According to Karyn, the walk-in transition can be quite a blow to the physical body, particularly, if this has occurred due to a car accident, coma, operation, or a lengthy illness. While my memory of actual energy shifting was scant, I recall my experience being far from horrifying.

It was the aftermath at home that was most troubling.

She went on to explain: as a newly embodied soul, you will feel somewhat alienated from everyone close to you, although you keep the memories of your body's past history. This really made sense, because I was not able to relate to my family as I was before. This always made it very difficult to stay in a loving and kind mindset with my family; they seemed so strange to me and so worthy of criticism. After my coma, I felt more of an observer, rather than a participant with them. I didn't understand why they did what they did, or said what they said—and I resented all the pettiness and the emptiness they sometimes displayed.

In such a process, Karyn also explained, the other soul continues on its journey, either to reunite with a loved one that had already crossed over, or to be sent by Spirit to another place to continue soul learning on earth, or another plane of consciousness.

I became more and more curious the deeper I read and reflected during my walk with Karyn. I did a great deal of research into the concept of a "walk-in." I wanted to know what I could find out and how it might help me navigate my life more easily.

"Be unique. Be different. Be yourself."

—Debasish Mridha

In her book Karyn states, that a walk-in soul agrees to complete the contract, or the purpose, left by the walk-out soul. Like in reincarnation—the soul travels on!

In my case, perhaps the previous soul left my body because *she* could not carry out her soul purpose within that particular family. This was a perfect situation for the new me; it allowed me to take my journey here. Sure, I found the family quite difficult to navigate, but I now know that it served an important function in my development.

Some walk-in souls may just have serious karma they feel they have to complete (in Hinduism and Buddhism the sum of a person's actions in this and previous states of existence, viewed as deciding their fate in future existences).

As I understand it, some are just special souls that come for one thing: *to bring love or knowledge to the suffering.* When I heard this, I felt like it was me Karyn was talking about. THIS gift, or knowing, was all that I wanted, or felt that I needed to better understand my purpose on this earth.

Really, when I think about it, I believe we are all walk-ins.

Souls walk into the body of an infant, right?

The only difference with an "official" walk-in as Karyn describes is that the soul steps into the body of an older person or adult, who's already taken up residence on earth for a while. These souls can incarnate without having to spend time learning lessons brought about through babyhood or childhood. It's just another way the soul navigates a path of discovery and growth.

But still, it boggled my mind. *Was I a walk-in soul?*

I suspected I might be a walk-in soul. This greatly helped

me understand myself better, and the world around me. But one question that still bothered me was—if a walk-in has a specific mission, what was mine? Did I just come to play out some karmic script, to simply hang out, or did I come to serve?

Years after my time with Karyn, I was turned onto, and convinced of the idea of being a soul who had come to earth for the purpose of helping humanity shift into a more loving, advanced state of consciousness.

Is this why I had come? To offer love and compassion, and serve others by giving of myself? Was this the very reason why I felt like earth was too foreign and strange to me? Because it can often be the opposite of compassion and love—instead it can be unfeeling and cruel.

I always felt the need to help people, sometimes trying to "save" them at my own expense. This explained my fascination with meditation, energy—and the history of power and control humans inflict upon others, readily displayed on earth.

The walk-in generally cannot tolerate violence or anything that does not come from love; anything that is not balanced. This new knowledge further filled in the blanks for me. I was sure this was my answer.

Was I a walk-in? Ahh… and talking with Karyn, I now knew there were others like me. How refreshing. Not feeling so alone, this comforted me.

Most walk-ins retain life experiences of the previous soul without emotional strings. This could explain why I was often so detached from my immediate family and why I left home so early with no thought of going back.

At times, it was as if Bavaria never existed.

Memories of my previous soul's experiences were much like watching a movie—but with the "emotional sound" turned off. I often felt like I was acting, playing out different roles like a movie set with a cast of characters. My personality was completely malleable at that time. I can now see that the "new" soul was trying on fresh personality traits, until I found a good combination that would better serve the new life-goal I had.

How interesting it was to me that as unattached as I was, I still was so sensitive to the slightest things happening around me. Once, I remember standing in front of my closet and crying—over clothes! I was receiving a vision overlay of long rows of garments that belonged to me, as "Petra."

I was so devastated to see my clothes from another existence. Even my fashion sense was altered by the switch. I used to not care about the things I wore and what my mother dressed me in, and after my near-death experience, at thirteen and fourteen years old, I had a definite desire to wear more elegant clothes like dresses that were tailor made in my grandmother's attic.

My mother would have to tell me that I already had enough clothes when I'd beg her to take me shopping. I was constantly attempting to remake myself. My taste in food also changed drastically; I couldn't eat pork or beef anymore and later became a vegetarian. Death, including the killing of animals, or war, can be big triggers for a walk-in. If you are a walk-in this can be amplified, because a walk-ins personality traits seem gentler, more compassionate. I was no different.

A freshly arrived walk-in is like a newborn baby. The emotional and mental bodies are "new." They have not yet been imprinted from the environment. Like an infant, a walk-in is a sponge for the emotions, traits and beliefs of the people around them. It is so important that a new walk-in carefully choose their relations wisely; they will take on those people's qualities and biases, be them positive or negative.

Somehow, in retrospect, I can see that I knew this at the core of my being. I'd make sure to avoid certain kinds of people, yet gravitate towards others. Soon after my transitioning, I felt I had to protect myself from harsh language, arguments, and negative spaces and vibrations.

Karyn explained: "The most difficult situation for a new walk-in is to be around people who pressure them to be the exact same person they were before it all happened."

Of course, my family did not realize, nor would they have believed, in fact, I would have been institutionalized if had mentioned something like this, nor was I consciously aware at the time that a transfer like this could have happened to me, or that such things were even possible. Not in a long shot.

My family was Catholic, and didn't even believe in reincarnation. To talk about walk-ins would have been outrageous to them, and a sin in their minds, some form of demonic possession. I can't imagine how they would have responded if I had ever mentioned my discoveries about walk-ins.

For much of my younger years, I had to deal with well-meaning people projecting their emotions and pictures of the "old Petra." It hurt me physically, emotionally and spiritually. My family did a keen job "ghosting" me, as those close to the walk-in soul can do. It's almost like a multi-dimensional avoidance or denial of the fact that you are not that person you claim to be by being in that body. This can create immense stress on the physical body and the personality, to the point that it creates disease. Sometimes, you can feel like you're going crazy. At times, I certainly did.

Like for most walk-ins, I felt an innate sense of spirit around me. Fortunately, I had this to keep me sane. Walk-in spirituality assists in the integration process after inherently turning to prayer or meditation to sort out all of the "Who am I?" yearnings.

For the walk-in soul, it's like a code in the DNA knows that it has to seek knowledge and peace, even if it's human hosts can't provide this. For me, I now grasped from talking with Karen, that my true walk-in integration didn't take place until I received the initiation from my guru when I went to India in 1985.

The single thing that I have to say about walk-ins is that we must learn to be really gentle with our physical bodies. The physical is not a vehicle but a co-creative partner in our life experiences; it's where emotions are processed.

The physical body of a walk-in needs time to absorb life experiences, especially to process feelings related to dying, suffering, abandonment or heartbreak. Only when the body understands that the walk-in soul consciously chose this body, loves this body, and is willing to act as a partner with this physical structure, can true harmony occur. This happened for me, albeit a little too late in life.

It helped that someone like Karyn knew what I had gone through. We both dealt in energy medicine and prayer, which bonded us. And she could identify the pain and alienation I felt being a walk-in. Her book and literature helped me to not feel so all alone.

Until I found this information, even though I had meditated for so many years with the Masters of the East, a sense of separation still lingered. Once I practiced grounding meditation, much of my burden was released. The connecting to other dimensions, lightening the spirit and the flesh, and feeling a personal sense of connection to something greater soothed my walk-in soul.

I can pick-up things maybe other people cannot. My extra-sensory perception as a young child was always pretty well-tuned. I could make out, and get a sense of entities and spirits even then.

Most importantly, I feel I can see another person's true soul essence when I looked deep into their eyes. This gives me a sensation of understanding and kindness. I didn't always get a chance to experience this before going to India. Able to read beyond their personality and physical features, I feel closer to my true home in the stars, where anything is possible.

26

Will and the River of Life

It had been hard financially, while with Christopher. Though it had been fortunate for him that Susie, his ex-girlfriend and heir to a very large fortune, for some reason, had always been there for him. She had given him money to buy our property on Little River Road. When he first disappeared, I took my name off the home deed, and called Susie to let her know. She was kind enough to compensate me for all the years I had paid the mortgage.

I met William one year prior to Christopher's disappearance, and before his death. I will never forget that Sunday morning. I opened the door at our house on Little River Road—and standing there was a tall, slender and handsome young man, maybe nineteen, at my doorstep. He asked me if I was the Reiki Master that Christopher had told him about, and said:

"My mother had the same dream at least three times in the last few months. The dream was about an old Japanese man holding a rake in his hand, running over an ocean of gravel, repeating the word: Reiki… Reiki… Reiki…!"

Neither of us had any idea what it meant then. It would soon become clear.

William explained further, "I met Christopher at a neighbor's house, and he told me about you, and mentioned that you are a Reiki teacher, and that it is a form of healing arts from Japan. I immediately remembered my mother's dream and knew right away that I had to meet you and find out what this is!"

Shortly after our encounter, I was scheduled to teach a Reiki Level I Class. William and his mother chose to attend. We became fast friends and stayed in touch even after the class was over.

Little did I know that William was to become one of my allies in this lifetime. He was raised in Arizona with parents who were products of the sixties. His journey in life was highly influenced by his parent's alcohol abuse and addictions, as well as their neglect of him as a small boy, which all contributed to a lifetime of depression issues. Integrating socially, due to this model given by his parents, was also a challenge for him.

William's grandfather was very wealthy, so he and his brother were recipients of his generosity on a regular basis. In fact, every year in January a large deposit would arrive in his account, which wasn't always helpful. It somehow crippled him, and made him less productive. Over the next few years, William and his mother became close friends, and visited often.

When Christopher left, they could see that I was truly heartbroken over his sudden desertion. Because all the time we had been together, Christopher had always been my best friend. Of course, (I now knew there were things and patterns I chose not to see regarding Christopher. Some of those things ultimately contributed to his fatal car accident.)

Life has a way of going on, with or without us… and we lived among a community that knew us very well, and I felt their support.

It happened in the middle of a very hot summer, during my fortieth birthday party, my friends decided to throw at the river house.

It was such fun, with around seventy people, enjoying the live music and gourmet vegetarian dishes like enchiladas, casseroles, and desserts. William, too, attended the celebrations. He'd been a good friend, giving me moral support since Christopher had left.

As if life had turned into slow-motion, William drove into the property in his lemon-yellow sports car, two beautiful mixed bouquets of flowers, and many bags of gourmet cheese and crackers. Looking confident, dressed in khaki shorts and a black cotton tank and flip flops, he set down the flowers and the food, and walked straight up and kissed me on the lips in front of everyone. I was completely startled, my cheeks blushing bright red, as everyone looked at us. They didn't know him… but now they were sure to wonder who that handsome young man was!

The party went on, and it was amazing and memorable, with good friends from the area, much laughter, children played in the meadow, as adults jumped off large boulders into the perfect crystal-clear water of Little River.

After everyone had left that night, William stayed over and put his arms around me. We stood on the porch listening to the flow of the river in the moonlight and he said:

"Don't worry, I have your back!"

I was strangely relieved when William spoke those words to me. I somehow knew that he was there to protect John and me, and that was such incredible relief for me to know he cared about us.

Shortly after that, I was able to sell my restaurant to some lovely people from Florida, who literally just dropped in one day and decided to purchase it.

William and I purchased a wonderful house in Eugene, OR, and lived there together with my son for some years. Sadly, I didn't know the severity of William's struggle with depression and anxiety, and how taxing it would be on my son and me. The whole time we lived under the same roof, we kept our intimate relationship quiet, since we didn't want my son to know that we were lovers as well as roommates.

I don't know why I had such an issue about Will being seventeen years younger than me and being my lover. Maybe it was because it felt like it was taboo, and he had a tendency towards bisexuality.

I was in love with him. Nobody that I had ever been with equaled the energy that we had together. Everything was electric and my love for him was unconditional.

Over four years after we moved into the Eugene house, I was managing to help William's deal with his depression and anxiety, though emotional processing, Reiki, acupuncture, massage and many many different modalities of healing and diet. I had gotten my real estate license, and business was going great, and purchased my brand-new A6 Audi Quattro. We decided to go skiing one day, and were all on top of the world, excited! All three of us were on the road by 6:00 a.m. I skied down the mountain, with John and Will snowboarding side-by-side. The sun was bright and warm, as the light flakes of snow fell on the silvery edge of the forest. We were all feeling so lucky and so very happy that day. It reminded me of the magical days of time spent skiing the Alps as a child in Bavaria. I felt so free, so happy, and so alive.

Just one month after that trip, one morning William told me that he had to leave the house for a while and move in with his parents outside of Glide, Oregon, on 120 acres they owned.

John and I were so sad he was leaving, but understood. He needed to be out in nature and felt he needed to go. I always knew that it wouldn't likely last forever with William… but he brought much joy into my life while we were together.

After-the-fact, it is so strange how we can remember certain moments in our lives like they were just yesterday. That was such a day, the day Will left. I was getting ready to list a house for a friend; two months after William decided to move back to live in the hills of acreage with his parents.

I, along with a friend who did tile work, was in the middle of tiling the kitchen to increase the value of his house, when suddenly a phone call came in from William's mother, Wynona.

She announced herself with a quivering and weepy, hardly audible voice:

"Petra, it's Wynona! I am so sorry to have to tell you that Will is dead. He shot himself yesterday. Can you please come right away and help us?"

In an instant, my legs gave out and I collapsed on the floor crying. My two friends helped me up to the couch, stayed with me, and consoled me for a while—they were Terry, whose house I was listing and my friend, Mark, who was helping with the tile job.

Nothing could have prepared me for this next episode in my life.

It was one thing when Christopher died, at age 55, but to see a vibrant 25-year-old in a cold casket is almost unbearable.

I remember it so well. John was still at school. I left him a message that I had to go to Roseburg, but didn't tell him why. When I arrived at the Chapel of the Roses funeral home I saw William's mother and his aunt Cyndy in the lobby. His mother collapsed into my arms. We sat there and hugged, both sustaining the other, for a long time.

I wanted to see William—and a few moments later, William's brother walked me down the narrow hallway to the viewing room. As soon as he opened the door, I saw William laying there so peacefully—looking like he always did, with his gentle smile. His black beanie covered the gunshot wound in his head. I touched his hands, and held onto the side of the coffin so I wouldn't collapse. I talked to him for two or three hours.

William's parents were unable to plan the funeral, so I took on the responsibility. I planned a memorial service for William, and drove myself home feeling hopeless and extremely sad.

I had called my son and told him that I was on my way home, hinting that something terrible happened to William. There are moments in life we are reminded how wise children really are. I walked up the stairs and my John stood on top of the stairwell, moving towards me. John put his hands on my shoulders, his forehead up against mine, and said to me,

"Mommy it wasn't your fault, you tried to save him so many times. It wasn't your fault and I need you, so please don't be sad!"

I asked him later, how he knew that William was dead and he said: "I don't know. I just felt it!"

Not knowing what to do, I immediately called one of my

psychics who knew William and who had been working with me for many years. I told him what had happened.

"Yes," he said, "Please give me some time to meditate, and I will call you back."

Two hours later I received a phone call. He said, "It is really amazing, Petra. I just saw Will. He is in a holding pattern right now. There is this huge angel that is holding him, and he is curled up in an embryo position. There are wings around him. The most extraordinary part of it is, the angel looks exactly like Will. He has Will's face."

So I called Will's mom and told her about what Gary had said, and his vision.

Her response startled me: "You won't even believe it. His cousin, who was named after her aunt Wynona, dreamt about him the day before William died and told me that an angel came to her. He told her to accompany William across, to the other side." When people die in such an abrupt way as William did, it's believed that they sometimes don't know that they are dead, and they don't know the journey home. They get confused and trapped.

She was crying as she continued sharing Wynona's very revealing dream about William, the day *before* he committed suicide.

Apparently, she found herself walking along a forest path, together with Will, among lots of tall ferns. After a while she came to a cave, and in that cave, there were many beings in their light bodies. There was one being who looked quite familiar to her. He told her that William had chosen her to help him cross to the other side of the river of life, because of their relationship as children growing up together. The angel told her that the rest of the path was shielded from the living and she had to be blindfolded. It was the path for people who had already crossed over and no longer were in their physicality.

She walked along, holding hands with Will, who was next to her. The angel led the way until they came to the river of life, also called Mansarova Lake, which in the Eastern tradition is the water you have to cross when you die. This is where your soul gets washed clear from all of the karma of this life. Supposedly, Will didn't want to go into the water, even though they kept trying to encourage him to enter.

As the dream goes, Will said,

"I can't go in.

I don't want to go in.

If I go in, I will forget everything.

I don't want to forget."

The angel told Wynona to go into the river, and ask William to join her in the water. After some time, William finally went into the river where he lay in her arms, and became younger. As he lay in her arms in the river, he became younger and younger, until he morphed into his five-year-old self. She was holding him in her arms, when the angel fleet picked him up and took him further down the riverbank. At the end of that flow of water stood the Divine Mother Mary. She scooped him up and held him close to her breast, then turned around and walked away.

It was at that time the sky lit up with this fleet of angels from all traditions and religions descending down in this ethereal ship to the river. Finally, Will climbed into the ship.

This dream was so surreal and healing for all of us.

When the story of the dream had been told, this great sense of relief came over me. Can you imagine how happy we were that he made it? He was able to cross.

Will's mother said. "Oh my god. That angel with him is my brother. He died in a helicopter crash in Alaska when he was delivering food to the Eskimos. He looked exactly like Will."

This was a very tender moment for both of us.

My belief that people get stuck when they die so abruptly, is a reminder of why I feel it's important to burn candles for them, and to erect an altar with a picture of them. And prayer for them helps them move into the higher dimensions, to understand and to shift.

This dream touched me so deeply that I decided to share it at Will's funeral. I was in full tears with two hundred people listening.

Accepting Loss

About two months later, I was sitting in meditation. I had a dream that I was in a ballroom at a black-tie event with gigantic crystal chandeliers. I was dressed in a beautiful black silk gown, and was walking like a ghost through the crowd, when I suddenly spotted a swinging door. I entered through the door and walked into this other room where I saw William lying on a wooden platform; it was like the one he was on before they cremated him. He had a white sheet over him.

I stood in front of him, and he sat up straight. I looked at him and said: "You're supposed to be dead, you know." He said to me in the most loving way, "Look to the right of my head and you'll know why I had to leave!"

Suddenly, a crystal formation, the size of a grapefruit, of many colors, appeared next to his head; it was spinning in space. My consciousness was immediately drawn into it. A great blessing was given, a transfer of information, with mathematical code, from him to me. I suddenly understood why he could no longer be in his body; his energy was misaligned. After that, I was able to release my emotional attachment and fully recognize what a relief it was for William to be released from his physical body.

It was just a few days later when his mother called me to share that she had the most profound dream about William. She said that they were walking side by side, strolling through the forest on her property. She cried on the phone as she shared her dream with me. William had taken her hand, and smiled from ear to ear, announcing that he will be back to earth soon, but this time, *he'll be shorter*. We both laughed and cried some tears of relief, knowing he was well.

This is when you realize, as a healer, that you cannot help certain people, because they aren't meant to be helped. You can love them, you can want it for them, but if the healing is not supposed to take place, then it is not going to happen.

None of us can play God.

It's up to the Creator to do what needs to be done, and in Will's case, it wasn't my call. That's why my son said what he said to me, I believe—so intuitively and lovingly. But at the same time, for all of us who love someone, we always feel like we didn't do enough.

The lessons I learned about human behavior observing my grandfather, my father, and my brother, my first and second husband, and William, have all helped me to understand depression and anxiety.

I felt like I was cursed in the ways of love. The first man I was in love with was Walter, and I lost my virginity to him. He was about ten years older than me, and I was only seventeen. The next love in my life was Foad, whom I married, while in London, and before India. After that, was the master's arranged marriage to Jay. Then I fell in love with Chris, left with him to Mexico. That, too, became a toxic relationship. Then Will came when I was forty, and my relationship with him lasted only five years before he killed himself.

I had had enough!

After Will's death, I was alone for two years, grieving and drowning out my sorrow by writing a book, *Quantum Transformation: The Seven Insights.* This helped me avoid my emotional grief and sadness, and kept me focused on higher consciousness.

One day, I would be ready to try love again.

I built a website and posted information about *The Seven Insights,* and it wasn't long after that, that an astrologer found me. Perhaps through my website or she just picked me out of the clear blue sky, and sent me this eighty page reading that blew me away. How did this person know this about me?

I never really wanted to be in another relationship because I didn't think I could find what Will and I had ever again. I didn't want to try to replace him, but the Universe had different things in store for me.

Thankful

I am thankful for all of the experiences I've had with love and heartbreak. After all, I would have never learned what depression and anxiety truly meant. In the case of William, how could such a young and handsome, loving and kind person be so troubled by nightmares and depression? Until I had a firsthand experience, I did not understand the impact that depression makes on millions of Americans, and the drugs that are given can sometimes further destroy lives.

I felt my life has been, and still is, a gigantic school room of experiences that I had to witness and experience, in order for me to have more compassion, understanding and insights.

I am now on the threshold of such incredible expansion of my own consciousness. Every lesson throughout my life, no matter how difficult, dark, magical or bright has led me to this point to be a better teacher, a better lover, a better coach, a better business person. They say that it is not about the destination, it's the journey that counts!

At fifty-five years of age, I can say that I am finally free. Free of pretense and must-do; free in my spirit, free in my journey to have to please or impress anyone. And free to love.

Freedom comes in many forms, but my greatest freedom is that I can be just me. I have ridden myself of all the shackles of the paradigm of my upbringing and my self-imposed perfectionism.

I am going to live, live freely and ecstatically, and take in all that life has to offer. My destination matters not—as the journey I am on gets better every day. Why? Because I am a better receiver of all that people and God offer.

I experienced love with William, felt so loved by him, and yet once again, I had loved a man who was unable to continue our life together, which brought our story together to a tragic and sad end. Now at last, I can see my relationship stories more objectively and clearly.

They all blended together to speak an important truth to me. It was like *finally* I could see my repeated relationship patterns in full, living color. I recognized the challenge, and sadness, each important relationship had presented to me, and for the first time, I was done with repeatedly getting myself into difficult relationships with men like these.

I had to clear whatever it was that resided deep within me, those things that I needed to unblock and fully comprehend, which might have gone clear back to my father. And until I could do so, I avoided seeking further relationships.

I needed to clear this so I didn't re-attract people into my life that were incapable of loving me. So after William… I chose to move on with everything that was my life experience, to move purposefully forward… by allowing myself to feel the pain… learn and grow… gain knowledge… deepen spiritual insight… embrace people… develop higher consciousness… love myself and others—all of these are chapters in my life… but don't close the book on my life just yet… there's more.

27

Clarity About The Guru Takes Me Back To Oz

"There is only one Guru, that is God and there is no other Guru. We have to recognize Him as our only preceptor. He is the preceptor of preceptors. Realizing that God dwells within us, we must treat God as the universal Guru and the preceptor for mankind and contemplate on Him."

—Bhagavan Baba

I have joy in my heart and a smile on my face, because I can truly say that I am happier now than when I was as an active member of the organization of the master. I feel more contented with my life, living among people in the world. I no longer isolate myself within one community, or focus on a far-off goal of God-realization. I enjoy the here and now. I am in awe of my life the way it is today, and the people in it—and for that I am most grateful.

My whole concept of a master, a guru, had been shaken, but not shattered in my interactions with Thakar Singh. There were some extraordinary teachers and gurus that were a big part of influencing my life and my story. On the Path of the Masters, people such as Baba Sawan Singh or Saint Kirpal Singh served tirelessly, as they accomplished amazing things in this world. I can honestly say that being with a guru in my twenties saved my life and my sanity. Without their teachings about devoted and disciplined meditation, I don't know if I would've become the balanced person that I am today—spiritually, emotionally, mentally or physically.

What if I had chosen to focus only on the one incident of the master's indiscretion on that airplane flight to America? If so, I would have thrown away the entire experience, many of them amazing, that I had had in India and in the ashram, due to that one event. What a waste that would have been.

Instead, for decades, I have had the great benefits of light and sound meditation, adopted a peaceful and loving lifestyle, eaten a healthy diet, and have the advantages provided by the personal discipline I was taught. I know it myself, and must acknowledge it to you, the reader, because there was so much within that lifestyle and faith that positively influenced me, helping me to learn, grow and mature. I feel it was all in God's plan for my life.

I have since studied the works of Paramahansa Yogananda, Krishna Murti, Sai Baba and many more. Yes, I even became initiated into the Krishna faith, and was given the name Priya Sakhi.

I spent many years as a dedicated initiate —and it took me even more years to finally wake up and realize the function of the guru. And I often asked this question…

WHO IS THE REAL GURU?

"Who is a true guru? Is he the one that teaches worldly education? Is he one that that explores the properties of matter? No, they are only teachers. Is one who teaches a mantra or Vedanta a guru? No, we may call them Acharyas (teachers), not gurus. People consider a person who imparts knowledge as a preceptor (a teacher responsibility to uphold a certain law or tradition). But most of them are mere teachers, not preceptors. A teacher, who teaches others, has had a teacher himself. The one who has no guru above him is the true guru.

The true meaning of guru is "one who dispels darkness of ignorance."

"Gu" means "darkness of ignorance" and "Ru" means "one who removes." Another meaning for guru is, "One who reveals the guri (target) to the disciple." He does this by removing the darkness of ignorance.

Guri here refers to the Atmic principle (highest plane of existence) present in every human being. The real guru who can reveal the Atmic principle is a Jnaanamurthy (embodiment of wisdom); the very embodiment of divine principles; and He is one who takes upon himself a form to teach the same to the disciple; he is God himself.

Another meaning of the word guru is "one who is beyond attributes and forms. "Gu" stands for Gunaatheetha—one who transcends the three Gunas (Satva, Rajas and Thamas); Ru stands for Rupavarjitha—one who is formless. The One who is beyond all attributes and forms is none other than the Supreme Self (the Brahmam) who is resident within

> each of us. Only God can be regarded as One who is beyond attributes and forms.
>
> Guru is Brahma, who is the creator of the universe. Guru is Vishnu who is all pervasive and is also the doer in the universe. Guru is Maheshvara who commands and ordains everything in the universe in the right manner. Guru is not one who merely teaches. A real Guru is omnipotent, omniscient and omnipresent; He is God himself.
>
> Let us purify our hearts to let the divine dwell in it. Let us install God, our Sadguru, in our hearts. The vibrations that emanate from the heart will elevate us and confer divine wisdom on us." —Bhagavan Baba

I followed the teachings of Sai Baba for many years and have great admiration for his wise philosophy. Clarity about who a guru is, their function, and their humanness is vital—and accepting this truth, as Sai Baba states above… "A real Guru is omnipotent, omniscient, and omnipresent—He is God himself."

Recognizing this truth, perhaps does take me back to OZ—my childhood days of love, security, and dreams of happiness that can come true.

28

In Summary: Unraveling One Story Allows Gearing Up for Another

Discovering and accepting the truth of your life will set you free! Like me, I want you to see the truth of your life for yourself, so that you can better understand your purpose on this earth. *Because to understand something, is to be liberated from it!*

Writing this book about my life has helped me to achieve exactly that—I have been freed! I have stepped off the hamster wheel that persisted to cause unrest and chaos in my life, to at last rest, and be grateful for, the calmness of still waters. I literally see those waters each morning, from my home in Lake Oswego, Oregon.

My purpose is clear, and my passion sustains my desire to help and serve people. And like me, sometimes in life, we repeatedly get ourselves in certain *sticky* situations, until the lesson is learned—and the patterns are fully accepted and recognized. With it comes a great sigh of relief, and anticipation for good things that are yet to come.

I am at the end of one story and at the same time, I fully recognize it perpetuates the beginning of a new one… new chapters are already developing as I write the ending chapter of this book.

I was in search of answers as long as I can remember. A frustrated, lonely and sad teenager looking for a way to escape the tragic circumstances at home, to find a different life, one that provided answers, or at least provided the tools for me to help myself. And who knows? If my family had been able to provide those things, I might not have been ready to listen.

If my vibration creates my reality, then the vibration I want to create is that of beauty, joy and bliss, for me and others. Chaos and suffering is not on the agenda, and yet I must stay extremely focused to preserve peace within. As all who know me will attest, I love to throw a good party, and be surrounded by friends. But at the same time, I need quiet time to regularly meditate within, to be able to go out into the world and fulfill my purpose to serve others. None of it comes easy, so I encourage you not to expect *easy.*

What do I really want to do for you right now? I look around and see so many people, disillusioned and hopeless. Very few are truly happy and content and living in alignment with their true calling. I ask, *how can I give people hope?*

I wrote this book because I wanted to share my story, with the sincere wish that you might be inspired by it.

I have learned that the happiest times in my life have always been free. The many nights sitting around a fire and singing Jack Johnson or Beatles songs, climbing to a mountain top and singing from the top of my voice, jumping in the river and feeling the warm sun on my body. Just being still. *Simply being!*

All we truly have is our health and our spirit.

My father always said: "ignorance is bliss" when I was asking too many questions about his Catholic experience and the shame he experienced.

Nothing we witness gets lost in our psyche and I would rather fight to my death for truth, than die not knowing what is truly happening to our human race. Many people would rather live in the mass hypnotic state of media, over-eating and addiction, and that would be worse than a prison sentence to me. And it's not what I want for you!

I particularly want to talk to the younger generation. Those who are full of light and vigor, and who want to know the truth of our world, and their purpose in it. Until I left my home, my family, my life, my body, my paradigm—and went all the way down into the rabbit hole to find the answers for myself, I didn't realize that I always had the tools to get back to where I was supposed to be. The spirit supplies if we stop long enough, and take time to seek what we need deep within our body and soul. The importance of external things is diminished in the light of the spiritual truth that we seek.

When I was young, everyone around me was intoxicated with the new-found material hypnotism that spread like a disease in post war Germany and the world to them seemed fine as long as their middle-class needs were met. But now, with the middle class almost gone, the one's left are fighting harder to preserve their standard of living—and they are beginning to ask questions. The good thing about our species is that if we are suppressed for too long, there always emerges a group that creates an uprising for something better, no matter how much psychic warfare and hypnotic control is enforced on the population.

Ever since my coma at nine years old, I thought about death every day, saw the emptiness and superficiality of this existence and how someone somewhere had some practical answers. I needed more, and I knew it could be found. My story today confirms this truth. We can reach our highest potential, but first we need to recognize we start by knowing nothing.

I have lived over half of my life educating myself on the world, science, politics, language, philosophy, art and spirituality—and the more I learned, the more I realized that, in fact, I know nothing. After studying the science of light and sound "Sant Mat" with the masters from the east, and many other teachings, I know that we cannot bring about change on the physical plane through physical efforts alone. We must evolve or awaken to a higher state of consciousness. A consciousness that allows us to live in peace, in harmony, and to truly love one another. You may call this naïve. I believe that it is possible because love is the highest power of all—and all things must flow back to the vibration of love, darkness eventually must integrate with divine light, and become one with God and the Universe.

The Dalai Lama when asked what surprised him the most about humanity, answered:

"Man. Because he sacrifices his health in order to make money. Then he sacrifices money to recuperate his health and he is so anxious about the future that he does not enjoy the present; the result being that he doesn't live in the present or the future; he lives as if he is never going to die, and then he dies having never lived."

A few years ago I sold everything I owned, and rented

my house, so that I could be free from the burden of having to take care of things that were wasting my time. Eleven years of intense meditation, have benefitted me. It taught me extraordinary skills of how to focus and slow down, and allow things to unfold.

Sixteen years ago, my Vedic Astrologer in Bend, Oregon, told me that the second half of my life would be quite charmed and easy. I feel extremely fortunate to have inner peace and I am grateful for every lesson, every experience, difficult or easy, that has crossed my path. Every obstacle, every trial, every challenge has taught me compassion, understanding and gratitude. There is such freedom in becoming desire less, for it is only our desire for things to be different that cause the experience of pain and suffering. Today, I live in the most beautiful places in the world and am surrounded by beauty, love, and grace, and I am truly thankful.

At times, I can't help but think… *How did I get through all that I did in life?* Right now the purpose is to free me from the ashes…

I'm living the truth of this quote: *"Like a Phoenix, she will rise from the ashes of despair and soar."*

I am so grateful to be clear of strife and chaos; I can focus, and have been given the energy to make a difference for others in the world.

As I have stepped out to work with others as an Emotional Energy Coach, I accept the responsibility and also the honor that is to help others unravel and unveil the patterns that prevail in their lives, so that they can live to their highest potential.

I want you to tell your story, and in doing so you are able to see how the patterns have influenced the overall theme of your life—and how your story has taught you specific life lessons. How do lessons become positive, even in the midst of much darkness, despair and grief? My story is proof that it is possible, and I want nothing less for you.

My radio show, "Revealing Conversations" on Blog Talk Radio has given me a platform to share incredibly inspiring information with people all over the world. I love the many insights that are revealed during these interviews with my guests. I also teach Emotional Processing, Reiki, and Sacred Contract workshops, as well as organize wellness retreats and platforms for people to gather. Life is fun, very fun.

Thank you for reading about my life, as strange as it may seem.

I feel blessed. And I wish you peace and blessing, too!

About the Author

"Like a Phoenix, she will rise from the ashes of despair and soar."

Petra Nicoll is an "Emotional Energy Coach" who helps others unravel and unveil the patterns in their individual life story, so that they can live life to their highest potential. Her comfortable and unique process of having clients talk through their story, enables them to clearly see how particular patterns have influenced the overall theme of their life. Their stories, like yours, are distinctive ones that have taught specific life lessons. Today, her passion and purpose is to help all those she serves see how these specific patterns create significant lessons that become a positive influence for personal light and good, even in the midst of much darkness, despair and grief.

Petra Nicoll grew up in a middle-class family in the small village of Markt Schwaben, enjoying her years of childhood innocence in a place of picturesque beauty, just fifteen miles south of Munich, the capital of Bavaria, Germany.

Petra's real-life story could be fiction—only it's not. Readers will find her life thought-provoking, mesmerizing—and perhaps even remarkable.

Sheltered and protected by her Catholic family, her story begins with life altering changes that occur at nine years old, during a near death experience, which begins her lifelong journey of uncommon insights and unsettling discoveries.

The extreme pain and sorrow of her exposure to the tragic death of her mother, suicide, depression, and realities of war tell only part of Petra's story; one of a rare woman. All of her experiences lead her to the Masters of the Far East, the

Shaman's of North America and Mexico—through whom she awakens to the realization and vision that she has been given—to become transformed and more intuitive, authentic and soul-centered. Her extraordinary journey, and the practices and training that she has received throughout her life, has given her the tools to help others.

Petra studied psychology and art in London, has taught Emotional Energy Technique, Reiki, Gestalt and Reichian modalities to over 3500 students worldwide. As an author, certified life coach, transformational story coach, radio show host and public speaker, Petra has a wealth of information to share and skills to apply. Also a successful entrepreneur, she has facilitated hundreds of workshops and seminars, with proven, sustainable transformations in individuals for over thirty years.

"In the end, just three things matter: how well we have lived; how well we have loved; how well we have learned to let go."

—Jack Cornfield

"My near-death experience taught me the magic of life, how precious each moment is and how living in the NOW is the key to happiness. There is no death, there is only transformation."

Petra Nicoll

Contact information: www.petranicoll.com

List Of Website References

https://www.jewishvirtuallibrary.org/jsource/Holocaust/Lebensborn.html: The Nazi Party: The "Lebensborn" Program, 1935–1945. (page 8)

https://www.google.pt/search?q=Oberf%C3%BChrer&sa=X&ved=0ahUKEwiu4frQ6 tHLAhXGOxQKHUjgB-m0Q7xYIGSgA: Oberführer (page 15)

https://kar.kent. ac.uk/1179/1/NTQ%2002.doc: Karl Valentin and Liesl Karlstadt: Popular Entertainment in Munich (Oliver Double & Michael Wilson) (page 43)

http://buddhism.about.com/od/lifeofthebuddha/a/ buddhalife.htm: The Life of the Buddha (page 47)

http://www.creativespirits.info/aboriginalculture/spirituality: dreamtime-or-the dreaming: Aboriginal spirituality and beliefs. (page 116)

www.wildspeak.com/other/shapeshiftingintro.html: An Introduction to Shapeshifting (page 139)

www.nature.com/ physics/looking-back/Einstein/index.html: Wikipedia, the free encyclopedia. Albert Einstein. (page 141)

http://www.mrsikhnet.com/2010/04/09/words-of-power/: Words of Power, by Guruka Singh on Apr 9th, 2010 in Featured Articles, Gurbani, Meditation (page 168)

http://history-of-hinduism.blogspot.com/2008/09/hanuman-monkey-god.html Hanuman, The Monkey God (page 212) http://www.olrl.org/lives/germaine.shtml: SAINT GERMAINE: A Lesson in Humility and Meekness (page 252)

http://www.drunvalo.org/: Flower of Life and Merkaba Energy, Drunvalo Melchizedek (page 253)

https://en.wikipedia.org/wiki/Project_MKUltra: Wikipedia, the free encyclopedia: Project MKUltra (page 279)